The World's Greatest Books : Religion and Philosophy

Infinity Spectrum Books

Published by:

INFINITY SPECTRUM BOOKS

Email: infinityspectrumbooks@gmail.com

First published by Infinity Spectrum Books 2024

Copyright © Infinity Spectrum Books 2024

Title : **The World's Greatest Books (Religion and Philosophy)**
Paperback ISBN **:** 9789361901935
Hardback ISBN: 9789361901904

Religion

THE APOCRYPHA

Apocrypha is a Greek word, signifying "secret" or "hidden," but in the sixteenth century it came to be applied to a list of books contained in the Septuagint, or Greek translation of the Old Testament, but not in the Palestinian, or Hebrew Canon. Hence, by theological or bibliographic purists, these books were not regarded as genuine Scripture. That view was adopted by the early Greek Church, though the Western Church was divided in opinion. They appeared as a separate section in Coverdale's English Bible in 1538, and in Luther's German Bible in 1537. The Council of Trent in 1546 admitted them as canonical, except the First and Second Esdras and the Prayer of Manasses--a view rejected after the Reformation by Protestants, who recognised only the Palestinian Record as canonical. The Westminster Confession declared that they were only to be made use of as "human writings," and the Sixth Article of the Church of England states that they are "to be read for example of life and instruction of manners, but not to establish doctrine." As the result of a violent controversy in Scotland and America between 1825 and 1827, the Apocrypha was deleted from the copies of the Holy Scriptures issued by the British and Foreign Bible Society. The controversy was revived in 1862 when a quotation was engraved on the Prince Consort's Memorial in Kensington Gardens from the Wisdom of Solomon: "He, being made perfect in a short time, fulfilled a long time. For his soul pleased the Lord: Therefore hasted He to take him away from among the wicked." All the books bear evidence of having been written long after the date to which they are ascribed.

First Esdras

And Josias held the feast of the Passover in Jerusalem unto his Lord, the 14th day of the first month of the 18th year of his reign, and ordered the Levites, the holy ministers of Israel, to hallow themselves unto the Lord, and set the Holy Ark of the Lord in the house that King Solomon had built. And there were offered in sacrifices to the Lord on the altar 37,600 lambs and kids, and 4,300 calves. And they roasted the Passover with fire: as for the sacrifices, they sod them in brass pots and pans with a good savour, and set them before all the people. And such a Passover was not kept in Israel since the time of the Prophet Samuel. And the works of Josias were upright before his Lord with an heart full of godliness.

Now, after all these acts of Josias, it came to pass that Pharaoh, the King of Egypt, came to raise war at Carchamis upon Euphrates; and Josias, not regarding the words of the Prophet Jeremy, spoken by the mouth of the Lord, went out against him and joined battle with him in the plain of Magiddo. Then said the king unto his servants: Carry me away out of the battle; for I am very weak. And being brought back to Jerusalem he died and was buried in his father's sepulchre. And in all Jewry the chief men, with the women, yea Jeremy the prophet, made lamentation for him unto this day.

And the people took Joachaz, the son of Josias, and made him king; but the King of Egypt deposed him, and made Joacim, his brother, King of Judea and Jerusalem, who did evil before the Lord. Wherefore, against him, Nabuchodonosor, King of Babylon, came up and bound him with a chain of brass, and carried him into Babylon. Nabuchodonosor also took of the holy vessels of the Lord and carried them away, and set them in his own temple at Babylon, and made Zedechias king. Zedechias reigned eleven years, but did evil also in the sight of the Lord.

The governors of the people and of the priests did likewise many things against the Lord, and defiled the Temple of the Lord, who, being wrath with his people for their great ungodliness, commanded the Kings of the Chaldees to come up against them. This they did, and slew and spared neither young man nor maid, old man nor child, among them. And they took all the holy vessels of the Lord, both great and small, with thevessels of the Ark of God and the king's treasures, and carried them away into Babylon. As for the House of the Lord, they burnt it, and broke down the walls of Jerusalem and set fire upon her towers. And the people that were not slain with the sword were carried unto Babylon, who became servants to Nabuchodonosor, till the Persians reigned, to fulfil the word of the Lord spoken by the mouth of Jeremy.

In the first year of Cyrus, King of the Persians, the Lord raised up his spirit, and he made proclamation through all his kingdom, saying: The Lord of Israel, the most high Lord, hath made me king of the whole world, and commanded me to build him an house at Jerusalem in Jewry. If there be any of you that are of his people, let the Lord, even his Lord, be with him; let him go up to Jerusalem and build the house of the Lord of Israel.

Then the chief of the families of Judea and of the tribe of Benjamin, the priests also, and the Levites moved up to Jerusalem to build an house for the Lord there. And they were helped in all things with silver and gold, with horses and cattle, and with very many free gifts. King Cyrus also brought forth the holy vessels which Nabuchodonosor had carried away from Jerusalem and had set up in his temple of idols. The vessels of gold and of silver which were brought back by Sanabassar, together with them of the captivity from Babylon to Jerusalem, were, in number, five thousand four hundred three score and nine.

But in the time of Artaxerxes, the building of the Temple ceased. Now, when Darius reigned, he made a great feast unto all the governors and captains that were under him from India unto Ethiopia, of an hundred and twenty-seven provinces. And when they had eaten and drunken, three young men that were of the guard that kept the king's body strove to excel each other in |wise speeches. Every one wrote his sentence and referred the writings to the judgment of the king. The first declareth the strength of wine; the second declareth the power of a king; the third the force of women and of truth. The third, who was Zorobabel, was judged to be wisest; and all the people then shouted: Great is Truth, and mighty above all things.

Then said the king unto him: Ask what thou wilt, and we will give it to thee, because thou art found wisest. Then Zorobabel said unto the king: Remember thy vow which thou hast vowed to build Jerusalem in the day when thou camest into thy kingdom, and to build up the Temple, which the Edomites burned when Judea was made desolate by the Chaldees.

Then Darius the king stood up and kissed him, and wrote letters for him unto all the treasurers and governors that they should safely convey on their way both him and all those that went with him to build Jerusalem. He also wrote letters unto the lieutenants in Celosyria, Phenice, and Libanus, that they should bring cedar wood from Libanus to Jerusalem; and that they should build the city. Then the families and tribes with their men-servants and maid-servants and singing men and women, escorted by a thousand horsemen which Darius sent with them, were brought back to Jerusalem.

On the first day of the second month, in the second year after they were come back to Jerusalem, the foundation of the House of God was laid; and the Temple was finished in the three and twentieth day of the month of Adar, in the sixth year of Darius, and dedicated with a great feast and sacrifices.

After these things, when Artaxerxes, the King of the Persians, reigned, came Esdras of the family of Aaron, the chief priest, from Babylon, and with him certain priests, Levites, holy singers and ministers of the Temple unto Jerusalem. He brought commission from the king to look into the affairs of Judea and Jerusalem, agreeably to that which is in the Law of the Lord, and giftsof vessels of gold and silver for the use of the Temple of the Lord.

Then Esdras made proclamation in all Jewry and Jerusalem to all them who were of the captivity, that they should be gathered together at Jerusalem. Three days after all the multitude gathered in the broad court of the Temple, and they gave their hands to put away their heathen wives and children, and to offer rams to make reconcilement for the errors they had committed. And Esdras stood up upon a pulpit of wood, which was made for that purpose, and opened the Law of Moses to the people.

So Esdras blessed the Lord God, most High, the God of Hosts, Almighty. And all the people answered: Amen; and, lifting up their hands, they fell to the ground and worshipped the Lord, saying: This day is holy unto the Lord; for they all wept when they heard the Law. So the Levites published all things to the people, saying: This day is holy to the Lord; be not sorrowful. Then went they their way every one to eat and drink, and make merry and to give to them that have nothing, and to make great cheer.

Second Esdras

The word of the Lord came unto the prophet Esdras, saying: Go thy way, and show my people their sinful deeds which they have done against me, for they have forgotten me, and have offered unto strange gods. I gathered you together, as a hen gathereth her chickens under her wings: But now I will cast you out from my face. Then Esdras willed to comfort Israel, but they refused, and despised the commandments of the Lord; therefore he announced that the heathen were called to the heavenly kingdom. After that, Esdras saw upon the Mount Sion a great people who praised the Lord with songs; and the angel said unto him: These be they thathave put off the mortal clothing, and put on the immortal, and have confessed the name of God. Now are they crowned, and receive palms in their hands from the Son of God in their midst.

In the thirtieth year after the ruin of the city, Esdras was in Babylon and troubled because of the desolation of Sion. He acknowledged to God the sins of the people, yet complained that the heathen who were lords over them were more wicked than they. Uriel, the angel, then said that when Adam transgressed God's statutes the way was made narrow, and the days few and evil; but, behold, the time shall come when my son Jesus shall be revealed and shall die, and all men that have life. And after seven days of silence, the earth shall restore those that are asleep, and the most High shall appear upon the seat of judgment; and misery shall pass away but judgment shall remain; truth shall stand; and faith wax strong.

Then Esdras said: I know the most High is called merciful, and he pardoneth; for if he did not so that they which have committed iniquities might be eased of them, the ten thousandth part of men should not remain living; there should be very few left, peradventure, in an innumerable multitude. And the angel answered: There be many created, but few shall be saved. Every one that shall be saved shall be able to escape by his works and by faith, and then they shall be shown great wonders. And it came to pass that a voice out of a bush called Esdras, which prophesied that God would take vengeance upon Egypt, Syria, Babylon, and Asia; that the servants of the Lord must look for troubles, and not hide their sins but depart from evil, and they would be delivered because God is their guide.

Tobit

This is the Book of Tobit, of the tribe of Nephthali, who in the time of Enemessar, King of the Assyrians, was led captive to Nineve. Tobit in captivity still remembered God with all his heart, and was deprived of his goods under King Sennacherib for privily burying fellow-captives who had been killed. Then Tobit, who became blind, remembered that he had in the days of his prosperity committed to Gabael in Rages of Media the sum of ten talents; and he called his son Tobias to go forth and seek Gabael, giving him handwriting. Tobias sought a guide and found Raphael, who was an angel though Tobias knew it not, and who said he knew and had lodged with Gabael. So they went forth both.

When Tobias and Raphael came to the River Tigris, a fish leaped out of the water and would have devoured him, but the young man laid hold of it, and drew it to land. The Angel bade Tobias open the fish, and take the heart and the liver and the gall, and put them up safely. The young man said to the Angel: To what use are these? And the Angel said: Touching the heart and the liver, if an evil spirit trouble any, we must make a smoke thereof, and the party shall be no more vexed. As for the gall: it is good to anoint a man that a whiteness in his eyes shall be healed.

When they came near to Rages, the Angel said: To-day we shall lodge with Raguel, who is thy cousin and hath an only daughter named Sara. The maid is fair and wise, and I will speak that she may be given thee as a wife. Then the young man answered the Angel, that he had heard that this maid had been given to seven men who all died in the marriage chamber, and he feared lest he should also die. But the Angel said: Fear not, for she is appointed unto thee from the beginning.

Now they came to the house of Raguel, and Sara met them and brought them therein. Raguel and Edna his wife recognised Tobias as a kinsman, and kissed and blessed him. Tobias and Raphael were entertained cheerfully; and after Raphael had communicated with Raguel, Edna, his wife, was called and an instrument of covenants of marriage between Sara and Tobias were written and sealed. And a chamber was prepared for them by Edna, who blessed Sara and asked the Lord of Heaven and Earth to give her joy. And when they had all supped, Tobias was brought in unto Sara. And, as he went he remembered the words of Raphael, and put the heart and liver of the fish upon the ashes of the perfume, and made a smoke therewith. When the evil spirit had smelled the smoke he fled into the utmost parts of Egypt, where an angel bound him. Then Tobias and Sara arose and prayed that God would have pity upon them, and bless them, and mercifully ordain that they might become aged together. So they slept both that night.

Raguel praised God because the Lord had had mercy upon two that were the only begotten children of their fathers, and prayed that they might finish their life in health and joy. Raphael then went to Rages to Gabael for the money, and the two returned to Raguel's house with the bags sealed up.

Now Tobit and his wife longed for their son, and Tobias said to Raguel: Let me go, for my father and mother look no more to see me. Then Raguel gave him Sara, his wife, and half his goods, servants, cattle and money. And he and Edna blessed them and sent them away.

After a prosperous journey, they drew near unto Nineve. Then Raphael told Tobias to make haste before his wife to prepare the house, and to take in his hand the gall of the fish. Now Anna sat looking about toward the way for her son, and when she espied him coming, she said to his father: Behold, thy son cometh and the man that went with him. And Anna ran forth, and fell upon the neck of her son and said: From henceforthI am content to die. Tobias met his father at the door, and strake of the gall on his father's eyes, saying: Be of good hope, my father. And Tobit recovered his sight. When he saw his son, he fell upon his neck and wept, and blessed God. Then Tobit went out to meet his daughter-in-law at the gate of Nineve, and welcomed and blessed her; and there was joy among all his brethren which were at Nineve.

Tobit offered to Raphael half of all that had been brought from Rages; but Raphael called him and Tobias apart and exhorted them to praise and magnify the Lord for all the things which he had done unto them; and told them that he, Raphael, was one of the seven holy angels which present the prayers of the saints, and which go in and out before the glory of the Holy One. Then they were both troubled and fell upon their faces; but he said: Fear not, for it shall go well with you. I go up to him that sent me; but write all the things which were done in a book. And when they arose they saw him no more.

Tobit wrote a prayer of rejoicing, saying: In the land of my captivity do I praise thee, O Lord, and declare thy might and majesty to a sinful nation. For Jerusalem shall be built up, her walls and towers and battlements restored. And all her streets shall say: Alleluia.

And when he was very aged, Tobit called his son and the six sons of his son, and bade them go into Media, for he was ready to depart out of this life, and he surely believed that which Jonas the prophet spake of Nineve, that it should be overthrown. When he had said these things he gave up the ghost. Tobias departed with his wife to Media, and died there; but before he died he heard of the destruction of Nineve, which was taken by Nabuchodonosor.

Judith

In the days of Arphaxad, which reigned over the Medes in Ecbatane, he fortified Ecbatane with great stone walls, and towers and gates, for the going forth of his mighty armies. Nabuchodonosor, who reigned in Nineve, made war with King Arphaxad, and sent ambassadors to Cilicia, Damascus and Syria, and the land of Moab and Ammon and Judea and all Egypt asking aid; but the inhabitants thereof made light of the commandment, and sent away his ambassadors with disgrace. Therefore, Nabuchodonosor was very angry, and sware by his throne that he would be avenged upon all the inhabitants of these countries, and would slay them with the sword. Nabuchodonosor, in the seventeenth year of his reign, marched in battle array against Arphaxad and overthrew his power and, all his horsemen and chariots, and took his cities even unto Ecbatane, and spoiled the streets thereof, and turned the beauty of the city into shame. He also took Arphaxad in the mountains of Ragau and smote him. So he returned to Nineve with all his company of sundry nations and feasted. In the eighteenth year, Nabuchodonosor called the chief captain of his army, Holofernes, and commanded him to take one hundred and twenty thousand footmen and twelve thousand horsemen and go against all the west country because they had disobeyed his commandment. He charged also Holofernes to spare none that would not yield, and put them to the slaughter, and spoil them. And the army went forth with a great number of allies like locusts into Cilicia, and destroyed Phud and Lud, and all the children of Rasses and Ishmael. Then the army went over Euphrates and went through Mesopotamia, and destroyed all the high cities on the river Arbonai to the sea, and then to Japheth over against Arabia, and Media and Damascus, and burned up their tabernacles, destroyed their flocks and herds, utterly wasted their countries, and smote all their young menwith the edge of the sword. Then fear fell upon the inhabitants of Tyrus and Sidon, on the sea coasts, who sent ambassadors unto Holofernes, and made submission. He received them, yet he cast down their frontiers, cut down their groves, destroyed all the gods of the land, and decreed that all the nations should worship Nabuchodonosor only, and call upon him as God.

Now, the children of Israel that dwelt in Judea, who were newly returned from captivity, were exceedingly afraid for Jerusalem and for the Temple of the Lord their God. Therefore, they possessed themselves of all tops of the high mountains, and fortified the villages, and laid up victuals for the provision of war. And Joacim and all the priests ministered unto the Lord in the Temple, and offered sacrifices and prayed that he would not give the children of Israel for a prey, their wives for a spoil, the cities of their inheritance to destruction, and the sanctuary to profanation.

Holofernes was very angry when he heard this. And Achior, captain of the sons of Ammon, told Holofernes what the Jews were, their history, and what their God had done for them; and advised Holofernes not to meddle with them. There was then tumult in the council of the Assyrian host, and Holofernes despised the God of the people of Israel, and sent Achior to the children of Israel that were in Bethulia, in the hill country. Then Holofernes with all his army besieged Bethulia, and took possession of the fountains of water, so that the inhabitants fainted for thirst, and there was no longer any strength in them. They murmured against the governors, and called upon them to deliver the city to Holofernes and his army. Ozias, the chief of the city, said: Brethren, be of good courage; let us yet endure five days, in which space the Lord our God may turn his mercy towards us; for he will not forsake us utterly.

Now Judith heard thereof. She was a widow and was of a goodly countenance and very beautiful to behold, and she feared God greatly. Judith sent for the ancients of the city, and blamed them for provoking the Lord to anger by their lack of trust, and she promised that she would do a thing within the days before the city was to be delivered to their enemies which should go throughout all generations to the children of the nation. Then Judith went to the House of the Lord and fell upon her face and called upon the Lord who breakest the battles to bless her purpose. She went thereafter to her house, put off the garments of widowhood and of sackcloth, and bathed, and anointed herself with precious ointment, and put on the garments of gladness, with bracelets and chains and rings and ornaments to lure the eyes of all the men that should see her. Then she went forth with her maid out of the city of Bethulia into the camp of the Assyrians, and was taken by the guard to the tent of Holofernes, who marvelled at her beauty. Holofernes asked Judith the cause of her coming, and she declared that if he would follow her words, he and his army would be led by her through the midst of Judea unto Jerusalem wherein he would set op his throne.

Holofernes and all his servants were pleased, and said there was not such a woman in all the earth for beauty of face and wisdom of words. Judith would not eat of the meats and wine which Holofernes offered her, but partook only of the provisions which her maid had brought with her in a bag. Then she was brought into a tent and abode in the camp three days, going out every night into the valley of Bethulia to pray. In the fourth day Holofernes made a feast, and said to Bagoas, the eunuch, to go and persuade the Hebrew woman to come and eat and drink with him and his officers. Judith arose and decked herself, and went in and sat on the ground on soft skins over against Holofernes, whose heart was ravished with her, and his mind moved, and he desired greatly her company.

Now Judith took and ate and drank what her maid had prepared, and Holofernes was greatly delighted with her, and drank much more wine than he had drunk at any time in one day since he was born. Judith, when the evening was come, was left alone with Holofernes, and the servants were dismissed. Then she came to the pillar of the bed, which was at Holofernes's head, took down his fauchion, seized hold of the hair of his head, and said: Strengthen me, O Lord God of Israel, this day. And she smote twice upon his neck with all her might, and took away his head from him.

She put the head in her bag of meat and gave it to her maid, and the twain went forth together, according to their custom, as unto prayer, and passed the camp. Then came they to Bethulia, and were admitted into the city; and the people were astonished wonderfully and worshipped God, and said: Blessed be thou, O our God, which hast this day brought to nought the enemies of thy people. The head of Holofernes was hanged up on the highest place of the city walls, and the men of Israel went forth by bands into the passes of the mountain. When the Assyrians saw this, they sent to Holofernes's tent, and said that the slaves of Israelites had come forth against them in battle. Then Bagoas went into the tent and found the body of Holofernes cast upon the ground and his head taken away. When also he found not Judith, he leaped out to the people and told them; and great fear and trembling fell upon them, and they fled, being chased until past Damascus and the borders thereof by the children of Israel, who gat many spoils. Then Judith sang a song of thanksgiving in all Israel, and the people sang after her. She dedicated the spoil of Holofernes, which the people had given her, for a gift unto the Lord; and when she died in Bethulia, a widow of great honour, all Israel did lament.

The Book of Esther

These are the chapters of the Book of Esther, which are found neither in the Hebrew nor in the Chaldee.

In the second year of the reign of Artaxerxes the Great, Mardocheus, who was a Jew and dwelt in the city of Susa, had a dream. And the same night he overheard two eunuchs plotting to lay hands on Artaxerxes, and he, being a servitor in the king's court, told the king; and the eunuchs, after examination, were strangled.

Aman, because of this, induced Artaxerxes to write to all the princes and governors from India unto Ethiopia to destroy all the Jews, with their wives and children, without pity, on the fourteenth day of the twelfth month of Adar. Mardocheus and Queen Esther, being in the fear of death, resorted unto the Lord, and prayed for deliverance, and for the preservation of the children of Israel. On the third day, Queen Esther cometh unto the king's presence; and she was ruddy through the perfection of her beauty, but her heart was in anguish for fear. The king looketh angrily at her as she stood before his royal throne, and she fainteth. Then God changed the spirit of the king, who leaped from his throne, took her in his arms, saying: Be of good cheer, thou shalt not die, though our commandment be general. As he was speaking, she fell a second time for faintness, and the king was troubled and all his servants comforted her.

Artaxerxes then wrote a letter to all the princes wherein he taxed Aman, the Macedonian, with having by manifold and cunning deceits sought the destruction of Mardocheus, who had saved the king's life, and also of the blameless Esther, partaker of his kingdom, with their whole nation. The king revoked the decree procured by Aman, who, with all his family, was hanged at the gates of Susa. And the king commanded the day of their deliverance to be kept holy.

The Wisdom of Solomon

Love righteousness, ye that be judges of the earth, for into a malicious soul wisdom shall not enter. The spirit of the Lord filleth the world: therefore he that speaketh unrighteous things cannot be hid. Seek not death in the error of your life: for God made not death, and righteousness is immortal. The ungodly reason, but not aright: life is short and tedious, which, being extinguished, our bodies shall be turned into ashes, and our spirit vanish as the soft air. Come, therefore, let us enjoy the good things that are present. Their own wickedness hath blinded them, for God created man to be immortal.

Nevertheless, through envy of the devil came death into the world. The souls of the righteous are in the hands of God, and there shall no torments touch them. Having been a little chastised they shall be greatly rewarded. Better to have no children and to have virtue; for children begotten of unlawful beds are witnesses against their parents. Honourable age is not measured by number of years. He, being made perfect in a short time, fulfilled a long time. For his soul pleased the Lord: Therefore, hasted he to take him away from among the wicked. This the people saw and understood it not, neither laid they up this in their minds. That his grace and mercy are with his saints, and that he hath respect unto his chosen. The wicked wonder at the godly, and say: What hath pride profited us? And what good hath riches, with our vaunting, brought us? All those things are passed away like a shadow. The hope of the ungodly is like dust that is blown away: but the righteous live for evermore: their reward is a beautiful crown from the Lord's hand. Wisdom is easily found of such as seek her, therefore princes must desire her; for a wise prince is the stay of his people. He that hath Wisdom hath every good thing. Moreover, by her means man shall obtain immortality, and leave behind him an everlasting memorial.

The Wisdom of Jesus the Son of Sirach; or Ecclesiasticus.

There are two prologues to this book. The first is by an uncertain author, stating that the book is the compilation of three hands and is in imitation of the Book of Solomon. The second prologue is by Jesus, the son of Sirach and grandchild to Jesus of the same name, who had read the law and the prophets and other books of the fathers, and had been drawn himself to write something pertaining to wisdom and learning. Coming into Egypt when Euergetes was king, Jesus, son of Sirach, found a book of no small learning and bestowed diligence and travail to interpret it, and to bring it to an end. The following are among the precepts given:

All wisdom cometh from the Lord: she is with all flesh according to his gift. The fear of the Lord is the beginning of wisdom, and driveth away sins. My son, if thou come to serve the Lord, prepare thy soul for temptation. Set thy heart aright, and constantly endure. Woe be to fearful hearts; but they that fear the Lord shall be filled with the law. Whoso honoureth his father maketh an atonement for his sins. He that honoureth his mother layeth up treasure. Seek not out the things that are too hard for thee: profess not the knowledge that thou hast not. Defraud not the poor of his living: and be not fainthearted when thou sittest in judgment. Set not thy heart upon thy goods, for the Lord will surely revenge thy pride. Winnow not with every wind, and let thy life be sincere. Do not extol thy own conceit: if thou wouldst get a friend, prove him first. A faithful friend is a strong defence. Seek not of the Lord preeminence: humble thy soul greatly. Fear the Lord, and reverence his priests. Stretch thine hand unto the poor, and mourn with them that mourn. Strive not with a mighty man: kindle not the coals of a sinner. Lend not untohim that is mightier than thyself: be not surety above thy power. Go not to law with a judge: consult not with a fool. Judge none blessed before his death. He that toucheth pitch shall be denied therewith: like will to like. Say not thou: it is through the Lord that I fell away: He has caused me to err. The Lord made man from the beginning and left him in the hand of his counsel. He has commanded no man to do wickedly, neither has he given any man licence to sin. The knowledge of wickedness is not wisdom: neither at any time the counsel of sinners prudence. Whoso discovereth secrets loseth his credit and shall never find friend to his mind. Health and good estate of body are above all gold. There is no joy above the joy of the heart. Give not over thy mind to heaviness: the joyfulness of a man prolongeth his days. Envy and wrath shorten life: carefulness bringeth age before the time.

[Then follow praises of a good householder, a good physician, a wise interpreter of the law, and injunctions as to how a man should bear the miseries of life, and face the approach of death. And the book concludes with praises of the Patriarchs and the Prophets.

Baruch

Baruch, the son of Nerias, wrote a book in Babylon what time the Chaldeans took Jerusalem and burnt it with fire. Baruch read the words of his book in the hearing of Jechonias, the son of the King of Juda, and in the ears of all the people. The Jews wept at the reading of it, by the river Sud, and made a collection of money to send to Jerusalem, unto the High Priest Joachim, to buy burnt offerings and sin offerings and incense, and to prepare manna to be offered upon the altar of the Lord. The people at Jerusalem are asked also to pray for the life of Nabuchodonosor, King of Babylon, and his son Balthasar, and for those who sent the gifts and the book. The book begins with a prayer and confession which the Jews at Babylon make, acknowledging that they are yet this day in captivity for a reproach and a curse, and to be subject to payments according to all the iniquities of their fathers which departed from the Lord our God. Then beginneth the book:

Hear, Israel, the commandments of life: give ear to understand wisdom. Let them that dwell about Sion come, and remember the captivity of my sons and daughters, which the Everlasting hath brought upon them. Be of good cheer, O my children, crying unto the Lord, and He shall deliver you from the power and hand of the enemies. I sent you out with mourning and weeping: but God will give you to me again with joy and gladness for ever. Put off, O Jerusalem, the garment of thy mourning and affliction, and put on the comeliness of the glory that cometh from God for ever; for behold, thy children gathereth from the west and from the east and return out of captivity with glory.

[With this book of Baruch there is an Epistle of Jeremy, which he sent unto them that were to be led captive into Babylon because of their sins. The prophet describes the idols and the conduct of the priests and those who attend the heathen temples and warns the captives not to worship the false gods in Babylon.

Song of the Three Holy Children

[This Song is not in the Hebrew of the Book of Daniel.]

They walked in the midst of the fire praising God and blessing the Lord. Azarias opened his mouth in the midst of the flame and made confession of sins, and prayer for deliverance to the confusion of their enemies. Whereupon, the king's servants that put them in ceased not to make the oven hot with rosin, pitch, tow, and small wood, so that the flame passed through and burned those Chaldeans it found about the furnace. But the Angel of the Lord came down into the oven and made the midst of the furnace as it had been a moist whistling wind, so that the fire touched Azarias and his fellows not at all, neither hurt nor troubled them. Then the three, as out of one mouth, praised, glorified, and blessed God in the furnace, saying: The Lord hath delivered us from hell, and saved us from the hand of death: for his mercy endureth for ever.

The History of Susanna

There dwelt a man in Babylon called Joacim. And he took a wife whose name was Susanna, a very fair woman, and one that feared the Lord. The same year were appointed two of the ancients of the people to be judges; and they saw Susanna walking in her husband's garden, and their lust was inflamed towards her. Now, Susanna went into the garden to bathe, for it was hot, and dismissed her maids. The two elders, who had hidden in the garden, rose up and said: Consent and lie with us. If thou wilt not, we will bear witness against thee that a young man was with thee, and therefore thou didst send thy maids away. Then Susanna cried with a loud voice, and the two elders cried out against her, and declared their matter. The servants rushed in at the privy door and were greatly ashamed, for there was never such a report made of Susanna. It came to pass the next day when the people were assembled to her husband Joacim, with the two elders full of mischievous imagination against Susanna, these wicked men commanded Susanna to uncover her face that they might be filled with her beauty, and her friends and all that saw her wept. Then the elders made their charge which they had agreed upon against Susanna, and the assembled people believed them: so they condemned her to death. Then Susanna cried to the Everlasting God, saying: Thou knowest that they have borne false witness against me, and that I never did such things as these men have maliciously invented against me. And the Lord heard her voice.

When she was led to be put to death, the Lord raised up the holy spirit of a youth named Daniel, who said: Are ye such fools, ye sons of Israel, that without examination or knowledge of the truth ye have condemned a daughter of Israel? Then Daniel put the two elders aside, one far from the other, to examine them. To the first he said: If thou hast seen her, under what tree sawest thou them companying together? He answered: Under a mastic tree. Daniel said: Very well; and he put him aside and commanded the other to be brought. Tell me, he said, under what tree didst thou take them companying together? He answered: Under an holm tree. Then Daniel said: These men have lied against their own heads, for even now the Angel of God waiteth with the sword that he may destroy them. Then all the assembly arose against the two elders, for Daniel had convicted them of false witness by their own mouth; and they put them to death. Thus the innocent blood was saved the same day; and from that time forth was Daniel had in great reputation in the sight of the people.

The History of the Destruction of Bel and the Dragon

When Cyrus of Persia received his kingdom, Daniel conversed with him, and was honoured above all his friends. Now, the Babylonians had an idol called Bel, which the king worshipped, but Daniel worshipped his own God. The king said unto him: Why dost thou not worship Bel? Daniel answered: Because I may not worship idols made with hands, but the living God. Then the king said: Thinkest thou not that Bel is a living god? Seest thou not how much he eateth and drinketh every day? Then Daniel smiled and said: O king, be not deceived; for this is but clay within and brass without, and it never eateth or drinketh anything. Then trial was made by order of the king, and meat and wine were set in the temple, the door made fast, and sealed with the king's signet. The priests of Bel were three score and ten, besides their wives and children, and they little regarded the trial, for under the table they had made a privy entrance, whereby they entered the temple continually and consumed the meat and the wine. But Daniel had commanded his servants to strew the temple floor with ashes, before the door was shut and sealed. Now, in the night came the priests with their wives and children, as they were wont, and did eat and drink up all.

In the morning betimes the king arose, and Daniel with him. As soon as the door was opened, the king looked upon the table, and cried with a loud voice: Great art thou, O Bel, and with thee is no deceit at all. Then laughed Daniel, and said: Behold the pavement, and mark well whose footsteps are these. And the king saw the footsteps of men, women, and children, and was angry when he was shown the privy doors where they came in and consumed such things as were upon the table. Therefore the king slew them, and delivered Bel into Daniel's power, who destroyed the idol and the temple.

In the same place there was a great dragon, which they of Babylon worshipped. The king said to Daniel: Lo! this dragon liveth, eateth, drinketh; thou canst not say that he is no living god; therefore worship him. Then said Daniel: I will worship the Lord, for he is the living God. But give me leave, O king, and I shall slay this dragon without sword or staff.

The king gave him leave, and Daniel took pitch, and fat, and hair, and did seethe them together, and made lumps thereof. These he put in the dragon's mouth ,and the dragon burst in sunder. Then Daniel said: Lo, these are the gods ye worship!

When they of Babylon heard that, they conspired against the king, saying: The king is become a Jew. So they came to the king, and said: Deliver us Daniel, or else we will destroy thee and thine house. Being sore constrained, the king delivered Daniel unto them, and they cast him into the lions' den, where he was six days, during which the seven lions were given no carcases, to the intent that they might devour Daniel.

Now, there was in Jewry a prophet called Habakkuk who made pottage and broken bread to take to the reapers in the field. An Angel of the Lord said unto Habakkuk: Go, carry the dinner that thou hast into Babylon unto Daniel, who is in the lions' den. And Habakkuk said: Lord, I never saw Babylon; neither do I know where the den is. Then the Angel of the Lord took Habakkuk by the crown, and bare him by the hair of his head, and through the vehemency of his spirit set him in Babylon over the den. And Habakkuk cried: O Daniel, take the dinner which God has sent thee. And Daniel said: Thou hast remembered me, O God: neither hast thou forsaken them that seek thee and love thee. So Daniel arose, and did eat: And the Angel of the Lord set Habakkuk in his own place immediately. Upon the seventh day the king went to bewail Daniel; and when he came to the den, behold, Daniel was sitting. Then cried the king with a loud voice, saying: Great art thou, O Lord God of Daniel, and there is none other besides thee. And he drew Daniel out, and cast those that were the cause of his suffering into the den; and they were devoured by the lions in a moment before his face.

The Prayer of Manasses

The Prayer of Manasses, King of Juda, when he was holden captive in Babylon, is an enumeration of the attributes of the Almighty God of Abraham, Isaac, and Jacob, and of their righteous seed; a general confession of sins; and an entreaty that God would show him great mercy and goodness, forgive him, and condemn him not into the lower parts of the earth. Therefore, he would praise the Lord for ever, all the days of his life.

The First Book of the Maccabees

Antiochus, surnamed Epiphanes, reigned in the hundred and thirty-seventh year of the kingdom of the Greeks. In those days certain wicked men of Israel went to the king, who gave them licence to do after the ordinances of the heathen. Whereupon, they built a place of exercise at Jerusalem according to the custom of the heathen. Now, Antiochus made war against Egypt, and when he had smitten the strong cities, and taken the spoils thereof, he returned in the hundred forty and third year and went up against Israel and Jerusalem, and captured the city with great massacre and spoiled the Temple, and took away the vessels of gold and silver and hidden treasures which he found therein. Therefore, there was great mourning in Israel. Two years after, the king sent his chief collector of tribute unto the cities of Juda, and he fell suddenly upon Jerusalem, set fire to it, and pulled down the houses and walls thereof. And the women and children he took away captive, and defiled the sanctuary.

But the enemy builded the city of David, with a great and strong wall and mighty towers, and stored it with armour and victuals and the spoils of Jerusalem, so that it became a sore snare against the sanctuary and an evil adversary to Israel. Moreover, King Antiochus wrote to his whole kingdom that all should be one people, and sent letters unto Jerusalem and the cities of Juda commanding that the Israelites should abandon their own worship, cease to circumcise their children, and adore his idols. Then was the abomination of desolation set up in the Temple, and idol altars were builded throughout the cities of Juda, and the books of the law were burned. Howbeit many in Israel chose rather to die that they might not be defiled with meats and profane the Holy Covenant. In those days arose Mattathias, a priest of the sons of Joarib. He dwelt in Modin, and had five sons--Joannan, Simon, Judas who was called Maccabeus, Eleazar, and Jonathan. The king's officers came to Modin and asked Mattathias to fulfil the king's commandment; but Mattathias said: Though all the nations consent, yet will I and my sons walk in the covenant of our fathers. And he slew a Jew that did sacrifice to idols in his presence, and the king's messenger also. So he and his sons fled into the mountains, and, being joined by a company of mighty men of Israel, went round about, and pulled down idol altars and circumcised the children valiantly. And the work prospered in their hands, and they recovered the law out of the hands of the Gentiles. When Mattathias came to die he appointed Simon as a man of counsel, and Judas Maccabeus, who had been mighty and strong in battle even from his youth up, to be their captain to avenge the wrongs of their people. So he died in his hundred forty and sixth year, and was buried in the sepulchre of his fathers at Modin, and all Israel made great lamentation for him.

Now, Judas Maccabeus fought the battles of his people with great valiance, captured the cities of Juda, drove Apollonius and a great host out of Samaria, slew Apollonius, took their spoils, and Apollonius's sword also, and therewith he fought all his life long. Judas also overthrew Seron and the great army of Syria. Then Judas was renowned unto the utmost parts of the earth, and an exceeding great dread fell upon the nations round about. Now, when King Antiochus heard these things he was full of indignation; wherefore he sent and gathered together all the forces of his realm. And the king sent Lysias, one of the blood royal, with a great army to go into the land of Juda and destroy it. Judas and his brethren, when he heard this, assembled the Israelites at Maspha, over against Jerusalem, where they fasted; and Judas organised and armed them to battle, and camped at Emmaus. Gorgias, the lieutenant of Lysias, attempted to surprise Judas, but Judas joined him in battle and discomfited him, putting his host to flight and gaining great spoil. Next year Lysias gathered another army, that he might subdue the Israelites, and came into Idumea, and pitched tents at Bethsura. But Judas joined him in battle, and put Lysias and his army to flight. After this, Judas and his brethren came to Jerusalem, pulled down the altar which the heathen had profaned, and set up a new altar. He also builded up Mount Sion with strong towers and high walls. After that Judas smote the children of Esau, Bean, and Ammon, and sent Simon into Galilee, while he, with his brother Jonathan, went over Jordan, and captured the cities of Galaad. About that time Antiochus was in Persia, and heard of the doings of Judas. He was astonished and sore moved, and fell sick of grief and died. Lysias set up Antiochus, his son, as king, and called him Eupator, and brought a great army into Juda. The number of his army was an hundred thousand footmen, twenty thousand horsemen, and two and thirty elephants. Judas went out from Jerusalem and pitched in Bathzacharias over against the king's camp. Then a great battle was fought, when Judas was defeated. There being a famine in the city, he made peace with Eupator,who, however, ordered the wall round about Sion to be pulled down.

Demetrius came from Rome and attacked Eupator in Antioch, captured the city, and slew Eupator and Lysias. Alsimus, who wished to be high priest, complained to Demetrius of Judas, and the king sent Nicanor, a man that bare deadly hate unto Israel, to destroy the people; but he was defeated by Judas at Capharsalama with great slaughter, and in a second battle Nicanor's host was discomfited and he himself was slain, and his head and right hand were hanged up on the tower at Jerusalem. This was a day of great gladness to Israel, and the victory was kept holy every year after.

Now, Judas, being informed of the power and policy of the Romans, made a league with them of mutual help. Notwithstanding, Demetrius sent Bacchides and Alcimus a second time into Judea with a great host, and camped at Berea. Now, Judas had pitched his tent at Eleasa, where, seeing the multitude of the other army to be so great, his men began to desert him, whereupon Judas said: God forbid that I should flee away from the enemy; if our time be come, let us die manfully for our brethren, and let us not stain our honour.

The armies came to battle, and the earth shook at the noise thereof, and the fight continued from morning to night. Judas discomfited the right wing of the enemy under Bacchides and pursued them to Mount Azotus, but the left wing followed upon Judas and a sore battle took place, insomuch that many were slain on both sides. Judas was killed also, and the rest of his army fled. The body of Judas was taken to the sepulchre of his fathers at Modin by Jonathan and Simon, his brothers, and all Israel made lamentation for him, and mourned many days, saying: How is the valiant man fallen that delivered Israel!

Jonathan took command of the Israelites in the room of Judas, and made peace with Bacchides. Thereafter, Demetrius made large offers to have peace with Jonathan ,including freedom of worship and release of tribute, together with the rebuilding of the walls of Jerusalem and the towers thereof, and the repairs of the sanctuary; but Jonathan and the people gave no credit to these words because they remembered the great evil Demetrius had done in Israel. Jonathan made peace with Alexander, and joined him in battle against Demetrius, whose host fled, and he himself was slain.

After that Demetrius the younger came out of Crete, and sent a great host to Azotus. Here Jonathan attacked him, and with the help of Simon, his brother, defeated the enemy and set fire to Azotus, and the temple of Dagon therein. There were burned and slain with the sword eight thousand men. Now, King Alexander honoured Jonathan and sent him a buckle of gold such as is given to those of the king's blood. After these days, Jonathan did many wonderful exploits in Galilee and Damascus, and then returned to Jerusalem. Now, when Jonathan saw that the time served him, he renewed his league with the Romans and Lacedemonians, and pursued the Arabians unto Damascus. He strengthened the cities of Juda, but he was captured by fraud by Tryphon at Ptolemais. Simon was made captain in his brother Jonathan's room, and prepared to attack Tryphon and, rescue his brother, but Tryphon slew Jonathan, and returned into his own country.

The land of Juda was quiet all the days of Simon, and every man sat under his own vine and fig-tree. When Simon was visiting the cities that were in the country, Ptolemeus, son of Abubus, the captain of Jerico, invited Simon and his two sons into his castle, called Docus. There a great banquet was given, at which Simon and his sons drank largely, and Ptolemeus and his men came into the banqueting place and slew them.

The Second Book of the Maccabees

The brethren, the Jews that were at Jerusalem and in the land of Judea, wrote a letter to the Jews that were throughout Egypt to thank God for the death of Antiochus. In his letter are recounted all the sayings of Jeremy, and the great deeds of Judas Maccabeus and his brother Simon, as recorded in the books of Jason, until Nicanor the blasphemer was killed, and his head hanged upon the tower at Jerusalem, from which time forth the Hebrews had the city in their power.

ST. AUGUSTINE

The City of God

A French critic has said of Augustine's "City of God" that it is the earliest serious attempt to write a philosophy of history, and another has spoken of it as the encyclopaedia of the fifth century. These two remarks together characterise the work excellently. It is a huge treatise in twenty-two books, begun in the year 413, and finished in 426, and was given to the public in sections as these were completed. Augustine (see LIVES AND LETTERS) himself explains the origin of the work. The fall of Rome by Alaric's invasion in 410 had been ascribed to the desertion of the old gods of Rome and to the wide extension of Christianity, or the City of God, throughout the empire. It was to refute this calumny that the learned African bishop elaborated his great defense of Christ's kingdom, the "Catholic Church, which should include all nations and speak in all tongues." In Books 1-5 St. Augustine shows that the catastrophe of Rome was not due to the neglect of the old mythological superstitions; and in Books 6-10 that the heathen cult was helpless for the life after death. Books 11-14 deal with the origin of the two cities, namely, of God and the World; Books 15-18 with their respective histories, and Books 19-22 with their respective ultimate destinies.

I.-The Origin of the Two Cities

I write, dear Marcellinus, of that most glorious City of God, both in her present pilgrimage and life by faith, and in that fixed and everlasting seat which she awaits in patience. I write to defend her against those who place their gods above her Founder--a great and arduous work, but God is my aid. I well know what power a writer needs who would show the proud how great is the virtue of humility. For the law of our King and Founder is this: "God is against the proud but gives grace to the humble"; but the swollen and insolent soul loves herein to usurp the divine Majesty, and itself "to spare the subject and subdue the proud." Wherefore Imay not pass over in silence that earthly city also, enslaved by its lust of empire.

For it is from this City of the World that those enemies have arisen, against whom we have to defend the City of God; Romans, spared by the barbarians on Christ's account, are haters of the name of Christ. The shrines of the martyrs and the basilicas of the apostles received, in the devastation of the city, not their own people only, but every fugitive; and the fury and greed of the invaders were quenched at these holy thresholds. Yet with thankless arrogance and impious frenzy these men, who took refuge under that Name in order that they might enjoy the light of fugitive years, perversely oppose it now, that they may languish in sempiternal gloom.

Never has it been known, in so many wars as are recorded from before the foundation of Rome to the present day, that an enemy, having reduced any city, should have spared those who had fled to the temples of their gods; not even the Romans themselves, whose moderation in victory has so often been justly praised, have respected the sanctuary of vanquished deities. The devastation and massacre and pillage and conflagrations of the sack of Rome were nothing new. But this one thing was new and unheard of--these savages became suddenly so mild as to set apart spacious basilicas and to fill them with people on whom they had mercy; no one might be killed therein nor any dragged from thence. Who does not see that this is due to the name of Christ and to a Christian age? Who can deny that these sanguinary hordes were bridled by Him Who had said: "I will visit their sins with the rod, but will not take my mercy from them"?

All natures, because they exist and therefore have their manner and species and a certain peace with themselves, are good; and when they are in the places belonging to the order of nature, they preserve the being which they have received.

The truest cause of the felicity of the good angels is to be found in this, that they adhere to Him Who supremely is; and the cause of the misery of bad angels lies in this, that they have turned away from Him Who supremely is, to themselves, who have not supreme being. This vice has no other name but pride, which is the beginning of every sin. They refused to preserve their strength for Him, and so threw away that in which all their greatness consisted. It is vain to seek for an efficient cause for the bad will; we have to do, not with anything efficient, but with a deficiency. The mere defection from that which supremely is to things which are on a lower grade of being is to begin to have a bad will.

Now God founded mankind, not as the angels, so that even did they sin they should not die; but in such a way that did they obey, they should enter, without death, on a blessed eternity; but, did they disobey, they should suffer the most just penalty, both of body and of soul. For though the human soul is truly said to be immortal, yet is there a sense in which it dies when God forsakes it.

Only because they had begun inwardly to be evil did the first of mankind fall into overt disobedience. A bad will had preceded the bad action, and of that bad will the beginning was pride, or the appetite for an inordinate rank. To lift oneself up is in itself to be cast down and to fall. Wherefore humility is most highly of all things commended in and to the City of God, and in Christ her King; but the contrary vice of arrogance especially rules her adversary, the devil, and this is unquestionably the great difference by which the two cities are divided, and the society of the pious from the society of the impious. Thus two loves have founded two cities, the love of Self extending to contempt of God has made the City of the World; the love of God extending to contempt of Self has made the Heavenly City.

II.--The Growth of the Cities

This whole universal time or age, in which the dying give way and the newborn succeed them, is the scene and history of those two cities which are our theme. The City of the World, which lasts not for ever, has its good here below, and rejoices in it with such joy as is possible. The objects of its desire are not otherwise than good, and itself is the best of the good things of earth. It desires an earthly peace for lower ends, makes wars to gain this peace, wins glorious victories, and when victory crowns a just cause, who shall not acclaim the wished-for peace? These things are good indeed, and unquestionably are the gifts of God. But if, neglecting the better things, which belong to the supernal city, they covet these lower ends as if there were none higher, misery must inevitably follow.

All men, indeed, desire peace; but while the society which does not live by faith seeks its peace in the temporal advantages of the present life, that which lives by faith awaits the promised blessings, and makes use of earthly and temporal things only as pilgrims do. The earthly city seeks its peace in a harmony of the wills of men with respect to the things of this life. And the heavenly city also, or, rather, that part of it which travels in this mortality, must use that earthly peace while mortality remains. Living a captive life in the midst of the earthly city, it does not hesitate to respect its laws. Since this mortality is common to both cities, there is a concord between them in the things that belong to it. Only, the heavenly city cannot have common laws of religion with the earthly city, but has been forced to dissent, and to suffer hatred and the storms of persecution.

Therefore, this heavenly city, a pilgrim upon earth, calls out citizens from all peoples and collects a pilgrim society of all tongues, careless what differences there may be in manners, laws and institutions by which earthly peace is achieved and maintained, destroying none of these, but rather serving and fulfilling them. Even the celestial city, therefore, uses the earthly peace, and uses it as a means to the heavenly peace; for that alone can be called the peace of a rational creature which consists in a harmonious society devoted to the enjoyment of God and one another in God.

As for that uncertainty with regard to everything, which characterises the New Academy, the City of God detests all such doubting as a form of madness, since she has the most certain knowledge of those things which she understands by mind and reason, however that knowledge may be limited by our corruptible body. She believes also the evidence of the senses, which the mind uses through the body, for he is miserably deceived who regards them as untrustworthy. She believes also the holy Scriptures, which we call canonical.

It is no matter to the City of God what dress the citizen wears, or what manner of life he follows, so long as it is not contrary to the Divine commands; so that she does not compel the philosophers, who become Christians, to change their habit or their means of life, which are no hindrance to religion, but only their false opinions. As for these three kinds of life, the contemplative, the active, and that which partakes of both qualities, although a man living in faith may adopt any of them, and therein reach eternal reward, yet the love of truth and the duties of charity alike must have their place. One may not so give himself to contemplation as to neglect the good of his neighbour, nor be so deeply immersed in action as to neglect the contemplation of God. In leisure we ought to delight, not in an empty inertia, but in the inquisition or discovery of truth, in such a way that each may make progress without envying the attainments of another. In action we ought to seek neither the honours of this life nor power, since all that is under the sun is vanity; but only the work itself, which our situation enables us to do, and to do it rightly and serviceably.

According to the definitions which Scipio used in Cicero's "Republic," there never really existed a Roman republic. For he briefly defines a republic as the estate of the people--"res publica" as "res populi," and defines the people as a multitudinous assemblage, united by consent to law and by community of advantage. So, then, where justice is not, there can be no people; and if no people, then no estate of the people, but only of a confused multitude unworthy of the name of a people. Where no justice is, there is no commonwealth. Now, justice is a virtue distributing unto everyone his due. Where, then, is the justice of the man who deserts the true God and gives himself over to unclean demons? Is this giving everyone his due?

But if we define a people in another way, and consider it as an assemblage of rational beings united by unanimity as to the objects of their love, then, in order to ascertain the character of a people, we must ascertain what things they love. Whatever it loves, so long as it is an assemblage of rational creatures and not a herd of cattle, and is agreed as to the objects of its love, it is truly a people, though so much the better as its concord lies in better things, and so much the worse as its concord lies in inferior things. According to this definition, then, the Roman people is indeed a people, and its estate is a commonwealth. But what things that people has loved in its earlier and later times, and how it fell into bloody seditions and into social and civil wars, breaking and corrupting that concord which is the health of a people--of these things history is witness. Yet I would not on that account deny it the name of a people, nor its estate the name of a republic, so long as there remains some assemblage of rational persons associated by unanimity with regard to the objects of love. But in general, whatever be the nation in question, whether Athens, Egypt, Babylon, or Rome, the city of the ungodly--refusing obedience to the commandment of God that no sacrifice should be offered but to Him alone--is without true justice.

For though there may be an apparent mastery of the soul over the body, and of reason over vices, yet if soul and reason do not serve God as He has commanded, they can have no true dominion over the body and its passions. How can the mind which is ignorant of the true God, and instead of obeying Him is prostituted to impure demons, be true mistress of the body and the vices? Nay, the very virtues which it appears to itself to possess, by which it rules the body and the vices in order that it may obtain and guard the objects which it desires, being undirected to God, are rather vices than virtues. For as that which makes flesh to live is not flesh but above it, so that which enables man to live in blessedness is not of man, but above him.

III.--The Destiny of the Just

Who is able to tell of the creation, with its beauty and utility, which God has set before the eyes of man, though here condemned to labour and sorrow? The innumerable loveliness of sky, earth and sea, the abundance and wonder of light, the sun, moon and stars, the shade of trees, the colours and fragrance of flowers, the multitude of birds of varied hue and song, the many forms of animals, of which the smallest are more wonderful than the greatest, the works of bees more amazing than the vast bodies of whales--who shall describe them?

What shall those rewards, then, be? What will God give them whom He has predestined to life, having given such great things to those whom He has predestined to death? What in that blessed life will He lavish upon those for whom He gave His Son to death? What will the state of man's spirit be when it has become wholly free from vice; yielding to none, enslaved by none, warring against none, but perfectly and wholly at peace with itself?

Who can say, or even imagine, what degrees of glory shall there be given to the degrees of merit? Yet we cannot doubt that there will be degrees; and that in that blessed city no one in lower place shall envy his superior; for no one will wish to be that which he has not received, though bound in closest concord with him who has received. Together with his reward, each shall have the gift of contentment, so as to desire no more than he has. There we shall rest and see, we shall see and love, we shall love and praise. For what other end have we, but to reach the kingdom of which there is no end?

RICHARD BAXTER

The Saints' Everlasting Rest

Richard Baxter, the Puritan author of one hundred and sixty-eight volumes, of which "The Saints Everlasting Rest" was, and is, the most popular, was born in 1615 during the reign of James I., and died in 1691, soon after the accession of William III. His lifetime, therefore, was coincident with the troubles of the Stuart House. For fifty years Baxter was one of the best known divines in England. Throughout, his was a moderating influence in politics, the Church, and theology. His best known pastorate, one of extraordinary success, was at Kidderminster, between his twenty-sixth and forty-fifth years, and there, in an interlude of ill-health of more than customary severity--for all his life he was ailing--he wrote, anticipatory of death, "The Saints Everlasting Rest." The book, which was dedicated to his "dearly beloved friends the inhabitants of the Borrough and Forreign of Kederminster," was published in 1650 and had an immediate and almost unparallelled success. Twenty thousand copies were sold in the year after publication, and various editions are now in circulation. The saintliness of this broad-minded divine's character emerges unsullied from an age of contentious bigotry.

I.--The Nature of Rest

"There remaineth therefore a rest to the people of God."
--Heb. iv, 9.

It was not only our interest in God and actual fruition of Him which was lost in Adam's covenant-breaking fall, but all spiritual knowledge of Him, and true disposition towards such a felicity. Man hath now a heart too suitable to his low estate--a low state, and a low spirit. And when the Son of God comes with tenders of a spiritual and eternal happiness and glory, He finds not faith in man to believe it; but, as the poor man would not believe that any one man had such a sum as a hundred pounds--it was so far above what he possessed--so no man will hardly now believe that there is such a happiness as once he had, much less as Christ hath now procured.

The Apostle bestows most of his epistle against this distemper, and clearly and largely proves that the rest of Sabbaths and Canaan should teach men to look for further rest, which indeed is their happiness. What more welcome to men under personal afflictions, tiring duty, successions of sufferings, than rest? What more welcome news to men under public calamities, unpleasing employment, plundering losses, sad tidings, than this of rest?

Now let us see what this rest is. Though the sense of the text includes in the word "rest" all that ease and safety which a soul hath with Christ in *this life*--the rest of grace--yet because it chiefly intends the rest of eternal glory I shall confine my discourse to this last.

Rest is the end and perfection of motion. The saints' rest, here in question, is *the most happy estate of a Christian having obtained the end of his course.*

May we show what this rest containeth. Alas! how little know I of that whereof I am about to speak. Shall I speak before I know? If I stay till I clearly know I shall not come again to speak. Therefore will I speak that little which I do know of it rather than be wholly silent.

There is contained in this rest a cessation from motion or action. When we have obtained the haven we have done with sailing; when we are at our journey's end we have done with the way. There shall be no more prayer because no more necessity, but the full enjoyment of what we prayed for. Neither shall we need to fast and weep and watch any more, being out of the reach of sin and temptations. Nor will there be use for instructions and exhortations; preaching is done; the ministry of man ceaseth; sacraments useless; the labourer called in because the harvest is gathered, the tares burned, the work done.

This rest containeth a perfect freedom from all the evils that accompany us through our course, and which necessarily follow our absence from the chief good. Doubtless there is not such a thing as grief and sorrow known there; nor is there such a thing as a pale face, a languid body, feeble joints, unable infancy, decrepit age, peccant humours, dolorous sickness, griping fears, consuming care, nor whatsoever deserveth the name of evil. Indeed, a gale of groans and sighs, a stream of tears accompanied us to the very gates, and there bid us farewell for ever.

This rest containeth the highest degree of the saints' personal perfection, both of soul and body. This necessarily qualifies them to enjoy the glory and thoroughly to partake the sweetness of it. This is one thing that makes the saints' joy there so great. Here eye hath not seen, nor ear heard, nor heart conceived what God hath laid up for them that wait for Him; but there the eye and ear and heart are made capable, else how do they enjoy it? The more perfect the appetite the sweeter the food; the more musical the ear the more pleasant the melody; the more perfect the soul the more joyous those joys, and the more glorious to us is that glory.

This rest containeth, as the principal part, our nearest fruition of God, the chiefest good. And here, wonder not if I be at a loss. When I know so little of God, I cannot know how much it is to enjoy Him. When it is so little I know of mine own soul--either its quiddity or quality, while it is here in this tabernacle--how little must I needs know of the infinite majesty, or the state of this soul when it is advanced to that enjoyment. Nay, if I never saw that creature which contains not something unsearchable, nor the worm so small which afforded not matter for questions to puzzle the greatest philosopher that ever I met with, no wonder if mine eye fail when I look at God, my tongue fail me in speaking of Him, and my heart in conceiving. What strange conceivings hath a man born blind of the sun of its light;

or a man borndeaf of the nature of music; so do we want that sense by which God must be clearly known. But this we know, the chief good is for us to be near to God.

II.--How the Saints will be Employed

This rest containeth a sweet and constant action of all the powers of the soul and body in this fruition of God. It is not the rest of a stone which ceaseth from motion when it attains the centre. Whether the external senses, such as now we have, shall be continued and employed in this work is a great doubt. For some of them, it is usually acknowledged, they shall cease, because their being importeth their use, and their use implieth our state of imperfection--as there is no use for eating and drinking, so neither for taste. But do not all senses imply our imperfection? As the ore is cast into the fire a stone, but comes forth so pure a metal that it deserves another name, so far greater will the change of our body and senses be--even so great as now we cannot conceive. And, doubtless, as God advanceth our sense and enlargeth our capacity, so will He advance the happiness of those senses, and fill up with Himself all that capacity.

And if the body shall be thus employed, oh, how shall the soul be taken up! As the bodily senses have their proper aptitude and action, so doth the soul in its own action enjoy its own object--by knowing, by thinking, by remembering, by loving. This is the soul's enjoying.

Knowledge of itself is very desirable, even the knowledge of some evil, though not the evil itself. As far as a rational soul exceeds the sensitive, so far the delights of a philosopher in discovering the secrets of Nature, and knowing the mysteries of science, exceed the delights of the glutton, the drunkard, the unclean, and of all voluptuous sensualists whatsoever--so excellent is all truth. What, then, is their delight who know the God of truth! What would I not give so that all the uncertain, questionable principles in logic, natural philosophy, metaphysics, and medicine were but certain in themselves and to me, that my dull, obscure notions of them were but quick and clear. Oh, what then should I not either perform or part with to enjoy a clear and true apprehension of the most true God!

How noble a faculty of the soul is this understanding! It can compass the earth; it can measure the sun, moon, stars, and heaven; it can foreknow each eclipse to a minute many years before; yea, but the top of all its excellency is that it can know God, who is infinite, who made all these--a little here, and more, much more, hereafter. Oh, the wisdom and goodness of our blessed Lord! He hath created the understanding with a natural bias and inclination to truth as its object, and to the prime truth as its prime object; and lest we should turn aside to any creature, He hath kept this as His own divine prerogative, not communicable to any creature, namely, to *be* the prime truth.

And, doubtless, memory will not be idle or useless in this blessed work, if it be but by looking back to help the soul to value its enjoyment. Our knowledge will be enlarged, not diminished; therefore the knowledge of things past shall not be taken away. And what is that knowledge but a remembrance? Doubtless, from that height the saint can look behind him and before him; and to compare past with present things must needs raise in the blessed soul an unconceivable esteem and sense of its condition. To stand on that mount whence we can see the wilderness and Canaan both at once; to stand in heaven and look back on earth, and weigh them together in the balance of a comparing sense and judgment, how must it needs transport the soul and make it cry out: Have the gales of grace blown me into such a harbour! O, blessed way, and thrice blessed end!

And now if there be such a thing as indignation left how will it here let fly: O vile nature that resisted so much and so long such a blessing! Unworthy soul, is this the place thou camest so unwillingly towards? Was duty wearisome? Was the world too good to lose? Didst thou stick at leaving all, denying all, and suffering anything for this? Wast thou loth to die to come to this? O false heart, that had almost betrayed me and lost me this glory!

But oh, the full, the near, the sweet enjoyment is that of the affections--love and joy! It is near, for love is of the essence of the soul; love is the essence of God, for God is love. Oh, the high delights of this love! The content that the heart findeth in it! Surely love is both work and wages.

But, alas! my fearful heart scarce dares proceed. Methinks I hear the Almighty's voice saying to me, as to Job, "Who is this that darkeneth counsel by words without knowledge?" But pardon, O Lord, Thy servant's sin. I have not pried into unrevealed things, nor with audacious wits curiously searched into Thy counsels; but, indeed, I have dishonoured Thy Holiness, wronged Thine Excellency, disgraced Thy saints' glory by my own exceeding disproportionate pourtraying. I bewail that my conceivings fall so short, my apprehensions are so dull, my thoughts so mean, my affections so stupid, expressions so low, and unbeseeming such a glory. But I have only heard by the hearing of the ear. Oh, let Thy servant see Thee and possess these joys, and then I shall have more suitable conceivings, and shall give Thee fuller glory!

III.--How the Eternal Rest is Reached

Having thus opened to you a window towards the temple, and showed you a small glimpse of the back parts of that resemblance of the saints' rest which I had seen in the Gospel-glass, it follows that we proceed to view a little the adjuncts and blessed properties of this rest, and first consider the eminent antecedents, the great preparations, the notable introduction to this rest; for the porch of this temple is exceeding glorious, and the gate of it is called beautiful. And here offer themselves to our observation as the four corners of this porch the most glorious coming and appearing of the Son of God; His wonderful raising of our bodies from the dust, and uniting them again with the soul; His public and solemn proceedings in their judgment; His solemn celebration of their coronation, and His enthronising of them in their glory.

Well may the coming of Christ be reckoned into His people's glory and enumerated with those ingredients that compound this precious antidote of rest, for to this end it is intended, and to this end it is of apparent necessity. Alas, fellow Christians, what should we do if our Lord should not return? What a case are we here left in! It cannot be; never fear it, it cannot be. And O, fellow-Christians, what a day will that be when we, who have been kept prisoners by sin and the grave, shall be fetched out by the Lord Himself! It will not be such a coming as His first was--in meanness and poverty and contempt. He will not come, O careless world, to be slighted and neglected by you any more. To think and speak of that day with horror doth well beseem the impenitent sinner, but ill the believing saint. How full of joy was that blessed martyr Mr. Glover, with the discovery of Christ to his soul, after long doubting and waiting in sorrow, so that he cries out: "He is come! He is come!" If thou have but a dear friend returned, that hath been far and long absent, how do all run out to meet him with joy! "Oh," said the child, "My father is come!" Saith the wife, "My husband is come!" And shall not we, when we behold our Lord in His majesty returning, cry out: "He is come! He is come!"

The second stream that leadeth to Paradise is that great work of Jesus Christ in raising our bodies from the dust and uniting them again unto the soul. A wonderful effect of infinite power and love. "Yea, wonderful indeed," saith unbelief, "if it be true." "What," saith the Atheist and Sadducee, "shall all these scattered bones and dust become a man? A man drowned in the sea is eaten by fishes, and they by men again, and these men by worms. What is to become of the body of that first man? Shall it rise again?" Thou fool--for so Paul calls thee--dost thou dispute against the power of the Almighty? Wilt thou pose him with thy sophistry? Dost thou object difficulties to infinite strength? Thou blind mole, thou silly worm; thou little piece of creeping, breathing clay; thou dust, thou nothing, knowest thou who it is whose power thou dost question? If thou shouldst see Him, thou wouldst presently die. If He should come and dispute His cause with thee, couldst thou bear it? If thou shouldst hear His voice, couldst thou endure?

Come then, fellow-Christians, let us contentedly commit these carcasses to the dust, knowing that prison shall not long contain them. Let us lie down in peace and take our rest; it will not be an everlasting night or endless sleep. As sure as we awake in the morning when we have slept out the night, so sure shall we then awake. What if our carcasses become as vile as those of the beasts that perish, what if our bones are digged up and scattered about the pit brink, and worms consume our flesh, yet we know that our Redeemer liveth, and shall stand at the last on earth, and we shall see Him with these eyes.

The third part of this prologue to the saints' rest is the public and solemn process at their judgment. O terrible, O joyful day! Then shall the world behold the goodness and the severity of the Lord--on them who perish, severity; but to His chosen, goodness. Then, fellow-Christians, let the terror of that day be never so great, surely our Lord can mean no ill to us.

The fourth antecedent and highest step to the saints' advancement is their solemn coronation, enthronising and receiving into the kingdom. They that have been faithful unto death shall receive the crown of life, and according to the improvement of their talents here so shall their rule and dignity be enlarged.

IV.--Excellences of the Eternal Rest

A comfortable adjunct of this rest is the fellowship of the blessed saints and angels of God. Oh, when I look in the faces of the precious people of God, and believing, think of this day, what a refreshing thought is it! Shall we not there remember, think you, the pikes which we passed through here; our fellowship in duty and in sufferings; how oft our groans made as it were one sound, our conjunct tears but one stream, and our conjunct desires but one prayer. And now all our praises shall make up one melody, and all our churches one church; and all ourselves but one body; for we shall be one in Christ, even as He and the Father are one.

It is a question with some whether we shall know each other in heaven or no. Surely there shall no knowledge cease which we now have, but only that which implieth imperfection! And what imperfection can this imply? Nay, our present knowledge shall be increased beyond belief. It shall be done away, but as the light of candles and stars is done away by the rising of the sun, which is more properly a doing away of our ignorance than of our knowledge. Indeed, we shall not know each other after the flesh; nor by stature, voice, colour, complexion, visage, or outward shape, but by the image of Christ and spiritual relation, and former faithfulness in improving our talents we shall know and be known.

Again, a further excellence is this--it will be unto us a *seasonable* rest. When we have passed a long and tedious journey, and that through no small dangers, is not home then seasonable? When we have had a long and perilous war, and have lived in the midst of furious senemies, and have been forced to stand on a perpetual watch, and received from them many a wound, would not a peace with victory be now seasonable? Some are complaining under the pressure of the times--weary of their taxes, weary of their quarterings, weary of plunderings, weary of their fears and dangers, weary of their poverty and wants, and is not rest yet seasonable? Some of us languish under continual weakness, and groan under most grievous pains, weary of going, weary of sitting, weary of standing, weary of lying, weary of eating, weary of speaking, weary of waking, weary of our very friends, weary of ourselves. Oh, how oft hath this been mine own case--and is not rest yet seasonable?

A further excellence is that this is a *suitable* rest. Gold and earthly glory, temporal crowns and kingdoms could not make rest for saints. Such as their nature and desire such will be their rest.

It will, too, be absolutely *perfect and complete*--as there is no mixture of our corruption with our graces, so there will be no mixture of our sufferings with our solace. We shall know which was the right side and which the wrong. Then shall our understandings receive their light from the face of God, as the full moon from the open sun when there is no earth to interpose betwixt them. It is a perfect rest from perplexing doubts and fear, from all sense of God's displeasure, from all the temptations of Satan, the world, and the flesh. And it is an *eternal* rest. This is the crown of our crown. Mortality is the disgrace of all sublunary delights. But, O blessed eternity, where our lives are perplexed by no such thoughts, nor our joys interrupted by any such fears! Our first paradise in Eden had a way out, but none in again; but this eternal paradise hath a way in, but no way out again. The Lord heal our carnal hearts lest we enter not into His eternal rest because of our unbelief.

BOOK OF THE DEAD

This is probably the oldest religious book in the world. Properly speaking, indeed, it is no book at all, but rather a collection of hymns and litanies which have no more connection with each other than the Psalms. Like the Psalter, too, this so-called book has grown by degrees to the magnitude which it now usually assumes in European and other libraries--175 chapters of varying sizes. Its Egyptian name is "The Book of the Coming Forth by Day" (Renouf), or "The Coming Out of the Day" (Naville); the latter being probably more correct, "day" in this connection denoting man's life with its morning and evening. The hymns in this collection are supposed to be recited by the deceased person with whose body they were commonly buried, and by the recital of these and other sacred texts the departed was believed to be protected against injury in his journey to the underworld, and also to have secured for him a safe return in the form of a resurrection. It was Lepsius, the great German Egyptologist, who gave this compilation the name "Book of the Dead." Even this name, however, though more correct than any other, gives by no means an adequate account of that for which it stands. This, and other summaries of the sacred books of the East appearing in THE WORLD'S GREATEST BOOKS present in quite original ways the systems and philosophies of the great non-Christian religions.

Introductory

The Book of the Dead may be described as the soul's *vade mecum* in the journey from this world. It prescribes the forms the soul must have at command in order to ward off the dangers on the way to the underworld, during residence in the world, and on the journey back.

The ancient Egyptians considered this book as inspired by the gods, who caused their scribe, Thoth, to write it down. Every chapter is supposed to exist for the sake of persons who have died. Sometimes chapters had to be recited before the body was put down out of sight. Often a chapter, or more than one, was inscribed on the coffin, or sarcophagus, or mummy wrappings, this being thought a sure protection against foes of every kind.

This collection has been chiefly found written on papyrus in hieroglyphic or hieratic characters on coffins, mummies, sepulchral wrappings, statues, and on the walls of tombs. Complete copies have been found written on tombs of the time of the 26th Dynasty (about 800 B.C.).

There are many recensions, or editions, in the various libraries of Europe and also in the East, and no two of them are identical in the text. Lepsius translated from the Turin papyrus; Budge bases his translations on what is called the Theban recension. But in all the text is exceedingly corrupt, and translation is often no more than a guess. Owing to the number of proper names and technical terms which we have no means of understanding, it is often quite impossible to know the drift of large paragraphs, and even of whole chapters. Since many of the chapters were treated merely as having a magical efficacy either when recited or when inscribed on something buried with the body, it was of small consequence whether or not the words were understood. The bare recital or writing of names of gods, etc., had a magical efficacy according to the people who counted the Book of the Dead their sacred scriptures.

As regards date, the greater number of the hymns and prayers were recited by the people of Egypt on behalf of their deceased friends before the first dynasty had begun to reign. Birch says before 3000 B.C. The hymns and prayers were first of all preserved in the memory only, and their number was at an early time but small. They were written down when the priests had doubts with regard to the meaning of certain terms, and wished to hand them on unimpaired to posterity, being influenced by the belief that the words of this sacred book were, as such, magically potent. The oldest extant papyrus containing the Book of the Dead belongs to the 18th Dynasty, *i.e.*, about 1500 B.C.; but we do not come across a complete copy, with the chapters collected and set in order much as they are to-day, until the 26th Dynasty (about the 7th century B.C.). Previous to this the chapters seem to have been put together with no regard to order; probably they existed on different papyri, which were used as occasion required. Commonly they would be sold, and for that purpose stored up.

The translations which can be recommended to students are those by Renouf, with text and notes; Budge, with text and notes; and that by C.H.S. Davis, U.S.A. (based on Pièrre). All these editions include the vignettes, which are very helpful in understanding the text.

I.--The Scribe Ani Pleads with Osiris through Thoth for Admission to the Underworld and for a Safe Evit (Resurrection)

(Osiris) Ani the Scribe says: Praise be to thee, Osiris Bull [so he was often represented]. O Amentet [the lower world] the eternal king is here to put words into my mouth. I am Thoth, the great god in the sacred book, who fought for thee. I am one of the great gods that fought on behalf of Osiris. Ra, the sun-God, commanded me--Thoth--to do battle on the earth for the wronged Osiris, and I obeyed. I am among them moreover who wait over Osiris, now king of the underworld.

I am with Horus, son of Osiris, on the day when the great feast of Osiris is kept. I am the priest pouring forth libations at Tattu, I am the prophet in Abydos. I am here, O ye that bring perfected souls into the abode of Osiris, bring ye the perfected soul of (Osiris) the Scribe Ani, into the blissful home of Osiris. Let him see, hear, stand, and sit as ye do in the home of Osiris.

O ye who give cakes and ale to perfected souls, give yeat morn and at eve cakes and ale to the soul of Ani the Scribe.

O ye who open the way and prepare the paths to the abode of Osiris, open the way and prepare the path that the soul of (Osiris) Ani the Scribe may enter in confidence and come forth [on the resurrection] victoriously. May he not be turned back, may he enter and come forth; for he has been weighed in the scale and is "not lacking."

II.--The Prayer of Ani the Scribe

The chapter about coming forth by day and living after death.

Says (Osiris) Ani: O thou, only shining one of the moon; let me, departing from the crowd on earth, find entrance into the abode of shades. Open then for me the door to the underworld, and at length let me come back to earth and perform my part among men.

A chapter whereby the funeral statuettes (Shabti) may be made to work for a man in the underworld.

O thou statuette there! If in the underworld I shall be called upon to perform any tasks, be thou my representative and act for me--planting and sowing fields, watering the soil and carrying the sands of East and West.

A chapter concerning the piercing of the back of Apepi.

Tur, the overseer of the houses, says through his god Tmu: O thou wax one who takest thy victims captive and destroyest them, who preyest upon the weak and helpless, may I never be thy victim; may I never suffer collapse before thee. May the venom never enter my limbs, which are as those of the god Tmu. O let not the pains of death, which have reached thee; come upon me. I am the god Tmu, living in the foremost part of Tur [the sky]. I am the only one in the primordial water. I have many mysterious names, and provide myself a dwelling to endure millions of years. I was born of Tmu, and I am safe and sound.

About contending against fever with the shield of truth and good conduct.

Says (Osiris) Ani: I go forth against my foes endowed with the defence of truth and good conduct. I cross the heavens, and traverse the earth. Though a denizen of the underworld, I tread the earth like one alive, following in the footsteps of the blessed spirits. I have the gift of living a million years. I eat with my mouth and chew with my jaw, because I worship him who is master of the lower world.

III.--Nu Praises Ra (the Sun-God) for his Ability to go Down into the Grave and Return to Earth through the Magic Use of the Sacred Texts

About entering the underworld and coming forth therefrom.

Nu says: I cry aloud to thee, O Ra, thou guardian of the secret portals of Seb [the grave], which leads to where Ra in the underworld holds the balance which weighs every man's righteousness every day. I have burst the earth [returned to earth]; grant that I mayre main on to a good old age.

IV.--The Spirit of the Scribe Mesemneter Prays that Some Offended God may be Conciliated

About removing the anger of the god towards the departed one.

The scribe Mesemneter, chief deputy of Amon, says: Praise be to thee, O God, who makest the moments to glide by, who guardest the secrets of the life beyond that of the earth, and guidest me when I utter words. The god is angered against me. But let my faults be wasted away, and let the god of Right and Truth bear them upon me. Remove them wholly from me, O god of Right and Truth. Let the offended one be at peace with me. Remove the wall of separation from before us.

A hymn to Ra at his rising and setting.

(Osiris) the scribe says: Praise to thee, O Ra, when thou risest. Shine thou upon my face. Let me arise with thee into the heavens, and travel with thee in the boat wherein thou sailest on the clouds.

Thou passest in peace across the heavens, and art victorious over all thy foes.

Praise to thee who art Ra when thou risest, and Tmu when in beauty thou settest. The dwellers in the land of night come forth to see thee ascend the sky. I, too, would join the throng; O let me not be held back.

Hymn of praise to Osiris.

Praise be unto thee, Osiris, lord of eternity, who appearest in many guises, and whose attributes are glorious.

Thou lookest towards the underworld and causest the earth to shine as with gold.

The dead rise up to gaze on thy face; their hearts are at peace if they but look on thee.

V.--Litany to Osiris

Prayer. Praise to thee, O lord of the starry gods of Annu, more glorious than the gods hidden in Annu.

Answer (repeated after each prayer). Grant thou me a peaceful life, for I am truthful and just. I have uttered no falsehoods nor acted deceitfully.

Prayer. Praise to thee, O Ani; with thy long strides movest thou across the heavens.

Prayer. Praise to thee, O thou who art mighty in thy hour, great and mighty prince, lord and creator of eternity.

Prayer. Praise to those whose throne is Right and Truth, who hatest fraud and deceit.

Prayer. Praise to thee who bringest Hapi [the Nile]; in thy boat from his source.

Prayer. Praise to thee, O creator of the gods, thou king of the North and the South. O Osiris, the all-conquering one, ruler of the world, lord of the heavens.

VI.--Hymn of Praise to the Setting Sun

About the mystery of the underworld and about travelling through the underworld.

When he sets on the underworld the gods adore him. The great god Ra rises with two eyes [sun and moon]; all the seven gods (Kuas) welcome him in the evening into the underworld. They sing his praises, calling him Tmu. The deceased one says, "Praise be to thee, O Ra, praise be to thee, O Tmu. Thou hast risen and put on strength, and thou settest in glorious splendour into the underworld. Thou sailest in thy boat across the heavens, and thou establisheth the earth. East and West adore thee, bowing and doing homage to thee day and night."

VII.--About the Resurrection, or the Coming Backto Life (Day), of Departed Shades.

[This is one of the oldest (cir. B.C. 2700) and most remarkable chapters, though also one of the hardest to follow in its details. The vignettes reproduced in the editions of Davis, Renouf, and Budge help considerably in following the line of thought. An exact copy of this chapter has been found on the tomb of Horhotep.

The soul of the deceased encounters all manner of obstacles and opponents in the attempt to pass to the upper air, and he seeks constantly the help of Ra, etc., that he may be victorious].

Of the praises of entering the lower world and of coming out.

(Osiris) the scribe Ani says it is a good and profitable thing on earth for a man to recite this text, since all the words written herein shall come to pass.

I am Ra, who at my rising rule all things. I am the great self-made god.

I am yesterday and to-morrow. I gave the command, and a scene of strife among the gods arose [*i.e.*, the sun awakened all the forces of Nature into action]. What is this? It is Amentet, the underworld.

What is this? The horizon of my father Tmu [the setting sun]. All of my failings are now supplied, my sins cleansed as I pass through the two lakes which purify the offences which men offer the gods.

I advance on the path, descending to the realm of Osiris, passing through the gate Teser. O all ye who have passed this way in safety, let me grasp your hands and be brought to your abode.

O ye divine powers of Maert, the sworn foes of falsehood, may I come to you.

I am the great Cat [*i.e.*, Ra] himself, and therefore in his name which I bear, I can tread on all my enemies.O great Ra, who climbest the heavenly vaults and whosailest in thy boat across the firmament with undisputed authority, do thou save me from that austere god whose eyebrows are as menacing as the balance that weighs the deeds of men. Save me, I pray thee, from these guardians of the passages who will, if they-may, impede my progress. O Tmu, who livest in the august abode, god of gods, who thrivest upon damned souls, thou dog-faced, human-skinned one, devourer of shades, digester of human hearts, O fearful one, save me from the great soul-foe who gnaws and destroys shades of men.

O Chepera in thy bark, save me from the testing guardians into whose charge the glorious inviolate god has committed his foes; deliver thou me. May these never undo me, may I never fall helpless into the chambers of torture. O ye gods, in the presence of Osiris, reach, forth your arms, for I am one of the gods in your midst.

The (Osiris) Ani flies away like a hawk, he clucks like a goose, he is safe from destruction as the serpent Nehebkau. Avaunt, ye lions that obstruct my path. O Ra, thou ascending one, let me rise with thee, and have a triumphant arrival to my old earthly abode.

VIII.--A Litany Addressed to Thoth

The speech of Ammautef, the priest:

I have come to you, ye gods of heaven, earth, and the underworld, bringing with me Ani, the scribe, who has done no wrong against any gods, so that ye may protect him and give him good-speed to the underworld.

The speech of Ani himself:

Praise be to thee, O thou ruler of Amenta, Unneferu, who presides in Abydos. I have come to thee with a pure heart, free from sin. I have told no falsehoods nor acted deceitfully. Give thou me in the tomb the food I need for the journey, so let me have a safe entrance to the underworld and a sure exit.

The speech of the priest Samerif: I come to the gods residing at Restau. I have brought you (Osiris) Ani; grant him bread, water, and air, and also an abode in the Sechithotepu [Field of Peace].

The speech of Ani himself:

Praise be to Osiris, everlasting lord, and to the gods of Restau. I come to thee knowing thy goodwill and having learned those rites which thou requirest for entrance into the lower world. May I have a safe arrival, and find food in thy presence.

Litany to Thoth:

O thou who makest Osiris triumphant over his foes, make thou this scribe Nebenseri victorious over his foes.

O Thoth, make Ani triumphant over his enemies, etc., etc.

[If this chapter is recited over the deceased he shall come forth into the day and pass through the transformations which the departed one desires.]

IX.--A Magical Chapter

Chapter of the Crown of Triumph.

Thy father Tmu has made thee this beautiful crown as a magical charm so that thou mayest live for ever. Thy father Seb gives thee his inheritance. Osiris, the prince of Amenta, makes thee victorious over thy foes. Go thou as Horus, son of Isis and Osiris, and triumph ever on thy way to the underworld.

Yea (Osiris) Aufankh shall, through this recited text, live and triumph for ever and ever. Horus repeated these words four times, and his enemies fell headlong. And (Osiris) Aufankh has repeated these words four times, so let him be victorious.

This chapter is to be recited over a consecrated crown placed over the face of the deceased, and thou shalt cast incense into the flame on behalf of (Osiris) Aufankh, so securing triumph over all his foes. And food and drink shall in the underworld be reached him in the presence of Osiris its king.

Chapter about making the deceased remember his name in the underworld.

Nu triumphant, son of Amen-hotep, says: Let me remember my name in the great House below on the night when years are counted and months are reckoned up. If any god come to me, let me at once be able to utter his name and thus disarm him.

A chapter about not letting the heart of the deceased act against him in the underworld.

My heart, received from my mother, my heart, without which life on earth was not possible, rise then not up against me in the presence of the gods in the great day of judgment when human thoughts, words, and acts shall all be weighed in a balance.

These words are to be inscribed on a hard green, gold-coated scarab, which is to be inserted through the mouth into the bosom of the deceased.

Chapter about repelling the ass-eater.

Avaunt! serpent Hai, impure one, hater of Osiris. Get thee back, for Thoth has cut off thy head. Let alone the ass, that I may have clear skies when I cross to the underworld in the Neshmet boat. I am guiltless before the gods, and have wronged none. So avaunt! thou sun-beclouding one, and let me have a prosperous voyage.

Nu says: My seat, my throne, come ye to me, surround me, divine ones. I am a mummy-shaped person. O grant that I may become like the great god, successful, having seat and throne.

A chapter about coming forth by day from the underworld (i.e., the resurrection).

[One of the very oldest chapters in the Book of the Dead, as old at least as the first dynasty, say 4500 B.C. No chapter was regarded with greater reverence, or recited or copied with more confidence in its efficacy, probably because it is a summing up of the important chapters on the coming forth by day from the underworld. He who knows this chapter by heart is safe against danger in this world and in all other abodes.]

Nebseni, lord of reverence, says: I am yesterday and know to-morrow. I am able to be born again. Here is the invisible force which creates gods and gives food to denizens of the underworld. I go as a messenger to Osiris.

O goddess Aucherit, grant that I may come forth from the underworld to see Ra's blazing orb. O thou conductor of shades, let me have a fair path to the underworld and a sure arrival. May I be defended against all opposing powers. May the cycle of gods listen to me and grant my request.

BOOKS OF BRAHMANISM

Introductory

The religion of the ancient Persians and of the ancient Aryan Indians was at one time the same, and it is easy now to see the common basis of the beliefs and practices embodied in the Hindu Vedas and the Zend Avesta (see ZOROASTRIANISM), and their general resemblance. The religion of the ancient Aryan Indians has passed through three outstanding phases, designated by modern scholars: Vedism, or that taught by the Vedas; Brahmanism, based on the Brahmans, or ritual additions to the Vedas; and Hinduism (*q.v.*), the form which revived Brahmanism took after the expulsion of Buddhism. Though the latter is strictly an Indian religion, judged by its origin and characteristic features, it has for centuries almost ceased to exist in India proper. It will be found generally true that in Brahmanism there is, as compared with Vedism, an increase of the ritual, and a corresponding decrease of the moral element. The gods become more material, and the means of conciliating them ceremonial and magical. So also there is a growth in the power of the priesthood. One may compare this with the course of development among the Hebrews--the ritual and ceremonial bulking more and more, and the ethical receding, according to most modern scholars. It has to be remembered carefully, however, that the distinction between Vedism, Brahmanism, and Hinduism is more logical than actual. The seeds of Hinduism, even the doctrine of caste, may be traced in the Rig Veda, and a modern orthodox. Hindu will tell you that his principal scriptures are the Vedas, and that his creed and practice have their source in these scriptures. Brahmanism may be represented as a system of law and custom in the Laws of Manu; as a philosophy in the Upanishads; and as a mythology in the Ramayana and Mahabharata.

Mahabharata

The word "Mahabharata" means "The Great Bharata," the name of a well-known people in ancient India. The epic so called is a very long one, containing at least 220,000 lengthy lines. It is really an encyclopaedia of Hindu history, legend, mythology, and philosophy. Four-fifths of the poem consist of episodes, some of them very beautiful, as the tale of Nala and his wife Damayanti. These have no primary connection with the original, though they are worked in so deftly as to make the whole appear a splendid unity. For pathos, sublimity, and matchless language, no poem in the world exceeds this one.

It is arranged in eighteen books, all of which claim to have been composed by Vyasa--another name for the god Krishna--who is said also in the course of the epic to have composed the Vedas and the Puranas. This is, of course, mythology, and not literary history.

The historical nucleus underlying this poem is the conflict which raged in ancient India between two neighbouring tribes, the Kurus (or Kauravas) and the Pandavas. But this is worked up into another long tale into which and around which Brahman teachers and philosophers have woven a very network of religious, theosophic, and philosophic speculation. The tale is, in fact, made a vehicle for teaching Brahman ism as it existed in India in the first five centuries of our era, though much of the Mahabharata goes back to a thousand years or so B.C.

Outline of the Epic

The descendants of Bharata, the king of Hastinapura, about sixty miles north of Delhi, were divided into two branches, the Kauravas and the Pandavas, each of which occupied the territory which had come down to it by inheritance. They lived together in peace and prosperity, worshipping the gods, studying the Vedas, and spending much time in meditation about higher things. But there came a change for the worse. The Kauravas, not content with their own territory, looked with jealous eyes upon that of their kinsmen, the Pandavas. Soon their covetousness realised itself in action, for gathering their armed men together, they sprang suddenly upon the land of their neighbours, whom they disarmed previously by professions of friendship and goodwill The Pandavas were conquered and driven into a far country, where they wandered homelessly and yet filled with undying love for the old home of their fathers and with a resolve to regain at the first opportunity their ancestral territory.

With the help of as many princes and generals as they could win to their side they marched towards the land which they had lost, taking back by force what had been wrested from them by force. The two armies met face to face on the field of Kurukshetra (land of the Kurus), and the battle, which lasted eighteen days, was about to begin. The father and king of the Kauravas, called Dhritarashtra, aged and blind, felt that he could not stand to witness the bloody affray. He accordingly accepted the offer of Vyasa (Krishna), a relative of both the contending parties, to have the entire course of events described to him when all was over, one Sangara, being deputed to perform the task. The battle began and proceeded for ten long days when Bhrisma, the chief general of the Kauravas, fell.

At this point Sangara advanced to the old King Dhritarashtra to acquaint him with the course things had taken, and among the rest to recite to him a conversation which had taken place between Krishna and Arguna, the Pandavan prince and general. It is this dialogue which constitutes the Holy Song, known as the Bhagavad-Gita, or Krishna Song, the Krishna of this philosophic poem being, of course, the eighth avatara; or incarnation, of Vishnu.

The remaining books of the Mahabharata recount the subsequent incidents of the war, which, in all, lasted for eighteen days. The Kauravas were destroyed, the only survivors being the Pandavas and Krishna with his charioteer. The many dead that were left on the field were buried with the rites of religion, and amid many signs of touching affection and grief.

Bhrisma, leader of the Kauravas, instructs Yudhishthira on the duties of kings and other topics. The poem then ends.

The Bhagavad-Gita, or Holy Song of Brahmanism

This poem forms one of the finest episodes in the great Iliad of India, and, in fact, is hardly surpassed for profound thought, deep feeling, and exquisite phrasing, in the whole literature of India. Telang holds that the song is at least as old as the 4th century, and is inclined to regard it as an original part of the epic. According to most scholars, however, the "Divine Song" was added at a later period, and, in fact, in its present form it is scarcely older than 500 A.D. It is so thoroughly Brahmanicin its teaching that there can be little doubt but that this song was introduced in order to convey the teaching of Brahmanism prevalent at the time. The German scholar, Dr. Lorinser, has tried to prove that the author of this song had a knowledge of the New Testament and used it. The following passages are pointed out by him as dependent on New Testament passages.

BHAGAVAD-GITA

I am exceedingly dear to the
wise man; he also is dear
to me.

I am the way, supporter,
lord, witness, abode, refuge,
friend.

I never depart from him (the
true Yogis); he never departs
from me.

They who worship me with
true devotion, are in me
and I in them.

Be assured that he who worships
me perishes not.

I am the beginning and the
middle and the end of existent
things.

I will deliver thee from all
sin; do not grieve.

He who knows me as unborn
and without beginning, the
mighty Lord of the World,
he among mortals is undeluded,
he is delivered from
all sins.

What sacrifice, almsgiving, or
austerity is done without
faith is evil.

That man obtains the perfect
state who honours by his
proper work him from
whom all things have issued,
and by whom this All
was spread out.

NEW TESTAMENT

He that loveth Me shall be
loved of My Father, and I
will love him (John xiv.
21).

I am the way, the truth, and
the life (John xiv. 6) I am
the first and the last (Rev.
i. 17).

He that dwelleth in Me and I
in Him (John vi. 56).

I in them and thou in Me,
that they may be made perfect
in one (John xvii. 23).

Whosoever believeth in Him
shall not perish, but have
everlasting life (John iii.
16).

I am Alpha and Omega, the
beginning and ending (Rev.
i. 8).

Son, be of good cheer; thy
sins be forgiven thee (Matt.
ix. 2).

This is life eternal, that they
might know Thee, the only
true God, and Jesus Christ,
Whom Thou hast sent (John
xvii, 3).

Whatsover is not of faith is
sin (Rom. xiv. 23).

Whether therefore ye eat or
drink, or whatsoever ye do,
do all to the glory of God
(1 Cor. x. 31).

Outline of the Bhagavad-Gita

The blind old father of the Kauravas asked Sangara to tell him how the battle had gone. He replied that, just as the fighting began, Krishna, the Heaven-Born One, stationed his glorious chariot between the armies and entered into a long conversation, with Arguna, the prince-general of the Pandavas. Said Arguna, "My grief at seeing these kindred peoples at war is beyond bearing, and the omens are unfavourable. I long not for victory, but for peace and for the prosperity of all. Behold, in battle array grandfathers, fathers, sons, friends, and allies. We have resolved to commit a great sin, to slay our kindred and associates, and all for lust of wealth and power."

The Holy One (Krishna) said in reply, "Thou grievest for those who need no grief of thine; yet are thy words words of wisdom. The wise have no grief for dead or living; know thou, O Arguna, that the man who has knowledge of the Eternal and Absolute One will never more be born, nor will he know death. As one puts away an old used garment, putting on a new one, so the self in a man puts away the old body and assumes one that is new. He, the Everlasting One, is unchanging and inconceivable. Be not thou grieved and have no fear. If slain in the battle, thou shalt reach endless bliss in heaven. If victorious, thou shalt have happiness on the earth; get thee, therefore, honoured one, to the fight and have no care for pleasure or pain.

"Some obtain comfort from what the Vedas promise with reference to eternal bliss. But these very Vedas teach that a man should strive at self-mortification and advancement in virtue with no regard to any reward. The final good after which men are chiefly to aim is a state of supreme indifference and contempt."

"But," asked Arguna, "what, pray, is that state of equipoise of spirit which thou urgest?"

Said the Holy One, "There is a twofold law: that of Sankhyas, or intellectual devotion, and that of Yogis, or practical devotion. Men must strive after the highest knowledge, that of Brahma, and also seek after right conduct." "What," asked Arguna, "is the cause of sin?" To which the Holy One replied, "Love and hatred, for hatred is begotten of love, and ignorance of moral distinctions and of anger; from all this comes unreasonableness and resulting ruin. A man's knowledge carries always with it desire, as the fire smoke. The senses are great, the mind is greater, and the intellect still greater, but the greatest of all is the Eternal Essence, Brahma.

"Many," said the Holy One, "are my births, and I know them; many too, are thine, but thou knowest them not. I am born from age to age for the defence of the virtuous and the undoing of the wicked. He who believes in my divine birth and work has no second birth, but enters me and abides with me for ever. Know me as the creator of the cates, know me also as the Eternal one that creates nothing. Faith brings with it knowledge, and knowledge contentment. Without knowledge and faith the soul is lost."

Arguna asked, "How fares it with the man who is not able to suppress his lower instincts and to undergo the discipline of Yogis? Is he for this, to be undone for ever?"

"No," replied the Holy One, "neither in this world nor in the next is he lost. The virtuous man does not enter an evil state. He reaches that heaven provided for all the good, and is born thereafter with higher moral capacities, with which, and by means of the knowledge gained in his previous existence, he rises to greater perfection; so that after many births he reaches absolute perfection and is united for ever with Brahma. But learn thou my higher nature; what thou seest is my lower, for I am divine and human. All the world came forth from me, and I will at the last destroy it. Higher than I does not exist. I am taste, light, moon, sun; I am the mystic OM; I am the mystic seed from which all things grow. He that offers sacrifice to inferior gods goes after death to those gods, but they that worship me come to me."

"What," asked Arguna, "is Brahma, the supreme spirit, the supreme sacrifice?"

The Holy One answered, "He is the Supreme, the Indestructible One; I am the Supreme Sacrifice in my present body.

"Hear now, Son of Pritha," said the Holy One. "If thy heart be fixed on me, and thou seekest refuge in me, thou shalt know me fully, and I shall reveal to thee the perfect knowledge of God and man. There are countless myriads of men in this world, but few there are who seek after perfection, and fewer still there are who obtain it."

Other Parts of the Mahabharata

Though the husband die unhappy on account of his wife's ill-treatment and disobedience, yet if she consign herself to the flames after his death she is deserving of great praise. How much more should a woman be venerated who flings herself of her own accord into the flames after the death of a husband whom she has treated with affection and submission!

Let gifts be avoided; for receiving them is a sin. The silkworm dies of its riches.

It is not proper to rebuke or even blame wrong acts of gods or priests or seers; though no one is justified in following them in these acts.

Virtue is better than everlasting life; kingdom, sons, renown, and wealth all put together do not make up one-sixteenth part of the value of virtue.

The greatest sin that a king can commit is atoned for by sacrifices accompanied with large gifts [cows, etc.] to the priests.

SIR THOMAS BROWNE

Religio Medici

Sir Thomas Browne, English essayist, came of a Cheshire family, but was born in London on October 19, 1605. Educated at Oxford, where he graduated in 1626, he next studied medicine at the great universities of Montpelier, Padua, and Leyden, and in 1637 went to live at Norwich, where he remained until his death on October 19, 1682. He was happily married in 1641, and was knighted by Charles II. in 1671. Sir Thomas Browne is one of the greatest figures in English literary history. He had extraordinary learning, a magnificent style, a certain dry humour, and, above all, great power and nobility of mind. In his two most valued works, "Religio Medici," or "Religion of a Physician," published in 1643, and "Urn Burial," in 1658, he deals with the greatest of all themes, the mysteries of faith and of human destiny. The "Religio Medici," written about 1635, was not at first intended for publication; but the manuscript had been handed about and copied, and the appearance, in 1642, of private editions, forced the author to issue it himself.

I.--The Broad-Minded Christian

For my religion I dare, without usurpation, assume the honourable style of a Christian. Not that I merely owe this title to the font, my education, or the clime wherein I was born; but that having, in my riper years and confirmed judgment, seen and examined all, I find myself obliged, by the principles of grace and the law of mine own reason, to embrace no other name but this.

But, because the name of a Christian is become too general to express our faith--there being a geography of religion as well as lands--I am of that reformed new-cast religion, wherein I dislike nothing but the name: of the same belief our Saviour taught, the apostles disseminated, the fathers authorised, and the martyrs confirmed; but, by the sinister ends of princes, the ambition and avarice of prelates, and the fatal corruption of the times, so decayed, impaired, and fallen from its native beauty, that it required the careful and charitable hands of these times to restore it to its primitive integrity.

Yet do I not stand at sword's point with those who had rather promiscuously retain all than abridge any, and obstinately be what they are than what they have been. We have reformed from them, not against them, for there is between us one common name and appellation, one faith and necessary body of principles common to us both; and therefore I am not scrupulous to converse and live with them, to enter their churches in defect of ours, and either pray with them or for them.

I am naturally inclined to that which misguided zeal terms superstition; at my devotion I love to use the civility of my knee, my hat, my hand, with all those outward and sensible motions which may express or promote my invisible devotion. At the sight of a crucifix I can dispense with my hat, but scarce with the thought or memory of my Saviour. I could never hear the Ave-Mary bell without an oraison, or think it a sufficient warrant, because they erred in one circumstance, for me to err in all--that is, in silence and dumb contempt.

I could never divide myself from any man upon the difference of an opinion; I have no genius to disputes in religion. A man may be in as just possession of truth as of a city, and yet be forced to surrender; 'tis therefore far better to enjoy her with peace than to hazard her upon a battle. If, therefore, there rise any doubts in my way, I do forget them, or at least defer them, till my better settled judgment be able to resolve them. In philosophy, where truth seems double-faced, there is no man more paradoxical than myself; but in divinity I love to keep the road, and, though not in an implicit, yet an humble, faith follow the great wheel of the Church.

Heads that are disposed unto schism, and complexion allypropense to innovation, are naturally indisposed for a community, nor will be ever confined unto the order or economy of one body; and, therefore, when they separate from others, they knit but loosely among themselves; nor contented with a general breach or dichotomy with their church, do subdivide and mince themselves almost into atoms.

As for those wingy mysteries in divinity and airy subtleties in religion which have unhinged the brains of better heads, they have never stretched the membranes of mine. Methinks there be not impossibilities enough in religion for an active faith; I love to lose myself in a mystery, to pursue my reason to an *O altitudo!* I can answer all the objections of Satan and my rebellious reason with that odd resolution of Tertullian: "It is certain because it is impossible."

II.--The Divine Wisdom

In my solitary and retired imagination I remember I am not alone; and therefore forget not to contemplate Him and His attributes who is ever with me, especially those two mighty ones, His wisdom and eternity. With the one I recreate, with the other I confound, my understanding; for who can speak of eternity without a solecism, or think thereof without an ecstasy?

In this mass of Nature there is a set of things that carry in their front, though not in capital letters, yet in stenography and short characters, something of divinity; which, to wiser reasons, serve as luminaries in the abyss of knowledge, and to judicious beliefs as scales to mount the pinnacles of divinity.

That other attribute wherewith I recreate my devotion is His wisdom, in which I am happy; and for the contemplation of this only, do not repent me that I was bred in the way of study. The advantage I have of the vulgar, with the content and happiness I conceive therein,is an ample recompense for all my endeavours in what part of knowledge soever. Wisdom is His most beauteous attribute; no man can attain unto it; yet Solomon pleased God when he desired it. He is wise because He knows all things; and He knows all things because He made them all; but His greatest knowledge is in comprehending that He made not--that is, Himself. The wisdom of God receives small honour from those heads that rudely stare about, and with a gross rusticity admire His works. Those highly magnify Him whose judicious inquiry into His acts, and a deliberate research into His creatures, return the duty of a devout and learned admiration. Every essence, created or uncreated, hath its final cause and some positive end both of its essence and operation. This is the cause I grope after in the works of Nature; on this hangs the providence of God.

That Nature does nothing in vain is the only indisputable axiom in philosophy. There are no grotesques in Nature, nor anything framed to fill up unnecessary spaces. I could never content my contemplation with those general pieces of wonder, the flux and reflux of the sea, the increase of the Nile, the conversion of the needle to the north; but have studied to match and parallel those in the more obvious and neglected pieces of Nature which, without further travel, I find in the cosmography of myself. We carry with us the wonders we seek without us; there is all Africa and her prodigies in us.

Thus there are two books from whence I collect my divinity: besides that written one of God, another of His servant, Nature, that universal and public manuscript, that lies expansed unto the eyes of all. Surely the heathens knew better how to join and read these mystical letters than we Christians, who cast a more careless eye on these common hieroglyphics, and disdain to suck divinity from the flowers of Nature. Now, Nature is not at variance with art, nor art with Nature, they being both the servants of His providence. Art is the perfection of Nature. Nature hath made one world, and art another. In brief, all things are artificial, for Nature is the art of God.

This is the ordinary and open way of His providence, which art and industry have in good part discovered, whose effects we may foretell without an oracle. But there is another way, full of meanders and labyrinths, and that is a more particular and obscure method of His providence, directing the operations of individual and single essences. This we call fortune, that serpentine and crooked line whereby He draws those actions His wisdom intends in a more unknown and secret way.

This cryptic and involved method of His providence have I ever admired; nor can I relate the history of my life, the occurrences of my days, the escapes, or dangers, and hits of chance, with a bare grammercy to my good stars. Surely there are in every man's life certain rubs, doublings, and wrenches, which pass a while under the effects of chance; but at the last, well examined, prove the mere hand of God. 'Twas not dumb chance that, to discover the fougade, or powder plot, contrived a miscarriage in the letter. I like the victory of '88 the better for that one occurrence which our enemies imputed to our dishonour and the partiality of fortune: to wit, the tempests and contrariety of winds.

There is no liberty for causes to operate in a loose and straggling way, nor any effect whatever but hath its warrant from some universal or superior cause. 'Tis not a ridiculous devotion to say a prayer before a game at tables; for even in sortileges and matters of greatest uncertainty there is a settled and pre-ordered course of effects. It is we that are blind, not fortune. Because our eye is too dim to discover the mystery of her effects, we foolishly paint her blind, and hoodwink theprovidence of the Almighty.

'Tis, I confess, the common fate of men of singular gifts of mind to be destitute of those of fortune; which doth not any way deject the spirit of wiser judgments, who thoroughly understand the justice of this proceeding; and, being enriched with higher donatives, cast a more careless eye on these vulgar parts of felicity. It is a most unjust ambition to desire to engross the mercies of the Almighty.

I have heard some with deep sighs lament the lost lines of Cicero; others with as many groans deplore the combustion of the library of Alexandria; for my own part, I think there be too many in the world, and could with patience behold the urn and ashes of the Vatican, could I, with a few others, recover the perished leaves of Solomon. Some men have written more than others have spoken. Of those three great inventions in Germany, there are two which are not without their incommodities. Tis not a melancholy wish of my own, but the desires of better heads, that there were a general synod--not to unite the incompatible difference of religion, but for the benefit of learning, to reduce it, as it lay at first, in a few and solid authors; and to condemn to the fire those swarms and millions of rhapsodies, begotten only to distract and abuse the weaker judgments of scholars and to maintain the trade and mystery of typographers.

As all that die in the war are not termed soldiers, so neither can I properly term all those that suffer in matters of religion, martyrs. There are many, questionless, canonised on earth that shall never be saints in heaven, and have their names in histories and martyrologies who, in the eyes of God, are not so perfect martyrs as was that wise heathen Socrates, that suffered on a fundamental point of religion-- the unity of God. The leaven and ferment of all, not only civil but religious actions,is wisdom; without which to commit ourselves to theflames is homicide, and, I fear, but to pass through one fire into another.

III.--The Hope of Immortality

I thank God I have not those strait ligaments or narrow obligations to the world as to dote on life or tremble at the name of death. Not that I am insensible of the horror thereof, or, by raking into the bowels of the deceased and continual sight of anatomies, I have forgot the apprehension of mortality; but that, marshalling all the horrors, I find not anything therein able to daunt the courage of a man, much less a well-resolved Christian. Were there not another life that I hope for, all the vanities of this world should not entreat a moment's breath from me. Those strange and mystical transmigrations that I have observed in silkworms turned my philosophy into divinity. There is in these works of Nature which seem to puzzle reason, something divine, that hath more in it than the eye of a common spectator doth discover.

Some, upon the courage of a fruitful issue, wherein, as in the truest chronicle, they seem to outlive themselves, can with greater patience away with death. This seems to me a mere fallacy, unworthy the desires of a man that can but conceive a thought of the next world; who, in a nobler ambition, should desire to live in his substance in heaven rather than his name and shadow in the earth. Were there any hopes to outlive vice, or a point to be superannuated from sin, it were worthy our knees to implore the days of Methuselah. But age doth not rectify but brings on incurable vices, and the number of our days doth but make our sins innumerable. There is but one comfort left, that though it be in the power of the weakest arm to take away life, it is not in the strongest to deprive us of death.

There is no happiness within this circle of flesh, noris it in the optics of these eyes to behold felicity. But besides this literal and positive kind of death, there are others whereof divines make mention, as mortification, dying unto sin and the world. In these moral acceptations, the way to be immortal is to die daily; and I have enlarged that common "Remember death" into a more Christian memorandum--"Remember the four last things"--death, judgment, heaven, and hell. I believe that the world grows near its end; but that general opinion, that the world grows near its end, hath possessed all ages past as nearly as ours.

There is no road or ready way to virtue; it is not an easy point of art to disentangle ourselves from this riddle or web of sin. To perfect virtue, as to religion, there is required a panoplia, or complete armour; that whilst we lie at close ward against one vice, we lie not open to the assault of another. There go so many circumstances to piece up one good action that it is a lesson to be good, and we are forced to be virtuous by the book.

Insolent zeals that do decry good works, and rely only upon faith, take not away merit; for, depending upon the efficacy of their faith, they enforce the condition of God, and in a more sophistical way do seem to challenge heaven. I do not deny but that true faith is not only a mark or token, but also a means, of our salvation; but, where to find this is as obscure to me as my last end. If a faith to the quantity of a grain of mustard seed is able to remove mountains, surely that which we boast of is not anything, or, at the most, but a remove from nothing.

For that other virtue of charity, without which faith is a mere notion and of no existence, I have ever endeavoured to nourish the merciful disposition and humane inclination I borrowed from my parents, and regulate it to the written and prescribed laws of charity. I give no alms to satisfy the hunger of my brother, but tofulfil the command of my God; I draw not my purse for his sake that demands it, but His that enjoined it. Again, it is no greater charity to clothe his body than to apparel the nakedness of his soul; and to this, as calling myself a scholar, I am obliged by the duty of my condition.

Bless me in this life with but the peace of my conscience; command of my affections the love of Thyself and my dearest friends; and I shall be happy enough to pity Caesar! These are, O Lord, the humble desires of my most reasonable ambition, and all I dare call happiness on earth: wherein I set no limit to Thy hand or providence; dispose of me according to the wisdom of Thy pleasure. Thy will be done, though in my own undoing.

JOHN CALVIN

Institution of the Christian Religion

John Calvin was born on July 10, 1509, at Noyon, in Picardy, Northern France. Although the Calvins, his ancestors, had been bargemen on the Oise, his father was notary apostolic, procurator-fiscal of the county, clerk of the church court, and diocesan secretary. Young Jean Calvin was eight years old when Luther nailed his theses to the door of the castle church in Wittenburg. The new religion gaining very quickly a footing in France, the youth became influenced by it when studying in Paris at the College de la Marche. He held meetings with Protestants in a cave at Poitiers. His precocity was remarkable. At the age of twenty-three he wrote his first book, a commentary on Seneca's "Treatise on Clemency." At twenty-five he revised a translation of the French Bible. At twenty-seven he published the first edition of his mighty work, "The Institution of the Christian Religion," a treatise which has been styled "one of the landmarks of the history of Christian doctrine." At twenty-eight Calvin was the foremost man in Geneva, and was already one of the most remarkable reformers in the world. His career has rarely been paralleled. Calvin died on May 27, 1564.

I.--The Knowledge of God the Creator

Our wisdom consists almost exclusively of two parts: the knowledge of God, and of ourselves. But, as these are connected together by many ties, it is not easy to determine which of the two precedes, and which gives birth to the others. Our weakness, ignorance, and depravity remind us that in the Lord, and in none but Him only, dwell the two lights of wisdom, of virtue, and of piety. It is evident that man never attains to a true self-knowledge until after he has contemplated the face of God, and come down after such contemplation to look into himself.

It is beyond dispute that there exists in the humanmind, and indeed by natural instinct, some sense of deity. As Cicero, though a pagan, tells us, there is no nation so brutish as not to be imbued with the conviction that there is a God. Even idolatry is an evidence of this fact. But, though experience teaches that a seed of religion is divinely sown in all, few cherish it in the heart. Some lose themselves in superstitious observances; others, of set purpose, wickedly revolt from God; and many think of God against their will, never approaching Him without being dragged into His presence.

But since the perfection of blessedness consists in the knowledge of God, He has been pleased not only to deposit in our minds the seed of religion, of which we have already spoken, but so to manifest His perfections in the whole structure of the universe, and daily place Himself in our view, that we cannot open our eyes without being compelled to behold Him. His essence is, indeed, transcendent and incomparable, but on each of His works His glory is engraven in characters so bright that none, however dull and illiterate, can plead ignorance as an excuse.

Herein appears the shameful ingratitude of men, that, though they have in their own persons a factory where countless operations of God are carried on, instead of praising Him, they are the more inflated with pride. How few are there among us who, in lifting our eyes to the heavens, or looking abroad on the earth, ever think of the Creator! In vain, because of our dulness, does creation exhibit so many bright lamps lit up to show forth the glory of its Author. Therefore, another and better help must be given to guide us properly to God as our Creator, and He has added the light of His Word in order to make known His salvation.

Here it seems proper to make some observations on the authority of Scripture. Nothing can be more absurd than the fiction that the power of judging Scripture isin the Church. When the Church gives it the stamp of her authority, she does not thus make it authentic, but shows her reverence for it as the truth of God by her unhesitating assent. Scripture bears, on the face of it, as clear evidence of its truth as black and white do of their colour, sweet and bitter of their taste. It is preposterous to attempt, by discussion, to rear up a full faith in Scripture. Those who are inwardly taught by the Holy Spirit acquiesce in it implicitly, for it carries with it its own testimony.

It is foolish to attempt to prove to infidels that the Scripture is the Word of God. For it cannot be known to be, except by faith. Justly does Augustine remind us that every man who would have any understanding in such high matters must previously possess piety and mental peace. In order to direct us to the true God, the Scripture excludes all the gods of the heathen. This exclusiveness annihilates every deity which men frame for themselves, of their own accord. Whence had idols their origin, but from the will of man?

There was thus ground for the sarcasm of the heathen poet (Horace, Satires, I.8). "I was once the trunk of a fig-tree, a useless log, when the tradesman, uncertain whether he should make me a stool, etc., chose rather that I should be a god." In regard to the origin of idols, the statement of the Book of Wisdom has been received with almost universal consent, that they originated with those who bestowed this honour on the dead, from a superstitious regard to their memory.

II.--The Grace of Christ the Redeemer

Through the fall of Adam arose the need of a Redeemer, the whole human race having by that event been made accursed and degenerate. Man thereby became deprived of freedom of will and miserably enslaved. The dominion of sin, ever since the first man was broughtunder it, not only extends to the whole race, but has complete possession of every soul. Free will does not enable any man to perform good works unless he is assisted by grace. Yet, since man is by nature a social being, he is disposed, from natural instinct, to cherish and preserve society; and, accordingly, we see that the minds of all men have impressions of order and civil honesty. So that, in regard to the constitution of the present life, no man is devoid of the light of reason. And this gift ought justly to be ascribed to the divine indulgence. Had God not so spared us, our revolt would have carried with it the entire destruction of nature. But to the great truth, what God is in Himself, and what He is in relation to us, human reason makes not the least approach. The natural man has no capacity for such sublime wisdom as to apprehend God, unless illumined by His Spirit, and none can enter the kingdom of God save those whose minds have been renewed by the power of the spirit.

It is certain that after the fall of our first parent, no knowledge of God without a Mediator was effectual to salvation. Hence it is that God never showed Himself propitious to His ancient people, nor gave them any hope of grace without a Mediator. The prosperous and happy state of the Church was always founded in the person of Christ. The primary adoption of the chosen people depended on the grace of the Mediator, and Christ was always held forth to the holy fathers under the law as the object of their faith.

It deeply concerns us that He who was to become our Mediator should be very God and very man. The work to be by Him performed was of no common description, being to restore us to the divine favour so as to make us sons of God and heirs of the heavenly kingdom. In Him the divinity was so conjoined with the humanity that the entire properties of each nature remained entire, and yet the two natures constitute only one Christ.Everything needful for us exists in Christ.

When we see that the whole sum of our salvation, and every single part of it, are comprehended in Christ, we must beware of deriving even the minutest part of it from any other quarter. If we seek salvation, we are taught by the very name of Jesus that He possesses it; if we seek any other gifts of the Spirit, we shall find them in His unction; strength in His permanent government; purity in His conception; indulgence in His nativity, in which He was made like us in all respects, in order that He might learn to sympathise with us; if we seek redemption we shall find it in His passion; acquittal in His condemnation; remission of the curse in His cross; satisfaction in His sacrifice; purification in His blood; reconciliation in His descent into hell; mortification of the flesh in His sepulchre; newness of life in His resurrection; immortality also in His resurrection; the inheritance of a celestial kingdom in His entrance into heaven; protection, security, and the abundant supply of all blessings, in His kingdom; secure anticipation of judgment in the power of judging committed to Him. In fine, since in Him blessings are treasured up, let us draw a full supply from Him, and none from another quarter.

III.--The Merit of Christ as Our Saviour

It may be proved both from reason and from Scripture that the grace of God and the merit of Christ (the Prince and Author of our salvation) are perfectly compatible. Christ is not only the minister, but also the cause of our salvation, and divine grace is not obscured by this expression. Christ, by His obedience, truly merited this divine grace for us, which was obtained by the shedding of His blood, and His obedience even unto death, whereby He paid our ransom.

It is by the secret operation of the Holy Spirit thatwe enjoy Christ and all His benefits. In Christ the Mediator the gifts of the Holy Spirit are to be seen in all their fulness. As salvation is perfected in the person of Christ, so, in order to make us partakers of it, He "baptizes us with the Holy Spirit and with fire," enlightening us into the faith of His Gospel, and so regenerating us to be new creatures. Thus cleansed from all pollution, He dedicates us as holy temples to the Lord.

But here it is proper to consider the nature of faith. The true knowledge of Christ consists in receiving Him as He is offered by the Father, namely, as invested with His Gospel. There is an inseparable relation between faith and the Word, and these can no more be disconnected from each other than rays of light from the sun. John points to this fountain of faith thus: "To-day, if ye will hear His voice," to "hear" being uniformly taken for to "believe." Take away the Word and no faith will remain. Hence Paul designates faith as the obedience which is given to the Gospel.

The mere assent of the intellect to the Word is, according to some, the faith insisted on in Scripture, but this is a mere fiction. Such as thus define faith do not duly ponder the saying of Paul, "With the heart man believeth unto righteousness." Assent itself is more a matter of the heart than the head, of the affection than the intellect.

IV.--Of Repentance

Repentance follows faith and is produced by it. In the conversion of the life to God we require a transformation not only in external works, but in the soul itself, which is able only after it has put off its old habits to bring forth fruits conformable to its renovation. Repentance proceeds from a sincere fear of God, and it consists of two parts, the mortification of the flesh andthe quickening of the spirit. Both of these we obtain by union with Christ. If we are partakers in His resurrection we are raised up by means of it to newness of life, which conforms us to the righteousness of God. In one word, then, by repentance I understand regeneration, the only aim of which is to form us anew in the image of God, which was sullied and all but effaced by the transgression of Adam.

The apostle, in his description of repentance (2 Corinthians vii. 2), enumerates seven causes, effects, or parts belonging to it. These are carefulness, excuse, indignation, fear, desire, zeal, revenge. I stop not to consider whether these are causes or effects; both views may be maintained. The penitent will be careful not in future to offend God; in his excuses he will trust, not to his own apologies, but to Christ's intercession; his indignation will be directed against his own iniquities; his fear will be lest he cause God displeasure; his desire is equivalent to alacrity in duty; zeal will follow; and revenge will be practised in the censure passed on his own sins.

V.--Of Justification by Faith

A man is said to be justified in the sight of God when, in the judgment of God, he is deemed righteous, and is accepted on account of his righteousness. So we interpret justification as the acceptance with which God receives us into His favour as if we were righteous; and we say that this justification consists in the forgiveness of sins and the imputation of the righteousness to Christ. Since many imagine a righteousness compounded of faith and works, let it be noted that there is so wide a difference between justification by faith and by works that one necessarily overthrows the other. If we destroy the righteousness by faith by establishing our own righteousness, then, in order to obtain His righteousness,our own must be entirely abandoned. The Gospel differs from the law in this, that it entirely places justification in the mercy of God and does not confine it to works. It is entirely by the intervention of Christ's righteousness that we obtain justification before God.

The doctrine of Christian liberty is founded on this justification by faith. This liberty consists of three parts. First, believers renouncing the righteousness of the law look only to Christ. Secondly, the conscience, freed from the yoke of the law, voluntarily obeys the will of God. This cannot be done under the dominion of the law. Thirdly, under the Gospel we are free to use things indifferent. The consciences of believers, while seeking the assurance of their justification before God, must rise above the law, and think no more of obtaining justification by it. Our consciences being free from the yoke of the law itself, voluntarily obey the will of God.

VI.--On the Doctrine of Election

Ignorance of the doctrine of election and predestination impairs the glory of God and fosters pride. The covenant of life is not preached equally to all, and among those to whom it is preached does not always meet with the same reception. The reason of this discrimination belongs to the secret thing of God. This doctrine is cavilled at; yet when we see one nation preferred to another, shall we plead against God for having chosen to give such a manifestation of His mercy? God has displayed His grace in special forms. Thus of the family of Abraham He rejected some, and kept others within His Church, showing that He retained them among His sons.

Although the election of God is secret, it is made manifest by effectual calling. Both election and effectual calling are founded on the free mercy of God Calling is proved to be according to the free grace ofGod by the declarations of Scripture, by the mode in which it is dispensed, by the instance of Abraham's vocation, by the testimony of John, and by the example of all those who have been called. There are two species of calling. There is a universal call by which God, through the preaching of His Word, invites all men alike. Besides this, there is a special call, which, for the most part, God bestows on believers only, when by the internal illumination of His Spirit he causes the Gospel to take deep root in their hearts.

SAMUEL TAYLOR COLERIDGE

Aids to Reflection

This famous book, of which the full title is "Aids to Reflection in the Formation of a Manly Character on the several Grounds of Prudence, Morality, and Religion," was published in 1825, nine years before the author's death. Its influence on thoughtful minds was very great, and many of the first divines of that period owed to it their profoundest religious ideas. It has been said that the fame of Coleridge (see LIVES AND LETTERS) as a philosophic thinker is not so great as it was during the twenty years immediately after his death; but one imagines that this statement merely means that not so many people now read Coleridge as did fifty years ago. The book, at any rate, has not yet been written which exposes a fallacy in his argument or demolishes his system. It should be remembered that this poet and searching thinker, to whom men like Wordsworth and Haslitt listened with reverence, was for some time in his life a Unitarian, and won to faith in the divinity of Christ by the use of his reason.

I.--Introductory Aphorisms

It is the most useful prerogative of genius to rescue truths from the neglect caused by the very circumstance of their universal admission. Truths, of all others the most awful and interesting, are too often considered as so true that they lose the power of truth, and lie bedridden in the dormitory of the soul.

There is one sure way of giving freshness and importance to the most commonplace maxims--that of *reflecting* on them in direct reference to our own state and conduct, to our own past and future being. A reflecting mind, says an ancient writer, is the spring and source of every good thing. As a man without forethought scarce deserves the name of man, so forethought without reflection is but a metaphorical phrase for the instinct of a beast.

In order to learn, we must attend; in order to profitby what we have learnt, we must think; he only thinks who reflects.

To assign a feeling and a determination of their will as a satisfactory reason for embracing or rejecting an opinion is the habit of many educated people; to me, this seems little less irrational than to apply the nose to a picture, and to decide on its genuineness by the sense of smell.

In attention we keep the mind passive; in thought we rouse it into activity.

An hour of solitude passed in sincere and earnest prayer, or the conflict with and conquest over a single passion or "subtle bosom sin," will teach us more of thought, will more effectually awaken the faculty, and form the habit of reflection, than will a year's study in the schools without them.

Never yet did there exist a full faith in the Divine Word which did not expand the intellect, while it purified the heart; which did not multiply the aims and objects of the understanding, while it fixed and simplified those of the desires and passions. "Give me understanding," says David, "and I shall observe Thy laws with my whole heart."

It is worthy of especial observation that the Scriptures are distinguished from all other writings pretending to inspiration, by the strong and frequent recommendations of knowledge and a spirit of inquiry. The word "rational" has been strongly abused of late times. This must not, however, disincline us to the weighty consideration that thoughtfulness and a desire to rest all our convictions on grounds of right reasoning, are inseparable from the character of a Christian. He who begins by loving Christianity better than truth will proceed by loving his own sect and church better than Christianity, and end in loving himself best of all.

II.--Reflections Respecting Morality

Sensibility, that is a constitutional quickness, of sympathy with pain and pleasure, is not to be confounded with the moral principle. Sensibility is not even a sure pledge of a good heart. How many are prompted to remove those evils alone, which by hideous spectacle or clamorous outcry are present to their senses and disturb their selfish enjoyments? Provided the dunghill is not before their parlour window, they are well contented to know that it exists, and perhaps is the hotbed on which their own luxuries are reared. Sensibility is not necessarily benevolence.

All the evil of the materialists is inconsiderable besides the mischief effected and occasioned by the sentimental philosophy of Sterne and his numerous imitators. The vilest appetites and the most remorseless inconstancy towards their objects, acquired the titles of the "heart," "the irresistible feelings," "the too-tender sensibility"; and if the frosts of prudence, the icy chain of human law, thawed and vanished at the genial warmth of human nature, who could help it? It was an amiable weakness! At this time the profanation of the word "love" rose to its height; the muse of science condescended to seek admission at the saloons of fashion and frivolity, rouged like a harlot and with the harlot's wanton leer. I know not how the annals of guilt could be better forced into the service of virtue than by such a comment on the present paragraph as would be afforded by sentimental correspondence produced in courts of justice, fairly translated into the true meaning of the words, and the actual object and purpose of the infamous writers.

Do you in good earnest aim at dignity of character? I conjure you, turn away from those who live in the twilight between vice and virtue. Are not reason, discrimination, law, and deliberate choice the distinguishing characters of humanity? Can anything manly proceed from those who for law and light would substitute shapeless feelings, sentiments, impulses, which, as far as they differ from the vital workings in the brute animals, owe the difference to their former connection with the proper virtues of humanity? Remember that love itself, in its highest earthly bearing, as the ground of the marriage union, becomes love by an inward fiat of the will, by a completing and sealing act of moral election, and lays claim to permanence only under the form of duty.

All things strive to ascend, and ascend in the striving. While you labour for anything below your proper humanity, you seek a happy life in the region of death.

> Unless above himself he can
> Erect himself, how mean a thing is man!

III.--Prudential Aphorisms

With respect to any final aim or end, the greater part of mankind live at hazard. They have no certain harbour in view, nor direct their course by any fixed star. But to him that knoweth not the port to which he is bound, no wind can be favourable; neither can he who has not yet determined at what mark he is to shoot, direct his arrow aright.

It is not, however, the less true that there is a proper object to aim at; and if this object be meant by the term happiness, the perfection of which consists in the exclusion of all hap [*i.e.*, chance], I assert that there is such a thing as *summum bonum,* or ultimate good. What this is, the Bible alone shows certainly, and points out the way. "In Cicero and Plato," says Augustine, "I meet with many things acutely said, and things that excite a certain warmth of emotion, but in none of them do I find these words, 'Come unto Me, all ye that labour and are heavy laden, and I will give you rest!'"

In the works of Christian and pagan moralists, it isdeclared that virtue is the only happiness of this life. You cannot become better, but you will become happier; you cannot become worse without an increase of misery. Few men are so reprobate as not to have some lucid moments, and in such moments few can stand up unshaken against the appeal of their own experience. What have been the wages of sin? What has the devil done for you?

Though prudence in itself is neither virtue nor holiness, yet without prudence neither virtue nor holiness can exist.

Art thou under the tyranny of sin, a slave to vicious habits, at enmity with God, a fugitive from thy own conscience? Oh, how idle the disputes whether the listening to the dictates of prudence from self-interested motives be virtue, when the *not* listening is guilt, misery, madness, and despair! The most Christian-like pity thou canst show is to take pity on thy own soul. The best service thou canst render is to show mercy to thyself.

IV.--Aphorisms on Spiritual Religion

If there be aught spiritual in man, the will must be such. If there be a will, there must be spirituality in man.

There is more in man than can be rationally referred to the life of Nature and the mechanism of organisation. He has a will not included in his mechanism; the will is, in an especial sense, the spiritual part of our humanity.

I assume a something, the proof of which no man can *give* to another, yet every man may find for himself. If any man say that he cannot find it, I am bound to disbelieve him. I cannot do otherwise without unsettling the foundations of my own moral nature. If he will not find it, he excommunicates himself, forfeits his personal rights, and becomes a thing--*i.e.*, one who may be usedagainst his will and without regard to his interest. If the materialist use the words "right" and "obligation," he does it deceptively, and means only compulsion and power. To overthrow faith in aught higher than nature and physical necessity is the very purpose of his argument. But he cannot be ignorant that the best and greatest of men have devoted their lives to enforce the contrary; and there is not a language in which he could argue for ten minutes in support of his scheme without sliding into phrases that imply the contrary.

The Christian grounds his philosophy on assertions which have nothing in them of theory or hypothesis; they are in immediate reference to three ultimate facts-- namely, the reality of the law of conscience; the existence of a responsible will as the subject of the law; and lastly, the existence of evil--of evil essentially such, not by accident of circumstances, not derived from physical consequences, nor from any cause out of itself. The first is a fact of consciousness, the second a fact of reason necessarily concluded from the first, and the third a fact of history interpreted by both.

I maintain that a will conceived separately from intelligence is a non-entity, and that a will the state of which does in no sense originate in its own act is a contradiction. It might be an instinct, an impulse, and, if accompanied with consciousness, a desire; but a will it could not be. And this every human being knows with equal clearness, though different minds may reflect on it with different degrees of distinctness; for who would not smile at the notion of a rose willing to put forth its buds and expand them into flowers?

I deem it impious and absurd to hold that the Creator would have given us the faculty of reason, or that the Redeemer would in so many varied forms of argument and persuasion have appealed to it, if it had been useless or impotent. I believe that the imperfect human understanding can be effectually exerted only in subordinationto, and in a dependent alliance with, the means and aidances supplied by the supreme reason.

Christianity is not a theory, or a speculation, but a life. Not a philosophy of life, but life, and a living process. It has been eighteen hundred years in existence.

The practical inquirer has his foot on the rock when he knows that whoever needs not a Redeemer is more than human. Remove from him the difficulties that perplex his belief in a crucified Saviour, convince him of the reality of sin, and then satisfy him as to the fact historically, and as to the truth spiritually, of a redemption therefrom by Christ. Do this for him, and there is little fear that he will let either logical quirks or metaphysical puzzles contravene the plain dictate of his commonsense, that the Sinless One that redeemed mankind from sin must have been more than man, and that He who brought light and immortality into the world could not in His own nature have been an inheritor of death and darkness.

A moral evil is an evil that has its origin in a will. An evil common to all must have a ground common to all. Now, this evil ground cannot originate in the Divine will; it must, therefore, be referred to the will of man. And this evil ground we call original sin. It is a mystery--that is, a fact which we see, but cannot explain; and the doctrine a truth which we apprehend, but can neither comprehend nor communicate.

The article on original sin is binding on the Christian only as showing the antecedent ground and occasion of Christianity, which is the edifice raised on this ground. The two great moments of the Christian religion are, original sin and redemption; *that* the ground, *this* the superstructure of our faith. Christianity and redemption are equivalent terms.

The agent and personal cause of the redemption of mankind is--the co-eternal word and only begotten Sonof the living God. The causation act is--a spiritual and transcendent mystery, "that passeth all understanding." The effect caused is--the being born anew, as before in the flesh to the world, so now born in the spirit to Christ.

Now, albeit the causative act is a transcendent mystery, the fact, or actual truth, of it having been assured to us by revelation, it is not impossible, by steadfast meditation on the idea and supernatural character of a personal will, for a mind spiritually disciplined to satisfy itself that the redemptive act supposes an agent who can at once act on the will as an exciting cause, and in the will, as the condition of its potential, and the ground of its actual, being.

The frequent, not to say ordinary, disproportion between moral worth and worldly prosperity has at all times led the observant and reflecting few to a nicer consideration of the current belief, whether instinctive or traditional. By forcing the soul in upon herself, this enigma of saint and sage, from Job, David, and Solomon to Claudian and Boëtius, this perplexing disparity of success and desert, has been the occasion of a steadier and more distinct consciousness of a something in man, different in kind, which distinguishes and contra-distinguishes him from animals--at the same time that it has brought into closer view an enigma of yet harder solution--the fact, I mean, of a contradiction in the human being, of which no traces are observable elsewhere, in animated or inanimate nature.

A struggle of jarring impulses; a mysterious division between the injunctions of the mind and the elections of the will; and the utter incommensurateness and the unsatisfying qualities of the things around us, that yet are the only objects which our senses discover or our appetites require us to pursue; these facts suggest that the riddle of fortune and circumstance is but a form of the riddle of man, and that the solution of both problemslies in the acknowledgement that the soul of man, as the subject of mind and will, possesses a principle of permanence and is destined to endure.

Evidences of Christianity! I am weary of the word. Make a man feel the want of it; rouse him, if you can, to the self-knowledge of his need of it; and you may safely trust it to its own evidence--remembering only the express declaration of Christ himself, "No man cometh to Me, unless the Father leadeth him."

Christ's awful recalling of the drowsed soul from the dreams and phantom world of sensuality to actual reality--how has it been evaded! His word, that was spirit! His mysteries, which even the apostles must wait for the parable in order to comprehend! These spiritual things, which can only be spiritually discerned, were--say some--mere metaphors! Figures of speech! Oriental hyperboles! "All this means only morality!" Ah! how far nearer the truth to say that morality means all this!

CONFUCIANISM

The Lun Yu, or Sayings of Confucius

The so-called "Four Books" of Chinese literature are held in less esteem than the "Five Kings," or "Primary Classics," but they are still studied first by every Chinaman as a preparation for what is regarded as the higher and more important literature. It should be borne in mind that the four "Shus," as these books are called, tell us much more about the actual teaching and history of Confucius. The four books are: (i) The "Lun Yu," or the "Analects of Confucius," which contain chiefly the sayings and conversations of Confucius, and give, ostensibly in his own words, his teaching, and, in a subordinate degree, that of his principal disciples; (2) the "Ta-Hsio," or "Teaching for Adults," rendered also the "Great Learning," a treatise dealing with ethical and especially with political matters, forming Book 39 of the "Li-Ki," or "Book of Rites," the "Fourth Classic," (3) the "Chung Yung," or "Doctrine of the Mean," more correctly the State of Equilibrium or harmony, forming Book 28 of the "Li-Ki"; and (4) "Meng-tse," Latinised "Mencius," that is, the conversations and opinions of Mencius. The first, the "Lun Yu," or "Analects," is the most important of these, the next in importance being the teaching of Mencius. The book to which we are most indebted in the preparation of the following epitomes is "The Chinese Classics," edited by Dr. J. Legge. Other books are "The Sayings of Confucius," translated by S.A. Lyall; "Chinese Literature," by H.A. Giles; and "The Wisdom of Confucius," by G. Dimsdale Stacker.

Introductory

The original of the Chinese title of the "Lun Yu" is literally "Discourses and Dialogues." By Legge and most British Chinese scholars this work is called "The Confucian Analects," the word "analect" denoting things chosen, in the present case from the utterances of the master.

The "Lun Yu" is arranged in twenty chapters or books, and gives, ostensibly in his own words, the teaching of Confucius and that of his leading disciples. It is here that we learn nearly all that we know about Confucius.Since the work was composed, as we have it, within a century of the master's death, there seems good reason for believing that we have here a *bona-fide* record of what he thought and said. We may compare with the "Lun Yu" the Christian Gospels which profess to give the doctrines and sayings of Jesus, and also the traditional utterances of Mohammed edited by Al-Bokhari, who died in 870 A.D. The utterances which follow are by the master (Confucius) himself, unless it is otherwise stated. Other speakers are generally disciples of Confucius.

General Maxims

I care little who makes a nation's laws if I have the making of its ballads.

The young child ought to be obedient at home, modest from home, attentive, faithful, full of benevolence, spending spare time mostly upon poetry, music, and deportment.

A son ought to study his father's wishes as long as the father lives; and after the father is dead he should study his life, and respect his memory.

A man who is fond of learning is not a glutton, nor is he indolent; he is earnest and sincere in what he says and does, seeks the company of the good, and profits by it.

At fifteen my whole mind was on study. At thirty I was able to stand alone. At forty my speculative doubts came to an end. At fifty I understood Heaven's laws. At sixty my passions responded to higher instincts. At seventy my better nature ruled me altogether.

Mere study without thought is useless, but thought without study is dangerous.

Fine words and attractive appearances are seldom associated with true goodness.

If a man keeps cultivating his old knowledge and beever adding to it new, that man is fit to be a teacher of others.

The superior man is broad-minded, and no partisan. The mean man is biased and narrow.

Tze-chang studied with a view to official promotion. The master said, "This is wrong," adding, "Thou shouldest listen much, keep silent when there is doubt, and guard thy tongue. See much, beware of dangers, and walk warily. Then shalt thou have little cause for repentance."

I do not know how a man can get on without truth. It is easier for a waggon to go without a cross-pole, or a carriage to be drawn without harness.

Neither courtesy nor music avail a man if he has not virtue and love.

Worship the dead as though they stood alive before you. Sacrifice to the spirits as if they were in your immediate presence.

If I am not personally present when the sacrifice is being made, then I do not sacrifice. There can be no proxy in this matter.

Tze-kung wanted to do away with the offering of a sheep at the new moon. The master said, "Thou lovest the sheep, but I love the ceremony."

These things are not to be tolerated: Rank without generosity, ritual without reverence, and mourning without genuine sorrow.

It is better to have virtue with want and ignominy, than wealth and honour without virtue.

If a man in the morning learns the right way of life he may die at night without regret.

A scholar's mind should be set on the search for truth, and he should not be ashamed of poor clothes or of plain or even of insufficient food.

The superior man loves the good and pursues it; besides this, he has no likes or dislikes.

The good man considers what is right; the bad manwhat will pay.

As long as thy parents live thou must not go far from them. But if through necessity thou leavest them, let them know where thou art, and be ready to come to them when needed.

The man who governs himself, restraining his passions, seldom goes wrong.

The good man desires to be slow of speech, but active in conduct.

Virtue stands never alone. It will always make neighbours.

In my first dealings with men I listened to their words, and gave them credit for good conduct. Experience has taught me not to listen to their words but to watch their conduct. It was from Yu that I learned this lesson.

I have met no man of strong and unbending will; even Chang is passionate.

On being asked why Kung-wan was said to be cultured, the master replied, "Because he was quick to learn, fond of learning, and especially because he was not ashamed to ask questions of those below him." Of Tze-chang the master said that he had four characteristics of the gentleman: he was humble in his own life, respectful towards seniors, generous in supplying the needs of the people, and just in all his demands of them.

Yen Yuan and Chi Lu were once sitting by the master, who turned to them and said, "Come, I want each of you to tell me his wishes." Chi Lu said, "I should like to have carriages and horses and light fur robes to share with my friends that they, and I, may carelessly wear them out." Yen Yuan said, "My wish is to make no boast of moral or intellectual excellence." The master said, "My wish is this: to make the aged happy, to show sincerity towards friends, and to treat young people with tenderness and sympathy."

Nature preponderating over art begets coarseness; art preponderating over nature begets pedantry; art andnature united make a proper gentleman.

To men whose talents are above mediocrity we speak of superior things. To men whose talents are below the common we must speak things suited to their culture.

On being asked, "What is wisdom," the master replied, "To promote right thoughts and feelings among men; to honour the spirits of the dead." In reply to the question, "What is love?" the master answered, "Making most of self-sacrificing efforts but of success only in a subordinate degree."

Perfect virtue consists in keeping to the Golden Mean. He who has offended against Heaven has no one to whom he can pray.

Men should not murmur against Heaven, for all that Heaven does is good.

The master paid great attention to three things--piety, peace, and health.

If I have coarse rice to eat and pure water to drink, and my bent arm for a pillow, I am content and happy. But ill-gotten riches and honour are to me as a floating cloud.

If my life could be lengthened out by a few years, I would devote at least fifty years to the study of the "Yi King" [Book of Changes], then might I be purified from my sin.

On Poetry, History, and Propriety

The master constantly talked about poetry, history, and the rules of propriety.

Tze-lu, on being asked about Confucius, gave no answer. The master asked about being present, said, "Why didst thou not say to him, 'Confucius is a man so eager in the pursuit of knowledge that he forgets his food, so jubilant in its attainment that he forgets his grief and grows old without knowing it'?"

I was not born in the possession of knowledge, but Iam fond of the past and study it closely, and hence knowledge is coming to me.

My pupils, do not think that I hide anything from you. Whatever I think and do I tell you frankly and truly. I keep no secrets from my disciples.

The master used to teach four things: culture, morals, and manners, piety, and faithfulness.

In knowledge and in culture I am perhaps the equal of other men. I have not yet attained to perfection, nor are my knowledge and living consistent.

The master once being very ill, Tze-lu asked permission to pray for him. The master asked, "Is that customary?" "It is," replied the disciple, "for the memorials have it, 'Pray to the spirits in heaven above and on earth below.'" The master replied, "I have for long prayed for myself, and that is best."

The master was dignified, yet gentle. He was majestic, but inspired no fear. He was gentlemanly, but always at ease.

Poetry rouses the mind, the rules of propriety establish the character, music crowns a man's education.

It would be hard to meet a man who has studied for three years without learning something good.

Learn as though you felt you could never learn enough, and as though you feared you could not learn in your short life what is needful for conduct.

A man from a certain village once said, "Confucius is, no doubt, a very learned man, but he has not made himself a name in any special thing." When the master heard this, he said to his disciples, "What shall I undertake: charioteering, archery, or what? I think I shall become a charioteer, and thus get me a name."

A high officer asked Tze-kung, "May we not say that the master is a sage because he can do so many things?" To which Tze-kung replied, "Heaven has indeed highly endowed him, and he is almost a sage; and he is very many-sided."

On hearing this the master said, "Does the officer know me? Being of lowly birth when I was young, I learnt many a trade, but there was nothing great in that. The superior man may excel in one thing only, and not in many things."

Wishing to go and live among the nine wild tribes of the East, one of his friends remonstrated with the master and said, "They are low. How can you go and live among them?" To which he gave for answer, "Nothing that is low can survive where the virtuous and the good-mannered man is."

After I returned from Wei to Lu I found the music had been reformed, and that each song was given its proper place.

The master said, "To serve ministers and nobles when abroad, fathers and elder brothers when at home, to avoid neglect in offerings of the dead, and to be no slave to wine: to which of these have I attained?"

Confucius at Home and at Court

In his own village Confucius looked homely and sincere, as if he had no word to say; but in the ancestral temple and in the court he was full of words, though careful in using them.

When waiting at court he talked with the lower officers frankly, but to the higher officers more blandly and precisely. When the sovereign was present he used to be respectful but easy, solemn yet self-possessed. When the sovereign bade him receive visitors his countenance changed, and his legs appeared to bend. Bowing to those beside him, he straightened his robes in front and behind, hastening forward with his elbows extended like a bird's wings. When the guest had retired he used to report to the prince, saying, "The guest does not any more look back." When he entered the palace gatehe seemed to stoop as though it were not high enough for him. Ascending the dais, lifting up his robes with both hands, he held his breath as if he would cease breathing. As he came down his face relaxed after the first step, and looked more at ease. At the bottom of the steps he would hurry on, spreading out his elbows like wings, and on gaining his seat he would sit intent as previously.

He was never arrayed in deep purple or in puce-coloured garments. Even at home he wore nothing of a red or reddish colour. In hot weather he used to wear a single garment of fine texture, but always over an inner garment. Over lambs' fur he wore a garment of black, over fawns' fur one of white, and over foxes' fur one of yellow. His sleeping-dress was half as long again as his body. On the first day of the month he always went to court in court robes. On fast days he wore pale-hued garments, changed his food, and made a change in his apartment.

He liked to have his rice carefully cleaned and his minced meat chopped small. He did not eat rice that had been injured by heat or damp or that had turned sour, nor could he eat fish or meat which had gone. He did not eat anything that was discoloured or that had a bad flavour, or that was not in season. He would not eat meat badly cut, or that was served with the wrong sauce. No choice of meats could induce him to eat more than he thought right.

After sacrificing at the ancestral temple he would never keep the meat there overnight, nor would he keep it more than three days at home. If by any mishap it were kept longer, it was not eaten.

He never talked at meals, nor would he speak a word in bed. Though there were on the table nothing but coarse rice and vegetable soup, he would always reverently offer some of it to his ancestors. If his mat was not straight he would not sit on it.

On Learning and Virtue

Chung-kung asked about virtue. The master said: "It consists in these things: To treat those outside thine own home as if thou wert welcoming a great guest; to treat the people as if thou wert assisting at a high sacrifice; not to do to others what thou wouldest not have them do to thee; to encourage no wrongs in the state nor any in the home."

The master being once asked "Who is the virtuous man?" answered, "One that has neither anxiety nor fear, for he finds no evil in his heart. What, then, is there to cause anxiety or fear?"

The master, on being once asked by one of his disciples "On what does the art of government depend?" answered, "Sufficient food, troops, and a loyal people." "If, however," the same disciple asked, "one of them had to be dispensed with, which of the three could we best spare?" "Troops," said the master. "And which," the disciple then asked, "of the other two could be better spared?" "Food," said the master.

Tze-chang asked the master, "When may a scholar or an officer be called eminent?" The master asked, "What dost thou mean by being eminent?" To which the other answered, "To be famous throughout the state and throughout his clan."

"But that," said the master, "is fame, not eminence. The truly eminent man is genuine and straightforward; he loves righteousness, weighs people's words, and looks at their countenances. He humbles himself to others, and is sincerely desirous of helping all. That is the, eminent man, though he may not be a famous one."

If a ruler can govern himself, he is likely to be able to govern his people. But how can a man who has not control of himself keep his people in subjection?

Tze-kung asked, "Is it proper that a man should be liked by all his neighbours?" "Certainly not," said themaster. "Is it then proper," asked the same, "that a man should be hated by all his neighbours?" "Decidedly not," said the master. "The good man is loved by his good neighbours, and hated by his bad ones."

The virtuous man is hard to satisfy, but easy to serve. Nothing that thou doest to please him satisfies him unless it is strictly according to right. But in all his demands upon his servants he expects according to capacity, and is satisfied if the servant does his best, though it be little. The bad man is easy to satisfy, but hard to serve. He is satisfied with whatever pleases him, though it be not right; and he demands of his servants whatever he requires, making no allowance for capacity.

A scholar whose mind is set upon comfort is not worthy of the name.

"Where there's a will," said the master, "there's a way."

To refrain from speaking to a man who is disposed to hear is to wrong the man; to speak to a man not disposed to listen is to waste words.

"How can one in brief express man's whole duty?"

"Is not reciprocity such a word?" said the master; "that is, what thou dost not want others to do to thee, do thou not to others."

There are three things which the virtuous man has to guard against. In youth, lust; in full manhood, strife; and in old age, covetousness.

The highest class of men are those who are born wise; the next those who become wise by study; next and third, those who learn much, without having much natural ability. The lowest class of people are those who have neither natural ability nor perseverance. Men are very similar at birth; it is afterwards the great differences arise.

It is only the wisest and the silliest of men who never alter their opinions.

"My children," said the master once to his disciples,"Why do you not study the Book of Poetry [the Shih King]? It would stimulate your mind, encourage introspection, teach you to love your fellows, and to forbear with all. It would show you your duty to your fathers and your king; and you would also learn from it the names of many birds and beasts and plants and trees."

Ta-Hsio, or Teaching for Adults

Introductory

The "Ta-Hsio," or "Teaching for Adults," rendered also "The Great Learning," is really a treatise dealing with ethical, and especially with political, matters, the duties of rulers, ministers, etc. It is usually ascribed in part to "the master" himself, and in part to Tseng Tsan, one of the most illustrious of his disciples. This forms Book 39 of the "Li Ki," or "Book of Rites," and it is admitted by the best scholars to be a genuine specimen of the teaching of Confucius, though no one believes that "the master" is the author of the book as it now stands. The likeliest suggestion as to authorship is that which ascribes the present treatise, and also the "Chung Yung" (No. 28 of the "Li Ki") to Khung Chi, the grandson of Confucius.

The great Chinese philosopher Chang said of this book: "'The teaching for Adults' is a book belonging to the Confucian school, forming the gate through which youthful students enter the great temple of virtue. We should not have been able to ascertain the methods of learning pursued by the ancients if this book and the works of Mencius had not been preserved. Beginners ought to start their studies with this book, and then pass on to the harder books, after which the Five Classics should be read and pondered over."

The object of the "Ta-Hsio" is to illustrate outstandingvirtue, to promote love of the people and their improvement in morals and manners. In order that these results may be obtained, this treatise must be patiently calmly, and thoughtfully studied.

How the Empire is to be Improved

The ancients, wishing to make their empire perfect, first endeavoured to make their states perfect. For this last purpose they exerted themselves to improve their famines, and to this end they took great pains to improve their personal character. In order to improve their personal character, they endeavoured to purify their hearts and to make their thoughts sincere.

From the Son of Heaven [the Emperor] to the masses of the people, the cultivation of personal character was regarded as the root of all amelioration. To know this has been called knowing the "root," which is the perfection of knowledge.

On Thang's bathing-tub these words were inscribed:

"Renovate thyself day by day, yea, every day renovate thyself." At the opening of his reign, Thang was exhorted to renovate his people.

In the Book of Poetry it is said that although Kau was an ancient state, yet it regarded Heaven's commands as ever new. In the same book we read that the thoughts of the Emperor Wan were deep, and his conduct firm. In all his relationships he was reverent and true. As a sovereign he was benevolent; as a minister respectful; as a son he exhibited filial piety; as a father he was kind and considerate; towards his subjects he was steadfastly faithful. This virtuous and accomplished sovereign, Wan, took great pains to sharpen his intellect and to make his heart more sensitive to all obligations. How majestic, how glorious was he; he shall ever be remembered by his grateful people at the ancestral shrine.

"The cultivation of personal character depends uponthe regulation of the mind." What does this mean? If a man's passions are not kept under control, he will form wrong judgments about actions and never have a well-balanced mind. Therefore must man regulate his mind in order to cultivate himself. "The government of the family depends upon the cultivation of personal character." What does this mean? Where there is affection, judgment is distorted. We see the good qualities of those we love, but are blind to the bad ones. We see the bad qualities of those we hate, but are blind to the good ones. In order to be able to govern a family rightly, we must train our minds to judge fairly and impartially of those nearest to us--*i.e.*, it requires careful self-training to be able to train a family.

"We must be able to govern the family before we can rule a state." What means this? If a man fails to teach the members of his own family to be obedient and loyal to their head, how can he train a nation to be united, obedient, and loyal?

Yas and Shun ruled with love, and the people became loving. Kieh and Kau ruled with violence, and the people became violent. The sovereign must have and exhibit the same qualities that he wishes his subjects to cultivate. Nor has he the right to expect his people to be free from bad qualities which are in himself. The ruler must himself be what he wants his people to be. Thus it is that the government of the state rests upon the proper government of the family.

"That the empire should have peace and prosperity depends upon the government of the constituting states." What does this mean?

When ruler and ministers treat their aged ones as they ought to, the inhabitants in general become filial. Similarly, the inhabitants learn to show respect towards their seniors and sympathy towards the young when their superiors set them the right example in these matters.No man should treat his inferiors as he would not likehis superiors to treat him. What he disapproves of in his inferiors, let him not exhibit in his dealings towards his superiors.

In the Book of Poetry it is written, "The parents of the people are much to be congratulated. A sovereign whose loves and hates correspond with those of his people is his people's father." To gain the people is to gain the state; therefore a ruler's primary concern should be his own integrity, for thereby he wins his people's loyalty, and through that loyalty he obtains the state, and therewith the wealth of the whole country.

Virtue is the root, wealth but the branches. See first, therefore, to the root.

In the Records of Khu one reads, "The State of Khu values men, not gems nor robes."

A country is wealthy if it consumes less than it produces, and that man is rich whose income exceeds his expenditure.

The virtuous ruler gathers wealth on account of the reputation it can bring him. The wicked ruler seeks wealth for its own sake, sacrificing even virtue to obtain it.

A benevolent sovereign makes a just people. When the people are just the affairs of the sovereign prosper. The state's prosperity consists in righteousness, not in riches.

Chung Yung, or Doctrine of the Mean

Introductory

The "Chung Yung" is more correctly rendered "The state of equilibrium and harmony" (Legge, etc.) than by "The Doctrine of the Mean," its usual appellation. Other titles suggested have been "The Just Mean," "The True Mean," "The Golden Mean," and "The Constant Mean." The word "chung" means "middle," "yung"denoting "course" or "way." Hence, "Chung Yung" means literally, "The middle way." Compare Aristotle's doctrine of The Mean ("Ethics" Book II.).

This treatise occurs as Book 28 of the "Li-Ki" and by Chinese scholars has been declared to be the most valuable part of the Book of Rites. We have here the fullest account existing of the philosophy and ethics of the master. Apart from its value as such, the "Chung Yung" is exceedingly interesting as a monument of the teaching of the ancient Chinese. In its existing form the "Chung Yung" is arranged in five divisions, containing, in all, thirty-three chapters. No attempt is made in the epitomes that follow to retain these divisions and chapters. For the authorship and date of this third book see what is said in the introduction to the "Ta-Hsio."

The Good Man's Path

The sense of obligation has been implanted in man by Heaven. The path of duty is a life in accordance with this heaven-implanted intuition. Every man ought always to tread this path; the true doctrine teaches how this is to be accomplished. The good man will ever be on his guard lest he depart a hair's breadth from the right way.

The mental state of equilibrium is reached when a man is free from the distracting influences of anger and goodwill, joy and sorrow. When these emotions exist in due proportion and extent the state of harmony is attained. From the first proceed all great human enterprises. The state of harmony is the path along which all good men will go. When the states of equilibrium and harmony exist in their fulness gods and men receive their dues, and there is prosperity and happiness.

Kung-ni said, "The virtuous man embodies in himself the states of equilibrium and harmony, but the lowman knows neither of these states." This perfect condition of human character in which there is complete equilibrium and harmony is reached but by few. Why is this so? It is because those who are wise consider these ideal states too commonplace, and they aim at things which the world values more highly. The low man, on the other hand, grovels in the dust and never rises to higher thoughts or nobler aims. Men could, if they would, distinguish the worthy from the unworthy, just as with a healthy palate they can tell good food from bad.

But men's moral discernment has been blunted by a life of sensuality and sin, just as the physical palate loses its power of tasting when in a diseased condition.

In order to find out the Mean, our Father Shun, of blessed memory, used to question the people and study their answers, even the shallow ones. He used to encourage them to speak out by seeming to value the poorest answers. He would take the extremest sayings he heard, and from them deduce the Mean.

It is hard to keep in the middle way: men rule kingdoms and accept honours and emoluments who have yet signally failed to govern themselves by the rules of the Mean.

The good man's ambition is not to perform feats which startle the world and give him fame, but rather to live the life of the moderate and harmonious one; yet how often for lack of true discernment he fails! This middle path is not, however, hidden from the sincere and pure; even common men and women may know it, though in its highest reaches it baffles the wisest. The greatest and the wisest and the best find lodged within them unrealised ideals. Whoever strenuously aims at realising these ideals, though he fails, is near the right path.

"The good man has four difficulties," said the master,"and I have not myself been able to overcome them. (1) To serve my father as I should like my son to serve me. (2) To serve my ruler as I should like him to serve me were I his ruler. (3) To serve an elder brother as I should like him to serve me were he my younger brother. (4) To act towards a friend as I should like him to act towards me were our relations reversed."

The good man suits his conduct to his station in life. If he has wealth and high office he acts becomingly, never treating his inferiors with harshness or contempt. If he be poor and unrecognised, he never murmurs against heaven, or pines over his lot, or cringes before superiors, or does anything immoral for applause or gain. The virtuous man accepts heaven's allotments thankfully and uncomplainingly.

In order to attain to the middle path we must carefully perform the duties which lie nearest to us, not waiting to do great things. In the Book of Poetry we read of the love of wife, of children, and brothers. Cultivate this love on the home hearth, and thy charity will expand and take in mankind. [Note how charity, though beginning at home, travels far afield.]

Shun displayed his filial piety on a huge scale, and brought great honour to his parents and to himself. No wonder that such filial piety as his was rewarded with dominion, wealth, and fame. It is well said in the Book of Poetry, "The good man receives Heaven's benediction."

The Emperor Wan was the only man with no cause for grief, his father being the admirable Ki, and his son the equally admirable Wu. The father laid the foundation of all this excellence, the son transmitting it to his own son. The Emperor Wu retained the honour and distinction of his forebears Thai, Kai, and

Wan. He had the dignity of the true Son of Heaven, and owned allwithin the Four Seas. He sacrificed regularly in the ancestral temple, and after death his successors sacrificed to him. The Duke of Kau continued the glorious traditions handed on by Wu. Both these great rulers realised the aspirations and wishes of their forefathers, restoring and improving the ancestral temple, renovating the sacred vessels and offering sacrifices suited to each year. In other ways also they perpetuated the good deeds of their ancestors, observed their religious rites, encouraged the study of music and poetry, honoured the honourable, and loved the lovable. They showed due respect to their departed ones, and thus discharged their duty to the living and the dead.

The Works of Mencius

Introductory

Mencius is the Latinised form of "Mengtse," which means "the philosopher Meng," Meng (or Meng-sun) being the name of one of the three great Houses of Lu, whose usurpations gave so much offence to Confucius. His personal name was Ko, though this does not occur in his own works. He was born in B.C. 372, and died in B.C. 289 at the age of 83, in the twenty-sixth year of the Emperor Nan, with whom ended the long sovereignty of Kau (Chow) dynasty. He was thus a contemporary of Plato (whose last twenty-three years synchronised with his first twenty-three), Aristotle, Zeno, Epicurus, and Demosthenes, and he is well worthy of being ranked with these illustrious men.

Mencius was reared by his widowed mother, whose virtue and wisdom are still proverbial in China. Thefirst forty years of his life are virtually a blank to us, so that we know very little of his early education. He is said, however, to have studied under Khung Chi, the grandson of Confucius.

In the hundred and six years between the death of Confucius (B.C. 478) and the birth of Mencius (B.C. 372), the political and moral state of China had altered greatly for the worse. The smaller feudal states had been swallowed up by larger ones, the princes were constantly at war with one another, and there was but little loyalty to the occupant of the imperial throne; moreover, the moral standard of things had lowered very much. At about the age of forty-five Mencius became Minister under Prince Hsuan, of the Chi state. But as his master refused to carry out the reforms he urged, he resigned his post and travelled through many lands, advising rulers and ministers with whom he came in contact. In the year B.C. 319 he resumed his former position in the state of Chi, resigning once more eight years later. He now gave himself up to a life of study and teaching, preparing the works presently to be noticed. His main purpose was to expound and enforce the teaching of Confucius. But his own doctrine stands on a lower level than that of the master, for he views man's well-being rather from the point of view of political economy. He was justly named by Chao Chi "The Second Holy One or Prophet"--the name by which China still knows him.

The treatise called "The Works of Mencius" is a compilation of the conversation and opinions of Mencius, having a similar relation to that great philosopher that the Analects (or "Lun Yu") have to Confucius. It is arranged in seven books. According to tradition the work, in its existing form, is as it came from the philosopher himself.

Virtue, not Profit, to be the Chief Quest

When Mencius visited King Hui, of Liang, the latter asked him what counsel he could give to profit his kingdom. The philosopher replied, "Why does your majesty use the word profit? The only things which I have to counsel are righteousness and goodwill. If the king seeks mainly the *profit* of his kingdom, the great officers will seek the profit of their families and the common people that of theirs. The chief things to be aimed at by king and people are virtue and benevolence. All else is as nothing. No benevolent man has neglected his parents, nor has any virtuous man slighted his sovereign."

"How comes it," asked the king, "that my state Tsin has deteriorated since I became its ruler, and that calamities many and great have fallen on it?" Mencius answered, "With so great an extent of territory as thine prosperity ought to be within easy reach; but in order to procure it your majesty must govern thy subjects justly and kindly, moderating penalties, lightening taxes, promoting thus and otherwise their industries, increasing their comforts as well as lessening their burdens, deepening the faithfulness of the people to one another and to the throne. Then will thy people be loyal to thee and formidable towards thy foes. Thou shalt make thy subjects loyal friends, for the benevolent one has no enemy."

A Prosperous Ruler the Friend and Father of his People

On one occasion the Emperor Hsuan of Chi visited Mencius in the Snow Palace, and asked him, "Do the people find enjoyment in music and in the chase?" "Certainly," answered Mencius; "it is when ruler and people share each other's joys and sorrows that the sovereign attains to his highest dignity. Moreover, a ruler, when moving amongst his people ought to copy the ancientsovereigns. In the good old days, when the ruler made a tour of inspection among his people he was received with great acclamation everywhere, for joy and gladness came in his train. In the spring he inspected the ploughing and supplied all that was lacking in the way of seed. In the autumn he examined the reaping and made up for any deficiency in the yield. It was a common saying during the Hsia dynasty, 'If the Emperor visiteth not, what will become of us?' But now, may your majesty permit me to say, matters are very different, for, when in these days a ruler visits his people he is accompanied by a huge army, who with himself and suite have to be maintained by the people visited. And so it comes to be that the hungry are robbed of their food, and the toilers are wearied with the extra tasks imposed upon them. If a ruler wishes to have the hearts of his people, and to' be regarded as their father, he must consider their needs and endeavour to supply them."

Mencius uses Stratagem to Bring Home to the Emperor His Guilt

Mencius said on one occasion to Hsuan, King of Chi, "Suppose one of thy ministers were to entrust his family during his absence to a subordinate, and that the latter neglected his duty so that the wife and children were exposed to great suffering and danger. What should that minister do?"

"Dismiss him at once," was the royal reply.

"But," continued the philosopher, "suppose that the government of your own kingdom were bad, the people suffering and disunited and disloyal on account of their king's bad rule. What then should be done?" The king, looking this way and that, turned the conversation to other themes.

It May be Right to Kill a Sovereign

King Hsuan asked Mencius, "Is it true that Thang banished his own sovereign, Kieh [the last king of the Hsia dynasty], and that Wu attacked the tyrant Emperor Kau-hsin and slew him?" "It is true," said Mencius, "for it is so written in the 'Shu King.' But if a sovereign acts as Kieh did he is no longer a sovereign but a robber, and to be dealt with as such. And if a ruler is, like Kau-hsin, the enemy of his people, he is no longer their ruler, and therefore to be put out of the way, and how better than by death?"

The Gifts that May and Those that May Not be Accepted

Chan Tsin spoke to Mencius as follows:

"The King of Chi once offered thee a present and thou declinedst it, but didst accept gifts offered at Sung and at Hsieh. Why this inconsistency? If it were right to refuse in the first case it was equally right to refuse in the other two. If it were right to accept in the latter two cases, it was equally right to accept in the first case." The philosopher answered, "I acted rightly and consistently. The gifts at Sung were to provide me with what was needed for a long journey which I was about to undertake. Why should I refuse such gifts when needed? At Hsieh I was in some personal danger and needed help to procure the means of self-defence. The gifts were to enable me to procure arms. Why should I have refused such needed help? But at Chi I needed no money, and therefore refused it when offered, for to accept money when it is not needed is to accept a bribe. Why should I take such money?"

Wrong Conduct Should be Ended at Once

A distinguished officer of Sung, called Tai Ying-chib, called upon Mencius and said, "I am unable as yet to dispense with the tax on goods and the duties charged at the frontier passes and in the markets, though this is a right and proper thing to do. But it is my intention, until the next year, to lighten the tax and the duties, and then next year I shall remove them altogether." The philosopher replied, "Here is a man who daily steals a score of his neighbour's fowls. Someone remonstrates, and, feeling that he is guilty of acting dishonestly, he says, 'I know that this stealing is wrong, but in the future I shall be content with stealing one fowl a month. But next year I will stop stealing fowls altogether.' If," continued Mencius, "this task and these duties are, as you admit, wrong, end them at once. Why should you wait a year?"

The Inherent Goodness of Human Nature

Kao Tzu said to Mencius, "Human nature resembles running water, which flows east or west according as it can find an outlet. So human nature is inclined equally to what is good and to what is bad." "It is true," answered Mencius, "that water will flow indifferently to the east or to the west. But it will not flow indifferently up or down; it can only flow down. The tendency of human nature is towards what is good, as that of water is to flow downwards. One may, indeed, by splashing water, make it spurt upwards, but that is forcing it against its true character. Even so, when a man becomes prone to what is evil it is because his Heaven-implanted nature has been diverted from its true bent."

People First, Kings Last

"The people," said Mencius, "are first in importance; next come the gods. The kings are last and least."

What the Good King Delights in Most

"The virtuous king," said Mencius, "is glad to have a large extent of territory and a numerous people to rule over; but his heart is not on these things. To be at the head of a great kingdom and to see his people loyal, united, and flourishing, gives the good king joy; but his heart is not on these things. It is on benevolence, justice, propriety, and knowledge that the good king's heart is set."

The Influence of Example

Mencius said, "In the good days of old, men of virtue and talent abounded in the land, and their influence for good was great upon their fellows. But now, alas, the masses of the people are ignorant, and depraved, and their dominant influence is bad."

Counsellors Should Love Righteousness Rather Than Riches

Mencius said, "Those who counsel men in high places should feel contempt for their pomp and display. I have no wish for huge and gorgeous halls, for luxurious food with hundreds of attendants, or for sparkling wine or bewitching women. These things I esteem not; what I esteem are the rules of propriety handed down by the ancients."

FÉNELON

The Existence of God

François de Salignac de la Mothe Fénelon was born at the château of Fénelon, in the ancient territorial division of Périgord, France, August 6, 1651. At twenty-four he became a priest. He was for many years a friend of his celebrated contemporary Bossuet, but later Bossuet attacked a spiritual and unworldly work of Fénelon, who was condemned by the Pope. He died on January 17, 1715, leaving behind him many books, of which the "Treatise on the Existence of God," first published in 1713, is the masterpiece. This noble and profound work, though it accepts the "argument from design," which the discovery of universal evolution necessarily modifies, does so with such rare philosophical insight as to stand for ever far above any other works of the kind. Fénelon can scarcely be called a mystic, for his reason was of the finest, and never surrendered its claims; but, though a strictly rational thinker, he had the insight of the mystic or the idealist who sees in external nature, and in the mind of man alike, what Goethe called "the living garment of God."

I.--The Hand that Makes Everything

I cannot open my eyes without admiring the art that shines throughout all nature; the least cast suffices to make me perceive the Hand that makes everything.

Men the least exercised in reasoning, and the most tenacious of the prejudices of the senses, may yet with one look discover Him who has drawn Himself in all His works. The wisdom and power He has stamped upon everything He has made are seen, as it were, in a glass by those that cannot contemplate Him in His own idea. This is a sensible and popular philosophy, of which any man free from passion and prejudice is capable.

If a great number of men of subtle and penetrating wit have not discovered God with one cast of the eye upon nature, it is not matter of wonder, for either thepassions they have been tossed by have still rendered them incapable of any fixed reflection, or the false prejudices that result from passions have, like a thick cloud, interposed between their eyes and that noble spectacle.

A man deeply concerned in an affair of great importance, that should take up all the attention of his mind, might pass several days in a room treating about his concerns without taking notice of the proportions of the chamber, the ornaments of the chimney, and the pictures about him, all of which objects would continually be before his eyes, and yet none of them make any impression upon him. In this manner it is that men spend their lives. Everything offers God to their sight, and yet they see Him nowhere.

They pass away their lives without perceiving that sensible representation of the Deity. Such is the fascination of worldly trifles that obscure their eyes. Nay, oftentimes they will not so much as open them, but rather affect to keep them shut, lest they should find Him they do not look for. In short, what ought to help most to open their eyes serves only to close them faster. I mean the constant duration and regularity of the motions which the Supreme Wisdom has put in the universe.

But, after all, whole nature shows the infinite art of its Maker. When I speak of an art, I mean a collection of proper means chosen on purpose to arrive at a certain end; or, if you please, it is an order, a method, an industry, or a set design. Chance, on the contrary, is a blind and necessary cause, which neither sets in order nor chooses anything, and has neither will nor understanding. Now, I maintain that the universe bears the character and stamp of a cause infinitely powerful and industrious; and, at the same time, that chance--that is, the fortuitous concourse of causes void of reason--cannot have formed this universe.

Who will believe that so perfect a poem as Homer's"Iliad" was not the product of the genius of a great poet, but that the letters of the alphabet, being confusedly jumbled and mixed, were by chance, as it were by the cast of a pair of dice, brought together in such an order as is necessary to describe, in verses full of harmony and variety, so many great events; to place and connect them so well together; to paint every object with all its most graceful, most noble, and most affecting attendants; in short, to make every person speak according to his character in so natural and so forcible a manner? Let people subtilise upon the matter as much as they please, yet they never will persuade a man of sense that the "Iliad" was the mere result of chance. How, then, can a man of sense be induced to believe, with respect to the universe, what his reason will never suffer him to believe in relation to the "Iliad"?

II.--Earth, the Mother of All Living

After these comparisons, about which I only desire the reader to consult himself, without any argumentation, I think it is high time to enter into a detail of nature. I do not pretend to penetrate through the whole. Who is able to do it? Neither do I pretend to enter into any physical discussion. Such way of reasoning requires a certain deep knowledge, which abundance of men of wit and sense never acquire; and therefore I will offer nothing to them but the simple prospect of the face of nature. I will entertain them with nothing but what everybody knows, which requires only a little calm and serious attention.

Let us, in the first place, stop at the great object that first strikes our sight--I mean the general structure of the universe. Let us cast our eyes on this earth that bears us.

Who is it that hung and poised this motionless globeof the earth? Who laid its foundation? Nothing seems more vile and contemptible, for the meanest wretches tread it under foot; but yet it is in order to possess it that we part with the greatest treasures. If it were harder than it is, men could not open its bosom to cultivate it; and if it were less hard it could not bear them, and they would sink everywhere as they do in sand, or in a bog. It is from the inexhaustible bosom of the earth we draw what is most precious. That shapeless, vile, and rude mass assumes the most various forms, and yields alone, by turns, all the goods we can desire. That dirty soil transforms itself into a thousand fine objects that charm the eye. In the compass of one year it turns into branches, twigs, buds, leaves, blossoms, fruits, and seeds, in order, by those various shapes, to multiply its liberalities to mankind.

Nothing exhausts the earth; the more we tear her bowels the more she is liberal. After so many ages, during which she has produced everything, she is not yet worn out. She feels no decay from old age, and her entrails still contain the same treasures. A thousand generations have passed away, and returned into her bosom.

Everything grows old, she alone excepted; for she grows young again every year in the spring. She is never wanting to men; but foolish men are wanting to themselves in neglecting to cultivate her. It is through their laziness and extravagance they suffer brambles and briars to grow instead of grapes and corn. They contend for a good they let perish. The conquerors leave uncultivated the ground for the possession of which they have sacrificed the lives of so many thousand men, and have spent their own in hurry and trouble. Men have before them vast tracts of land uninhabited and uncultivated, and they turn mankind topsy-turvy for one nook of that neglected ground in dispute. The earth, if well cultivated, would feed ahundred times more men than she does now. Even the unevenness of ground, which at first seems to be a defect, turns either into ornament or profit. The mountains arose and the valleys descended to the place the Lord had appointed for them. Those different grounds have their particular advantages, according to the divers aspects of the sun. In those deep valleys grow fresh and tender grass to feed cattle. Next to them opens a vast champaign covered with a rich harvest. Here, hills rise like an amphitheatre, and are crowned with vineyards and fruit-trees. There, high mountains carry aloft their frozen brows to the very clouds, and the torrents that run down from them become the springs of rivers. The rocks that show their craggy tops bear up the earth of mountains just as the bones bear up the flesh in human bodies.

There is scarce any spot of ground absolutely barren if a man do not grow weary of digging, and turning it to the enlivening sun, and if he require no more from it than it is proper to bear. Amidst stone and rocks there is sometimes excellent pasture, and their cavities have veins which, being penetrated by the piercing rays of the sun, furnish plants with most savoury juices for the feeding of herds and flocks. Even sea-coasts that seem to be the most sterile and wild yield sometimes either delicious fruits or most wholesome medicines that are wanting in the most fertile countries. Besides, it is the effect of a wise over-ruling Providence that no land yields all that is useful to human life. For want invites men to commerce, in order to supply one another's necessities. It is therefore that want which is the natural tie of society between nations; otherwise, all the people of the earth would be reduced to one sort of food and clothing, and nothing would invite them to know and visit one another.

All that the earth produces, being corrupted, returns into her bosom, and becomes the source of a new production.Thus she resumes all she has given in order to give again. Thus the corruption of plants, and of the animals she feeds, feed her, and improve her fertility. Thus, the more she gives the more she resumes; and she is never exhausted, provided they who cultivate her restore to her what she has given. Everything comes from her bosom, everything returns to it, and nothing is lost in it. Nay, all seeds multiply there.

Admire the plants that spring from the earth; they yield food for the healthy, and remedies for the sick. Their species and virtues are innumerable. They deck the earth, yield verdure, fragrant flowers, and delicious fruits. Do you see those vast forests that seem as old as the world? Those trees sink into the earth by their roots, as deep as their branches shoot up to the sky. Their roots defend them against the winds, and fetch up, as it were by subterranean pipes, all the juices destined to feed the trunk. The trunk itself is covered with a tough bark that shelters the tender wood from the injuries of the air. The branches distribute, by several pipes, the sap which the roots had gathered up in the trunk. In summer the boughs protect us with their shadow against the scorching rays of the sun.

The farther we seek through the universe the more sure is her teaching. That which we learnt from the earth and from plants is taught us again by water, by the air, and by fire. It is the lesson of the skies, and of the sun and the stars. The whole animal world teaches us the same. If we turn from things that are large, we shall find wonders no less in the infinitely little; if we turn from the bodies of animals to the study of their instincts, their sleep, their food, the persistence of their races from age to age--though all individuals are mortal--again we find evidence of the skill and power of the Author of all things.

Still more wonderful is the body of man, his skin and veins, his bones and joints, his senses, tongue andteeth, the proportions of his body, and, above all things, his soul, which alone among all creatures thinks and knows and is sovereign master over the body.

It is this reason that is in man which, above all, demonstrates the residence of God in us.

III.--God in the Mind of Man

It cannot be said that man gives himself the thoughts he had not before; much less can it be said that he receives them from other men, since it is certain he neither does nor can admit anything from without, unless he finds it in his own foundation, by consulting within him the principles of reason, in order to examine whether what he is told is agreeable or repugnant to them. Therefore, there is an inward school wherein man receives what he neither can give himself, nor expect from other men who live upon trust as well as himself.

Here, then, are two reasons I find within me, one of which is myself, the other is above me. That which is myself is very imperfect, prejudiced, liable to error, changeable, headstrong, ignorant, and limited; in short, it possesses nothing but what is borrowed. The other is common to all men, and superior to them. It is perfect, eternal, immutable, ever ready to communicate itself in all places, and to rectify all minds that err and mistake; in short, incapable of ever being either exhausted or divided, although it communicates itself to all who desire it.

Where is that perfect reason which is so near me, and yet so different from me? Surely it must be something real, for nothing cannot either be perfect or make perfect imperfect natures. Where is that supreme reason? Is it not the very God I look for?

We have seen the prints of the Deity, or, to speak more properly, the seal and stamp of God Himself, inall that is called the works of nature. When a man does not enter into philosophical subtleties, he observes with the first cast of the eye a hand, that was the first mover, in all the parts of the universe, and set all the wheels of the great machine agoing. Everything shows and proclaims an order, an exact measure, an art, a wisdom, a mind superior to us, which is, as it were, the soul of the whole world, and which leads and directs everything to His ends, with a gentle and insensible, though ever an omnipotent force.

We have seen, as it were, the architecture and frame of the universe; the just proportion of all its parts; and the bare cast of the eye has sufficed us to find and discover even in an ant, more than in the sun, a wisdom and power that delights to exert itself in polishing and adorning its vilest works.

This is obvious, without any speculative discussion, to the most ignorant of men; but what a world of other wonders should we discover should we penetrate into the secrets of physics, and dissect the inward parts of animals, which are framed according to the most perfect mechanics.

Let a man study the world as much as he pleases; let him descend into the minutest details; dissect the vilest of animals; narrowly consider the least grain of corn sown in the ground, and the manner in which it germinates and multiplies; attentively observe with what precautions a rose-bud blows and opens in the sun, and closes again at night; and he will find in all these more design, conduct, and industry than in all the works of art. Nay, what is called the art of men is but a faint imitation of the great art called the laws of nature, which the impious did not blush to call blind chance. Is it, therefore, a wonder that poets animated the whole universe, bestowed wings upon the winds, and arrows on the sun, and described great rivers impetuously running to precipitate themselves into the sea and trees shooting upto heaven to repel the rays of the sun by their thick shades? These images and figures have also been received in the language of the vulgar, so natural it is for men to be sensible of the wonderful art that fills all nature.

Poetry did only ascribe to inanimate creatures the art and design of the Creator, who does everything in them. From the figurative language of the poets those notions passed into the theology of the heathens, whose divines were the poets. They supposed an art, a power, or a wisdom, which they called *numen* [divinity], in creatures the most destitute of understanding. With them great rivers were gods, and spring naiads. Woods and mountains had their particular deities; flowers had their Flora; and fruits, Pomona. After all, the more a man contemplates nature, the more he discovers in it an inexhaustible stock of wisdom, which is, as it were, the soul of the universe.

What must we infer from thence? The consequence flows of itself. "If so much wisdom and penetration," says Minutius Felix, "are required to observe the wonderful order and design of the structure of the world, how much more were necessary to form it!"

If men so much admire philosophers because they discover a small part of the wisdom that made all things, they must be stark blind not to admire that wisdom itself.

IV.--A Prayer to God

O my God, if so many men do not discover Thee in this great spectacle Thou givest them of all nature, it is not because Thou art far from any of us. Every one of us feels Thee, as it were, with his hand; but the senses, and the passions they raise, take up all the attention of our minds. Thus, O Lord, Thy light shines ļin darkness; but darkness is so thick and gloomy thatit does not admit the beams of Thy light.

Thou appearest everywhere; and everywhere inattentive mortals neglect to perceive Thee. All nature speaks of Thee, and resounds with Thy holy name; but she speaks to deaf men, whose deafness proceeds from the noise and clatter they make to stun themselves. Thou art near and within them; but they are fugitive, and wandering, as it were, out of themselves. They would find Thee, O Sweet Light, O Eternal Beauty, ever old and ever young, O Fountain of Chaste Delights, O Pure and Happy Life of all who live truly, should they look for Thee within themselves. But the impious lose Thee only by losing themselves. Alas! Thy very gifts, which should show them the hand from whence they flow, amuse them to such a degree as to hinder them from perceiving it. They live by Thee, and yet they live without thinking on Thee or, rather, they die by the Fountain of Life for want of quenching their drought in that vivifying stream; for what greater death can there be than not to know Thee, O Lord? They fall asleep in Thy soft and paternal bosom, and, full of the deceitful dreams by which they are tossed in their sleep, they are insensible of the powerful hand that supports them.

If Thou wert a barren, impotent, and inanimate body, like a flower that fades away, a river that runs, a house that decays and falls to ruin, a picture that is but a collection of colours to strike the imagination, or a useless metal that glistens, they would perceive Thee, and fondly ascribe to Thee the power of giving them some pleasure, although in reality pleasure cannot proceed from inanimate beings, which are themselves void and incapable of it, but from Thee alone, the true spring of all joy. If, therefore, Thou wert but a lumpish, frail, and inanimate being, a mass without any virtue or power, a shadow of a being, Thy vain fantastic nature would busy their vanity, and be a proper object to entertain their mean and brutish thoughts. But because Thou art too intimately within them, and they never at home, Thou art to them an unknown God; for while they rise and wander abroad, the intimate part of themselves is most remote from their sight. The order and beauty Thou scatterest over the face of Thy creatures are like a glaring light that hides Thee from them and dazzles their sore eyes. In fine, because Thou art too elevated and too pure a truth to affect gross senses, men who are become like beasts cannot conceive Thee, though man has daily convincing instances of wisdom and virtue without the testimony of any of his senses; for those virtues have not sound, colour, odour, taste, figure, nor any sensible quality.

Why, then, O my God, do men call Thy existence, wisdom, and power more in question than they do those other things most real and manifest, the truth of which they suppose as certain, in all the serious affairs of life, and which, nevertheless, as well as Thou, escape our feeble senses? O misery! O dismal night that surrounds the children of Adam! O monstrous stupidity! O confusion of the whole man! Man has eyes only to see shadows, and truth appears a phantom to him. What is nothing is all; and what is all is nothing to him. What do I behold in all nature? God. God everywhere, and still God alone.

When I think, O Lord, that all being is in Thee, Thou exhaustest and swallowest up, O Abyss of Truth, all my thoughts. I know not what becomes of me. Whatever is not Thou disappears; and scarce so much of myself remains wherewithal to find myself again. Who sees Thee not never saw anything; and who is not sensible of Thee, never was sensible of anything. He is as if he were not. His whole life is but a dream. Arise, O Lord, arise, Let Thy enemies melt like wax and vanish like smoke before Thy face. How unhappy is the impious soul who, far from Thee, is without God, without hope, without eternal comfort! How happy he who searches, sighs, and thirsts after Thee. But fully happy he on whom are reflected the beams of Thy countenance, whose tears Thy hand has wiped off, and whose desires Thy love has already completed.

When will that time be, O Lord? O fair day, without either cloud or end, of which Thyself shalt be the sun, and wherein Thou shalt run through my soul like a torrent of delight! Upon this pleasing hope I cry out: "Who is like Thee, O Lord? My heart melts and my flesh faints, O God of my soul, and my eternal wealth."

GALILEO

The Authority of Scripture

Galileo's treatise on "The Authority of Scripture in Philosophical Controversies" was written at a time when the Copernican theory of the constitution of the universe was engaging the attention of the world. A Benedictine monk, Benedetto Castelli, called upon to defend the theory at the grand-ducal table of Tuscany, asked Galileo's assistance in reconciling it with orthodoxy. His answer was an exposition of a formal theory as to the relations of physical science to Holy Writ. This answer was further amplified in the "Authority of the Scripture," addressed in 1614 to Christina of Lorraine, Dowager Grand-Duchess of Tuscany, an able and acute defence of his position. A year later another monk laid Galileo's letter to Castelli before the Inquisition, whereupon the philosopher was summoned by Pope Paul V. to the palace of Cardinal Bellarmine, and there warned against henceforth holding, teaching, or defending the condemned doctrine. Nevertheless, in a few years Galileo (see SCIENCE, vol. XV) had to suffer trial and condemnation by the Inquisition for publishing his "Dialogues on the System of the World," which gave the Ptolemaic theory its death-blow.

I.--The Defenders of Fallacy

Some years ago I discovered many astronomical facts till then unknown. Their novelty and their antagonism to some physical propositions commonly received by the schools did stir up against me many who professed the vulgar philosophy, as if, forsooth, I had with my own hand placed these things in the heavens to obscure and disturb nature and science. These opponents, more affectionate to their own opinion than to truth, tried to deny and disprove my discoveries, which they might have discerned with their own eyes; and they published vain discourses, interwoven with irrelevant passages, not rightly understood, of the sacred Scriptures. From this folly they might have been saved had they rememberedthe advice of St. Augustine, who, dealing with celestial bodies, writes: "We ought to believe nothing unadvisedly in a doubtful point, lest in favour of our error we conceive a prejudice against that which truth hereafter may discover to be nowise contrary to the sacred books."

Time has proved every one of my statements, and proving them has also proved that my opponents were of two kinds. Those who had doubted simply because the discoveries were new and strange have been gradually converted, while those whose incredulity was based on personal ill-will to me have shut their eyes to the facts and have endeavoured to asperse my moral character and to ruin me.

Knowing that I have confuted the Ptolemaic and Aristotelian arguments, and distrusting their defence in the field of philosophy, they have tried to shield their fallacies under the mantle of a feigned religion and of scriptural authority, and have endeavoured to spread the opinion that my propositions are contrary to the Scriptures, and therefore heretical. To this end they have found accomplices in the pulpits, and have scattered rumours that my theory of the world-system would ere long be condemned by supreme authority.

Further, they have endeavoured to make the theory peculiar to myself, ignoring the fact that the author, or rather restorer, of the doctrine was Nicholas Copernicus, a Catholic, and a much-esteemed priest, who was summoned to Rome to correct the ecclesiastic calendar, and in the course of his inquiries reached this view of the universe.

The calendar has since been regulated by his doctrine, and on his principles the motions of the planets have been calculated. Having reduced his doctrine to six books, he published them under the title of "De Revolutionibus Coelestibus," at the instance of the Cardinal of Capua, and of the Bishop of Culma; and, sincehe undertook the task at the order of Pope Leo X., he dedicated the work to his successor Paul III., and it was received by the Holy Church and studied by all the world.

In the end of his dedicatory epistle Copernicus writes: "If there should chance to be any mateologists who, ignorant in mathematics yet pretending to skill in that science, should dare, upon the authority of some passage of Scripture wrested to their purpose, to condemn and censure my hypothesis, I value them not, and scorn their inconsiderate judgment. For it is not unknown that Lactantius (a famous author though poor mathematician) writes very childishly concerning the form of the earth when he scoffs at those who affirm the earth to be in form of a globe. So that it ought not to seem strange to the intelligent if any such should likewise now deride us. The mathematics are written for mathematicians, to whom (if I deceive not myself) these labours of mine shall seem to add something, as also to the commonweal of the Church whose government is now in the hands of Your Holiness."

It is such as Lactantius who would now condemn Copernicus unread, and produce authorities of the Scripture, of divines, and of councils in support of their condemnation. I hold these authorities in reverence, but I hold that in this instance they are used for personal ends in a manner very different from the most sacred intention of the Holy Church. I am ready to renounce any religious errors into which I may run in this discourse, and if my book be not beneficial to the Holy Church may it be torn and burnt; but I hold that I have a right to defend myself against the attacks of ignorant opponents.

The doctrine of the movement of the earth and the fixity of the sun is condemned on the ground that the Scriptures speak in many places of the sun moving and the earth standing still. The Scriptures not being capableof lying or erring, it followeth that the position of those is erroneous and heretical who maintain that the sun is fixed and the earth in motion.

It is piously spoken that the Scriptures cannot lie. But none will deny that they are frequently abstruse and their true meaning difficult to discover, and more than the bare words signify. One taking the sense too literally might pervert the truth and conceive blasphemies, and give God feet, and hands, and eyes, and human affections, such as anger, repentance, forgetfulness, ignorance, whereas these expressions are employed merely to accommodate the truth to the mental capacity of the unlearned.

This being granted, I think that in the discussion of natural problems we ought to begin not with the Scriptures, but with experiments and demonstrations. Nor does God less admirably discover Himself to us in nature than in Scripture, and having found the truth in nature we may use it as an aid to the true exposition of the Scriptures. The Scriptures were intended to teach men those things which cannot be learned otherwise than by the mouth of the Holy Spirit; but we are meant to use our senses and reason in discovering for ourselves things within their scope and capacity, and hence certain sciences are neglected in the Holy Writ.

Astronomy, for instance, is hardly mentioned, and only the sun, and the moon, and Lucifer are named. Surely, if the holy writers had intended us to derive our astronomical knowledge from the Sacred Books, they would not have left us so uninformed. That they intentionally forbore to speak of the movements and constitution of the stars is the opinion of the most holy and most learned fathers. And if the Holy Spirit has omitted to teach us those matters as not pertinent to our salvation, how can it be said that one view is *de Fide* and the other heretical? I might here insert the opinion of an ecclesiastic raised to the degree of Eminentissimo:That the intention of the Holy Ghost is to teach us how we shall go to Heaven, and not how the heavens go.

II.--Scriptural and Experimental Truth

Since the Holy Writ is true, and all truth agrees with truth, the truth of Holy Writ cannot be contrary to the truth obtained by reason and experiment. This being true, it is the business of the judicious expositor to find the true meaning of scriptural passages which must accord with the conclusions of observation and experiment, and care must be taken that the work of exposition do not fall into foolish and ignorant hands. It must be remembered that there are very few men capable of understanding both the sacred Scriptures and science, and that there are many with a superficial knowledge of the Scriptures and with no knowledge of science who would fain arrogate to themselves the power of decreeing upon all questions of nature. As St. Jerome writes: "The talking old woman, the dotard, the garrulous sophist, all venture upon, lacerate, teach, before they have learnt. Others, induced by pride, dive into hard words, and philosophate among women touching the Holy Scriptures. Others (oh, shameful!) learn of women what they teach to men."

I will not rank among these same secular writers any theologists whom I repute to be men of profound learning and sober manners, and therefore hold in great esteem and veneration; yet it vexes me when they would constrain science by the authority of the Scriptures, and yet do not consider themselves bound to answer reason and experiment. It is true that theology is the queen of all the sciences, but queen only in the sense that she deals with high matters revealed in noble ways, and if she condescends not to study the more humble matters of the inferior sciences she ought not to arrogate to herself the right to judge them; for this would be as if anautocratic prince, being neither physician nor architect, should undertake to administer medicines and erect buildings to the danger of the lives of his subjects.

Again, to command the professors of astronomy to confute their own observations is to enjoin an impossibility, for it is to command them not to see what they do see, and not to understand what they do understand, and to find what they do not discover. I would entreat the wise and prudent fathers to consider the difference between matters of opinion and matters of demonstration, for demonstrated conclusions touching the things of nature and of the heavens cannot be changed with the same facility as opinions touching what is lawful in a contract, bargain, or bill of exchange. Your highness knows what happened to the late professor of mathematics in the University of Pisa--how, believing that the Copernican doctrine was false, he started to confute it, but in his study became convinced of its truth.

In order to suppress the Copernican doctrine, it would be necessary not only to prohibit the book of Copernicus and the writings of authors who agree with him, but to interdict the whole science of astronomy, and even to forbid men to look at the sky lest they might see Mars and Venus at very varying distances from the earth, and discover Venus at one time crescent, at another time round, or make other observations irreconcilable with the Ptolemaic system.

It is surely harmful to souls to make it a heresy to believe what is proved. The prohibition of astronomy would be an open contempt of a hundred texts of the Holy Scriptures, which teach us that the glory and the greatness of Almighty God are admirably discerned in all His works, and divinely read in the open book of the heavens.

III.--Fact and Faith

It may be said that the doctrine of the movement of the sun and the fixity of the earth must *de Fide* be held for true since the Scriptures affirm it, and all the fathers unanimously accept the scriptural words in their naked and literal sense. But it was necessary to assign motion to the sun and rest to the earth lest the shallow minds of the vulgar should be confounded, amused, and rendered obstinate and contumacious with regard to doctrines of faith. St. Jerome writes: "It is the custom for the pen-men of Scripture to deliver their judgments in many things according to the common received opinion that their times had of them." Even Copernicus himself, knowing the power of custom, and unwilling to create confusion in our comprehension, continues to talk of the rising and setting of the sun and stars and of variations in the obliquity of the zodiac. Whence it is to be noted how necessary it is to accommodate our discourse to our accustomed manner of understanding.

In the next place, the common consent of the fathers to a natural proposition should authorise it only if it have been discussed and debated with all possible diligence, and this question was in those times totally buried.

Besides, it is not enough to say that the fathers accept the Ptolemaic doctrine; it is necessary to prove that they condemned the Copernican. Was the Copernican doctrine ever formally condemned as contrary to the Scriptures? And Didacus, discoursing on the Copernican hypothesis, concludes that the motion of the earth is not contrary to the Scriptures.

Let my opponents, therefore, apply themselves to examine the arguments of Copernicus and others; and let them not hope to find such rash and impetuous decisions in the wary and holy fathers, or in the absolute wisdom of him that cannot err, as those into which they have suffered themselves to be hurried by prejudice or personal feeling. His holiness has certainly an absolute power of admitting or condemning propositions not directly *de Fide*, but it is not in the power of any creature to make them true or false otherwise than of their own nature and *de facto* they are.

In my judgment it would be well first to examine the truth of the fact (over which none hath power) before invoking supreme authority; for if it be not possible that a conclusion should be declared heretical while we are not certain but that it may be true, their pains are vain who pretend to condemn the doctrine of the mobility of the earth and the fixity of the sun, unless they have first demonstrated the doctrine to be impossible and false.

Let us now consider how we may interpret the command of Joshua that the sun should stand still.

According to the Ptolemaic system, the sun moves from east to west through the ecliptic, and therefore the standing still of the sun would shorten and not lengthen the day. Indeed, in order to lengthen the day on this system it would be necessary not to hold the sun, but to accelerate its pace about three hundred and sixty times. Possibly Joshua used the words to suit the comprehension of the ignorant people; possibly--as St. Augustine says--he commanded the whole system of the celestial spheres to stand still, and his command to the moon rather confirms this conjecture.

On the Copernican system interpretation is simplified; for if we consider the mobility of the sun and how it is in a certain sense the soul and heart of the universe, it is not illogical to say that it gives not only light, but also motion to the bodies round it. In this manner, by the standing still of the sun at Joshua's command, the day might be lengthened without disturbing the order of the universe or the mutual positions of the stars. This interpretation also explains the statement that the sun stood still *in medio coeli.* Had the sun been in themiddle of the heavens in the sense of rising and setting, it had hardly been necessary to check its course; but *in medio coeli* probably signifies in the middle or centre of the universe where it resides.

I have no doubt that other passages of the Scriptures could be likewise interpreted in accordance with the Copernican system by divines with knowledge of astronomy. They might say that the word "firmament" very well agrees, *ad literam,* with the starry sphere. *Ad literam,* if they admit the rotation of the earth, they might understand its poles, when it is said *Nec dum terram fecerat, et flumina, et cardines orbis terrae.* [Nor yet had He created the earth, or the rivers, or the hinges for the globe of the earth.] Surely *cardines,* or "hinges," are ascribed to the earth in vain if it be not to turn upon them.

GEORG WILHELM FRIEDRICH HEGEL

The Philosophy of Religion

Hegel's "Philosophy of Religion" was published the year following the philosopher's death, at Berlin, in 1832; and the rugged shape and uneven construction of some of it may fairly be attributed to the fact that, as it stands, it is largely an editorial compilation. Such faults, however, as Dr. Edward Caird has remarked, "if they take from the lectures as expressions of their author's mind, and from their value as scientific treatises, have some compensating advantages if we regard them as a means of education in philosophy; for in this point of view their very artlessness gives them something of the same stimulating, suggestive power which is attained by the consummate art of the Platonic dialogues." The importance of the work is evidenced by the influence it has exercised over the mind of a later generation; and many readers, to whom Hegel (see Vol. XIV) is little more than a name, will certainly find here the sources of much that has become familiar as an essential part of the religious atmosphere of a later day, and of the apologies of modern speculative theology.

I. The Relation of Philosophy to Religion

The object of religion is the same as that of philosophy; it is the external verity itself in its objective existence; it is God--nothing but God and the unfolding of God. Philosophy is not the wisdom of the world, but the knowledge of things which are not of this world. It is not the knowledge of external mass, of empirical life and existence, but of the eternal, of the nature of God, and of all which flows from His nature. For this nature ought to manifest and develop itself. Consequently, philosophy in unfolding religion merely unfolds itself, and in unfolding itself it unfolds religion. In so far as philosophy is occupied with the eternal truth, the truth which is in and for itself; in so far as it is occupied with this as thinking spirit, rather than in an arbitrary fashion and in view of a particular interest,philosophy has the same sphere of activity as has religion. And if the religious consciousness aspires to abolish all that is peculiar to itself and to be absorbed in its object, the philosophic spirit likewise plunges with the same energy into its object and renounces all particularity.

Religion and philosophy are thus at one in having one and the same object. Philosophy, in fact, also is the adoration of God, it is religion; for, seeing that God is its object, it involves the same renunciation of every opinion and every thought that is arbitrary and subjective. Philosophy is, in consequence, identical with religion. Only it is religion in a peculiar manner, and this it is which distinguishes it from religion commonly so called. So philosophy and religion are both religion, and that which distinguishes one from the other is no more than the characteristic mode in which respectively they consider their object, God.

100

Here is the difficulty of understanding how philosophy can make but one with religion, a difficulty which has even been mistaken for impossibility. Thence also arise the fears which philosophy inspires in theology and the hostile attitudes which they assume towards each other. What brings about this attitude is, on the side of theology, that for her philosophy does nothing but corrupt, pull down, and profane the content of religion, and that she understands God in a totally different manner from that after which religion understands Him. It is the same opposition which long ago among the Greeks caused a free and democratic people like the Athenians to burn books and to condemn Socrates. In our own day, however, this opposition is considered a thing which it is natural to admit--more natural indeed than the other opinion concerning the unity of religion and philosophy.

Diverse religions offer us, it is true, only too often the most bizarre and monstrous representations of thedivine essence. But we must not confine ourselves to a superficial consideration and consequent rejection of these representations and the religious practices which follow upon them as being engendered by superstition, by error, or by imposture, or even by a simple piety, and so neglect their essential value. There is need to discover in these representations and in these practices their relation with truth.

II.--God the Universal

For us, who have religion, God is a familiar being, a substantial truth existing in our subjective consciousness. But, scientifically considered, God is a general and abstract term. The philosophy of religion it is which develops and grasps the divine nature and which teaches us what God is. God is a familiar idea, but an idea which has still to be scientifically developed.

The result of philosophic examination is that God is the absolute truth, the universal in and for itself, embracing all things and in which all things subsist. And in regard to this assertion, we may appeal in the first place to the religious consciousness, and to its conviction that God is the absolute truth whence all things proceed, whither they all return, upon which all things depend, and in respect of which nothing can possess a true and absolute independence.

The heart may very well be full of this representation of God, but science is not built up of what is in the heart. The object of science is that which has arisen to the level of consciousness, and of thinking consciousness that is, in other words, that which has attained to the form of thought.

In so much as He is the universal, God is, for us, in relation to development, Being enclosed in itself, Being at unity with itself. When we say God is Being enclosed in itself, we enunciate a proposition which isbound to a development which we await. But this envelopment of God in Himself which we have called His universality we must not conceive, relatively to God Himself and His content, as an abstract universality, outside of which, and as opposed to which, the particular has an independent existence.

So we must consider this universal as an absolutely concrete universal. This sense of fulness is the sense in which God is one, and there is but one God--that is to say, God is not one merely by contrast with other gods, but because it is He that is the One, that is, God.

The things which are, the developments of the worlds of nature and of mind, show a multiplicity of forms and an infinite variety of existences. But whatever may be their difference of degree, of force, of content, these things have no true independence; their being is consequent, and, so to speak, contingent. When we predicate being of particular things, it is not of Being which is absolute that we speak--Being of and from itself; that is, God--but a borrowed being, a semblance of being.

God in His universality--that is, this universal Being which has no limit, no bounds, no particularity--is a Being which subsists absolutely, and which subsists alone; all else which subsists has its root in this unity, and by this alone subsists. In thus representing to ourselves this first content we may say that God is absolute substance, the only veritable reality. For not everything which has a reality has a reality of its own, or subsists by itself. God is the only absolute reality, and thereby the absolute substance.

If we stop at this abstract thought we have Spinozism, for in Spinozism subjectivity is not yet differentiated from substantiality, from substance as such. But in the presupposition just made there is also this thought--God is spirit, absolute and eternal; spirit which comes not forth from itself in differentiation. This ideality, this subjectivity of spirit, which is transparency, ideality excluding all particular determination, is precisely the universal, pure relation to self, Being which remains absolutely within itself.

If we halt at substance, we fail to grasp this universal under its concrete form. In its concrete determination spirit always preserves its unity, this unity of its reality which we call substance. But one should add that this substantiality, the unity of the absolute reality with itself, is but the foundation, but a moment in the determination of God as spirit. Hence, principally, arises the reproach which is directed against philosophy--to wit, that philosophy, to be consistent with itself, is necessarily Spinozism, and consequently atheism and fatalism. But at the beginning we have not yet determinations distinguished one from another as aye and nay. We have the one but not the other.

Consequently, what we have here is, to start with, content under the form of substance. Even when we say, "God," "spirit," we have only words, indeterminate representations. The essential point is to know what has been produced in the consciousness. And that is, first, the simple, the abstract. Here, in this first simple determination, we have God only under the form of universality. Only we do not halt at this moment.

Nevertheless, this content remains the foundation of all further developments, for in these developments God comes not forth from His unity. When God creates the world--to use the expression of every day--there comes not into existence an evil, a contrary, existing in itself independently of God.

III.--God Exists for Thought

This Beginning is an object for us or a content in us. We possess this object. Immediately the question arises, Who are we? We, I, spirit--here also isa complex being, a multiplied being. I have perceptions; I see, I hear, etc. Seeing, hearing; all this is I. Consequently, the precise sense of this question is, Which among these determinations is it in accordance with which this content exists for our minds? Idea, will, imagination, feeling--which is the seat, the proper domain of this content, of this object?

If we accept the common answers to this question, God will abide in us as the object of faith, of feeling, of representation, of knowledge.

We shall have to examine more closely later on in a special fashion with respect to this point, these forms, faculties, aspects of ourselves. In this place we shall not seek a reply to this question; nor shall we say, basing our answer on experience and observation, that God is in our feeling, etc. But, to begin with, we will confine ourselves to what we have actually before us, to this One, to this universal, to this concrete Being.

If we take this One, and ask for what power, for what activity of our mind does this One, this absolutely universal Being, exist, we cannot but name the one activity of mind which corresponds to it as constituting its proper natural domain. This activity, which corresponds to the universal, is thought.

Thought is the field in which this content moves; it is the energising of the universal, or the universal in the reality of its activity. Or, if we say that thought embraces the universal, that for which the universal is will still be thought.

This universal which can be produced by thought, and which is for thought, may be a quite abstract universal. In this sense it is the unlimited, the infinite, the being without bounds, without particular determination. This universal, negative to begin with, has its seat not elsewhere than in thought.

To think of God is to rise above the things of sense,exterior and individual, above simple feeling into theregion of pure being; being at unity with itself--that is to say, into the pure region of the universal. And this region is thought.

Such is the substratum for this content considered on the subjective side. Here the content is that Being in which is no difference, no schism; Being which abides in itself, the universal; and thought is the form for which this universal is.

Thus we have a difference between thought and the universal which we have called God. It is a difference which in the first place belongs only to our reflection, and is by no means to be found in the content on its own account. There is the result to which philosophy comes--a result already comprised in religion as under the form of faith--to wit, that God is the sole veritable reality, the Being without which no other reality would exist.

In the unity of this reality, in this cloudless shining, the reality and the distinction which we call thinking-being have as yet no place.

What we have before us is this absolute unity. This content, this determination we cannot yet call religion because to religion belongs subjective spirit consciousness. Thought is the seat of this universal, but this seat is, to begin with, absorbed in this being which is one, eternal, in and for itself.

This universal constitutes the beginning and the point of departure, but only as unity which so abides. It is not a mere substratum whence differences are born; rather, all differences are included in this universal. No more is it an abstract and inert universal, but the absolute principle of all activity, the matrix, the infinite source whence all things proceed, whither all things return, and in which they are eternally preserved.

Thus the universal is never separated from this ethereal element, from this Unity with itself, this concentration within itself.

IV.--What is Evil?

As the universal, God could not find Himself faced by a contrary whereof the reality should pretend to rise above the phantasmal level. For this pure unity and this perfect transparency matter is nothing impenetrable, and spirit, the ego, is not so independent as to possess a true, individual, substantiality of its own.

There has been a tendency to label this idea pantheism. It would be more exact to call it the conception of substantiality. God is first determined as substance only. The absolute subject spirit is also substance; but it is determined rather as subject. This is the difference generally ignored by those who assert that speculative philosophy is pantheism. As usual, they miss the essential point and disparage philosophy by falsifying it.

Pantheism is commonly taken to mean that God is all things--the whole, the universe, the collection of all existences, of things infinite and infinitely diverse. From which notion the charge is brought against philosophy that it teaches that all things are God; that is to say, that God is, not the universal which is in and for itself, but the infinite multiplicity of individual things in their empirical and immediate existence.

If you say God is all that is here, this paper, etc., you have indeed committed yourself to the pantheism with which philosophy is reproached; that is, the whole is understood as equivalent to all individual things. But there is also the genus, which is equally the universal, yet is wholly different from this totality in which the universal is but the collection of individual things, and the basis, the content, is constituted by these things themselves. To say that there has ever been a religion which has taught this pantheism is to say what is absolutely untrue. It has never entered any man's mindthat everything is God; that is to say, that God is things in their individual and contingent existence. Far less has philosophy ever taught this doctrine.

Spinozism itself, as such, as well as Oriental pantheism, contains this doctrine: that the divine in all things is no more than that which is universal in their content, their essence; and in such sense that this essence is conceived of as a determinate essence.

When Brahma says, "In the metal I am the brightness of its shining; among the rivers I am the Ganges; I am the life of all that lives," he thereby suppresses the individual. He says not, "I am the metal, the rivers, the individual things of various kinds as such, nor in the fashion of their immediate existence."

Here, at this stage, what is expressed is no longer pantheism; but rather that of the essence in individual things.

In the living being are time and space. But in this individual being it is only the changeless element that is made to stand out. "The life of being that lives" is in this latter sphere of life the unlimited, the universal. But if it be said "God is all things," here we understand individuality with all its limitations, its finity, its passing existence. This notion of pantheism arises out of the conception of unity, not as spiritual unity but abstract unity; and then, when the idea takes its religious form, where only the substance, the One, is possessed of true reality, there is a tendency to forget that it is precisely in presence of this unity that individual and finite things are effaced, and to continue to place these in a material fashion side by side with this unity. They will not admit the teaching of the Eleatics, who, when they say "There is only One," add expressly that non-entity is not. All that is finite would be limitation, a negation of the One, but non-entity, the boundary, term, limit, and that which is limited, exist not at all.

Spinozism has been accused of atheism. But Spinozismdoes not teach that God is the world, that He is *all things*. Things have indeed a phenomenal existence--that is, an existence as appearances. We speak of our existence, and our life is indeed comprised in this existence, but to speak philosophically the world has no reality, it has no existence. Individual things are finite things to which no reality can be attributed; it may be said of them that they have no existence.

Spinozism--this is the accusation directed against it--involves by way of consequence that, if all things make but one, good and evil make but one; there is no difference between them; and thereby all religion is destroyed. In themselves, it is said there is no difference between good and evil; consequently it is a matter of indifference whether one be righteous or wicked. It may be granted that in themselves--that is, in God, who is the sole veritable reality--the difference between good and evil disappears. In God there is no evil. But the difference between good and evil can exist only on condition that God is the evil. But it cannot be allowed that evil is an affirmative thing, and that this affirmation is in God. God is good, and nothing else than good; the distinction between good and evil is not present in this unity, in this substance, and comes into existence only with differentiation.

God is unity abiding absolutely in itself. In the substance there is no differentiation. The distinction of good and evil begins with the distinction of God from the world, and particularly from man. It is the fundamental principle of Spinozism with regard to this distinction of God and the world that man must have no other end than God. The love of God, therefore, it is that Spinozism marks out for man as the law to be followed in order to bring about the healing of this breach.

And it is the loftiest morality that teaches that evil has no existence and that man is not bound to permit the substantial existence of this distinction, this negation.Yet it is possible for him to desire to maintain the difference and even to push it to the point of sheer opposition to God, who is the universal, self-contained and self-sufficing. In this case man is evil. But, alternatively, he may annul this distinction and place his true existence in God alone and in his aspiration towards Him; and in this case he is good.

In Spinozism there is indeed the difference between good and evil, opposition between God and man; but side by side with it we have also the principle that evil is to be deemed a non-entity. In God as God, in God as substance, there is no distinction. It is for man that the distinction exists, as also for him exists the distinction of good and evil.

V.--The Determination of Unity

The superficial method of appraising philosophy is exemplified also in those who assert that it is a "system of identity." It is perfectly true that substance is this unity at one with itself, but spirit no less is this self-identity. Ultimately, all is identity, unity with itself. But when they speak of the philosophy of identity they have in view abstract identity or unity in general; and they neglect the essential point, to wit, the determination of this unity in itself; in other words, they omit to consider whether this unity is determined as substance or as spirit. Philosophy from beginning to end is nothing else than the study of determinations of unity.

In the sphere of the Notion many unities are comprised. The combination of water and earth is a unity, but this unity is mixture. If we bring together a base and an acid, we have as the result a crystal; also water; but water which cannot be discerned and which gives no trace of humidity. Here the unity of the water and of this matter is a unity different from the mixture of water and earth. The essential point is the differenceof these determinations. The unity of God is always unity, but what is of primary importance is to know the modes and forms of the determination of this unity.

Manifestation, development, determination do not go on to infinity, nor yet do they stop accidentally. But in the course of its true development the Notion completes its course by a return upon itself, whereby it has attained the reality adequate to it. So it is that the manifestation is infinite in nature, that the content is adequate to the Notion of spirit, and that the phenomenal world exists, like spirit, in and for itself. In religion, the Notion of religion has become its own object. Spirit which is in and for itself has now no longer in its development individual forms and determinations, it knows itself no longer as spirit in such determinability or such a limited moment; but it has triumphed over these limitations and this finiteness, and is for itself that which also it is in itself. This cognisance in which spirit is for itself what it is in itself constitutes the in-and-for of spirit which is in possession of knowledge, the perfect and absolute religion, in which is revealed what spirit is, what God is. That is the Christian religion.

THE BOOKS OF HINDUISM

The Vedanta Sutras

Hinduism, though usually understood to include Brahmanism (q.v.), is, in fact, a later development of it. Its central doctrine is the trinity, or Trimurti, which embraces the three-fold manifestation of the god-head as Brahma, the one supreme being, the Creator; Vishnu the Preserver; and Siva the Destroyer. The three principal books of Hinduism are the "Vedanta Sutras," the "Puranas," and the "Tantras," of which only the first is epitomised here. The "Sutras" are the earliest. The "Vedanta" (literally "goal" or "issue of the Veda") is a purely pantheistic and monastic philosophical system, and by far the most prevalent in Modern India. It is ascribed to Badarayana, sometimes called Vyasa, though this last is really a generic name denoting "a collector." The word "sutra" denotes literally "threads," and is used by Brahmanic writers for short, dry sentences, brief expositions. "Vedanta Sutras" means literally "compendious expressions of the Vedantic (not Vedic) doctrine." The second great division of Hindu sacred literature is the "Puranas," the last and most modern of the books of Hinduism. The word "Purana" means "old," and in ancient Sanscrit writings it has the same meaning as our "cosmology." The "Puranas," however, are ill-arranged collections of theological and philosophical reflections, myths and legends, ritual, and ascetic rules. They depend very much on the two great epics, especially the Mahabharata. The Sanscrit writings called "Tantras" are really manuals of religion, of magic, and of counter-charms, with songs in praise of Sakti, the female side of Siva.

Introductory

The Vedanta is sometimes called the Mimamsa (= philosophical reflections). The aphorisms of which the Vedanta Sutras consist are in themselves almost as unintelligible as the Confucian "Book of Changes," the compiler having been only too successful in aiding the memory of the Hindu student by a system of *multum in parvo.*

It is usual to accept the interpretation put on the Sutras by the Sanscrit commentator Sankara, commonlycalled Sankara Karya, who flourished about A.D. 700. There are, however, many other commentaries, notably that of Ramanuga. George Thibaut, in the "Sacred Books of the East" (vols. 34, 38, and 48), gives the interpretation of Sankara, and also that of Ramanuga when it differs essentially. On the whole it may be said that Sankara is a thorough-going Vedantist and pantheist. Ramanuga, on the other hand, has leanings towards the dualism of the Sankhya philosophy, and endeavours to make the Vedanta Sutras support his opinions.

The Vedanta Sutras embrace five hundred and fifty-five aphorisms, or Sutras, arranged in four books (*Adhyay*), each having four-chapters (*Pada*), the chapters being severally divided into sections (*Adhikarana*). These Sutras are of the utmost importance, as nearly all Hindu sects base their belief and practices on them. It should be remembered that these Sutras form a collection, and that they are the work of many hands, and belong to different periods.

Book I.--Brahman, the Sum and Substance of Everything

The ego and the non-ego differ in themselves and in their attributes. It will be found, however, that the non-ego depends on the ego, and is its product. Individual souls, on the other hand, representing so many egos, are themselves but manifestations of the supreme universal soul--Brahman; that is, Brahman and the Atman [the individual soul] are identical, the latter being the product of the self-revealing of the former. [With this one may compare the "ontological ideas" of Plato, the "absolute substance" of Spinoza, and the "absolute idea" of Hegel; all of them standing for the One only existing Being which manifests itself to thought and to sense in various forms.]

"What, then," asks the Vedantist, "is Brahman"? The word comes from *brih,* "to be great." Hence Brahman is something, or someone, transcendently great. The word may be defined as connoting that whence all things proceed. This implies absolute, unoriginated origin, absolute subsistence, and also reabsorption, for as all things go forth from Brahman, so shall all things return to that whence they started forth.

The Scriptures [Vedas] lay most stress on Brahman as the source and origin of all things. What qualities there are in the world inhere in Brahman, or they could not be in the world which has sprung from him. There could be no intelligent souls without a previously existing intelligent Brahman. That Brahman, the Supreme Being, is all-knowing is proved from the fact that the Veda itself, the source and centre of what is knowable, proceeds from Him as its one, only author.

This Brahman, as set forth in the Vedanta texts as the cause of the world, is therefore intelligent, and by no means to be identified with the non-intelligent Pradhâna (*Prakriti*) which the Sankhya [atheistic] philosophy makes to be the world's cause. What looks like a separate, conscious, individual soul or mind is really but the outworking of Brahman, the highest and first of beings.

The difference is apparent, but not real. So teaches Sankara; but his rival commentator, Ramanuga, endeavours to show that Brahman, the supreme self of the universe, is absolutely free from the effects of conduct. But the individual selves, which we call souls, are not, for it is the effect of conduct in a previous state of existence [Karma] that decides the character and form of the new life to be lived, or whether there is to be a new life lived at all, since conduct sufficiently good entitles to absorption in the one all--Brahman.

It may be objected that Brahman cannot be the creator of this actual world, for there is in it suffering,injustice, and cruelty. He could not be the author of these. To which the commentator Sankara answers: "Brahman is himself, with all his greatness, subject to the operation of the great moral laws according to which virtue is rewarded and vice punished. All men are free, and it is their self-chosen conduct that determines their destiny. This is a law that pervades all existence, conditions existence, and without which there could be no existence."

It may be again asked: "How can a being with perfect life produce a world that is lifeless?" In other words, "How can the effect differ from its cause?" The same commentator replies: "Just as lifeless hair can grow out of a living man."

Again, it is said, "In the universe Brahman is at once he who enjoys and he who is enjoyed. How can he be both one and the other--agent and object?" To which Sankara replies: "It is as possible for these two to go together as for the ocean to be itself and to be at the same time foam, waves, billows, and bubbles. The same earth produces diamonds, rock crystal, and vermilion. Do they differ from the earth?

"The same sun causes plants of various kinds to grow, and the very same nourishment taken into the body is changed to flesh, hair, nails, etc. The spider spins its web from its own substance, and spirits assume many forms when they appear on the earth. All these are but images of the eternal world-process by which Brahman reveals Himself in souls and in material objects."

THE HIGHEST KNOWLEDGE INACCESSIBLE TO LOW CASTE MEN

No Sudra [or lowest caste man] is capable of such knowledge as leads to Brahmanhood [the state of being absorbed in Brahman]. Only the twice-born are allowedto study the Vedic Scriptures, a knowledge of which is essential to salvation. The twice-born are likewise alone permitted to offer sacrifice, for how can a man sacrifice aright who is ignorant of the sacred scriptures, which are alone adequate for a man's guidance? If the Sudras, or fourth-caste men, are excluded from the *summum bonum* of humanity--absorption in the one great all--how much more are Pariahs, or non-caste men, deprived of this great boon! Brahman is the material, as well as the efficient, cause of the world, which springs from him by way of modification, but is his manifested self and nothing more.

Book II.--Objections to Vedantic Doctrines Stated and Refuted

The Vedanta texts, the Vedas and the Upanishads, teach that Brahman is the one only source of whatever exists outside himself; that his nature is not only mighty, but also intelligent. The evidence for this supplied in Book I. is, for the most part, the authority of the above texts; that which they say must be accepted as "gospel," whatever human reason may see or say to the contrary.

Book II. begins by stating and answering speculative objections on the part of Sankhyaists. Though himself intelligence (not merely intelligent) Brahman may give birth to a non-intelligent world, seeing that like does not always spring from like [see above].

Atomists hold that there is apparent difference and separateness in things. "Where, then," they ask, "is the oneness, the monism, for which the Vedantists argue?" It is replied that it is only superficial thought that fixes itself upon the manifoldness of things, losing sight of their oneness. Deeper thought sees underneath the many a oneness which binds them, and of which they are only the outward expressions. The great ocean is one, but its waves and ripples are many. All at bottom is but one: the Universal Being.

A non-intelligent first cause (*Prakriti*), such as the Sankhyaists postulate, could never call into being an orderly world, for how could unreason produce reason? Nor could atoms set in motion produce a planned or intelligent universe, as the Atomists falsely say. There must be an intelligent power controlling the atoms and contemplating the result to be attained.

The view put forth by the Sankhya philosophers, that an external and internal world exists in mutual independence, is contrary to thought and experience--is, in fact, unthinkable. We know no external world: we have never had any experience outside the region of our own consciousness; yet what is regarded as external to the individual consciousness is not *Maya,* as is taught in some of the Upanishads, and maintained by later philosophers. This external world as a fact of consciousness is as real as that consciousness and as the individual mind which makes mental experience possible, and is the great All, of which the individual mind is the working and manifestation.

THE RELATION OF BRAHMAN TO ELEMENTS AND THE SOUL

Are the elementary substances (ether, air, etc) co-eternal, with Brahman, or do they issue from him? It can be shown, and is shown, that one elementary substance proceeds from another (*e.g.,* air from ether), andthat in the last resort all such substances have come forth from Brahman, who has not only produced them, but also guided and effected their evolution.

The individual soul is, according to the scriptures [Vedas and Upanishads], eternal and permanent, and has not been produced by Brahman; who is, however, as noted, the producer of the elementary substances. Like Brahman himself, the individual soul is uncreated and eternal. What is in time and belongs to time is the connection of the soul with the conditions of space and time. This is the interpretation given by Sankara. Ramanuga, however, holds that the soul is a creature of Brahman, though an eternal one, it having existed ever as a mode of the great All [compare the doctrine of the eternal procession of the Son].

WHAT IS SOUL?

What is soul? It is *gna*, or knowledge. [The etymology of both these latter words is identical--compare Greek *gnosco*, etc.] This means, according to Sankara, that knowledge is of the very essence of soul, and not a mere attribute of it. The soul is not merely a knower (*gnatri*), but it is knowledge. Ramanuga, on the other hand, explains that the knowledge spoken of in this Sutra means "the knower"; that the soul is not knowledge, but that which can and does know.

Is the soul limited in size, and capable, therefore, of occupying but a restricted space? Or is it, on the contrary, omnipresent?

Sankara maintains that the Sutra in question teaches the latter; the soul is everywhere. Ramanuga makes the same Sutra teach the very contrary. As a matter of fact, the Sutra in question seems to teach both these contradictory doctrines, perhaps because it registers different traditions. Sankara, however, explains further on that as long as the soul is passing through the changes involved in Samsara [= transmigration] it islimited and local, but on reaching Brahmanhood it becomes omnipresent. In this way the great commentator seeks to reconcile teaching apparently contradictory in this Sutra.

Is this soul an agent? Some of the Sutras say it is, others say it is not. How are the conflicting statements to be reconciled? Sankara does this in the following way. As long as the soul is tied down to material conditions--that is, is passing through the processes of Samsara--it is an agent. But as soon as it has escaped from this bondage of transmigration it dwells in a state of perfect repose, inactive and restful. In all its activities the soul is prompted by Brahman, without whose inspiration and guidance the soul could perform nothing, and could never, therefore, reach the true goal of all souls, absorption in the one All, which can be obtained in no other way than by the performance of good deeds, which means action.

Book III.--Of the Soul and its Summum Bonum

When at death the soul passes from the body its subtle material elements still cling to it. Good souls pass on to the moon, whence they afterwards descend in a form and state determined by their former actions [Karma]. If the previous life has been a moral failure, the new life now entered upon will belong to a lower level of being, *i.e.*, the man may become an animal, the higher, animal may become a lower one. On the other hand, there may be an ascent in the scale of being.

When the soul is a-dreaming, what it thinks it sees and hears, etc., is all illusion, for it does not see or hear, etc., what it thinks it does. In a state of profound dreaminess the soul leaves the body and lives in close fellowship with Brahman.

How is the soul to obtain final release from the thraldom of material conditions? By meditating on Brahmanas he is set forth in the sacred scriptures. Brahman must be thought about and meditated on in all his attributes, and this produces identity with the one great self of existence.

Though Sankara makes this to be the teaching of the Sutras, in another place he insists that Brahman is without attributes. He is not, therefore, consistent. The meditation on Brahman which leads to soul-freedom must have regard also to Brahman's negative qualities, *i.e.*, his not being gross, nor subtle, wise nor foolish, etc.

THE RELATION OF KNOWLEDGE AND CONDUCT

The knowledge of Brahman is independent of action, and not subordinate to it. It is *vidya* [compare *vision*, which has the same etymology], or knowledge, that is alone prescribed in the holy writings, not conduct. Where, however, there is right knowledge, there will be rightness of life. But mere rightness of life is nothing; it is that which leads to it and is the cause that is alone commanded and commended [compare the controversy among Christian theologians about faith and works]. The knowledge which saves and enfranchises may be reached by a man in this present life, and will be, if the appropriate means are employed.

OF BRAHMANHOOD

Meditation is a duty to be observed to the very close of life, and the amount and intensity of it are the measure of a man's virtue and piety. When he has reached the full knowledge of Brahman, a man is freed from the consequences [karma] of all his evil deeds, past, present, and future. [One would think that the state of Brahmanhood excluded the possibility of sin, but this Sutra seems to imply the contrary. The Sutras, however, make a distinction between a lower state of Brahmanhood and a higher. See below.]

What happens to the knowing one (*vidvan*) at death?The soul of him who has at death the lower Brahman knowledge merges into the subtler elements. But when the highest knowledge is attained there is complete absorption in Brahman. Whoever dies in possession of this highest knowledge is at once merged in Brahman, and rests eternally and perfectly in him.

The Upanishads describe the stations on the way which leads up to Brahman. These stations are to be understood not merely as terminuses of the various stages of the journey, but they denote also the divine beings who direct the soul in its progress and enable it to move forward and upward. According to some Sutras in this book the guardians of the path conducting to the gods lead the departed soul, not to the highest Brahman, but to the effected (*karya*), or qualified (*saguna*), Brahman. But in other Sutras in this book the opposite view is stated and defended, according to which the *vidvan*, or knower, goes direct to the highest Brahman without halting anywhere short of that god.

The Sutras teach, on the whole, the doctrine that the enfranchised soul, being identical with Brahman, is inseparable from him just as a mode of substance is incapable of existing apart from the substance of which it is a mode. Ramanuga points out, however, that some of the Sutras in this book give it clearly to be understood that the freed soul can exist in isolation and in separation from the great All.

The released soul can enter several bodies at the same time, since it is not subject to space relations as other souls are.

THOMAS À KEMPIS

The Imitation of Christ

Thomas à Kempis, whose family name was Haemmerlein, received the name of Kempis from Kempen, in Holland, the place of his birth. Either Thomas Haemmerlein or Thomas Kempensis would be a more correct name than the form "à Kempis," by which he is generally known; and "Musica Ecclesiastica" is the more correct title of the "Imitatio Christi." It is not even certain that Thomas was the author of it, for the names of other authors have been put forward with more or less probability; but he was certainly its copyist, and the balance of evidence is in favour of his authorship. Thomas was born in 1379, the son of a shoemaker; entered in 1400 a monastery at Agnetenberg, near Zwolle, and died in the monastery on August 8, 1471, with a great reputation for learning and for sanctity. The "Imitation" was completed about 1420. Editions and translations in all principal languages are innumerable; but the definitive edition is the Latin text by Dr. Carl Hirsche, of Hamburg (1874), from which the following epitome has been made. The "Imitation" consists of four books of meditations, which are among the most priceless treasures of Christian literature.

I.--Admonitions Useful to the Spiritual Life

"Whoever follows Me does not walk in darkness," says the Lord. These are the words of Christ by which we are admonished how far we should imitate His life and manners if we wish to be truly illumined and liberated from all blindness of heart. Let it, therefore, be our supreme study to meditate on the life of Jesus Christ.

Vanity of vanities, all things are vanity, except to love God and to serve Him only. The highest wisdom is to strive towards celestial kingdoms, through contempt of the world. It is, therefore, vanity to seek the riches that are about to perish, and to hope in them. It is vanity also to solicit honours, and to exalt oneself to high place. It is vanity to follow after the desires of the flesh, and to seek that for which we must soon be heavily punished. It is vanity to wish a long life, and to care little about a good life. It is vanity to attend only to the present life, and not to provide for things which are to come. It is vanity to love that which passes away so speedily, and not to hasten thither where eternal joy remains.

Remember often that proverb--"The eye is not satisfied with seeing nor the ear with hearing." Study, therefore, to withdraw your heart from the love of visible things, and turn yourself to the invisible. For those who follow their sensuality stain their conscience, and lose the grace of God.

Every man naturally desires to know, but what does knowledge signify without the fear of God? The humble peasant who serves God is far better than the proud philosopher who neglects himself and considers the courses of the stars. Whoever knows himself well contemns himself, and takes no delight in human praise. If I should know all things in the world, and yet not be in charity, what would it advantage me in the presence of God, Who is about to judge me for my deeds?

Desist from too much desire of knowing, because great distraction and deception are found in it. Those who know, desire to seem and to be called wise. There are many things of which the knowledge is of little or no value to the soul, and the man is very foolish who turns to other things than those which subserve his health. Many words do not satisfy the soul; but a good life cools down the mind, and a good conscience affords great confidence towards God.

We might have great peace if we did not occupy ourselves with the words and deeds which are no concern of ours. How can he remain long in peace who meddles with cares which are foreign to him, who seeks opportunities without, and recollects himself little or rarely? Blessed are the simple, for they shall havemuch peace.

Without charity, an outward work is of value; but whatever is done from charity, however small and trivial it may be, becomes wholly fruitful. For God weighs more the source from which an action comes than the work which it does. He does much who loves much. He does much who does the deed well. He does well who serves the community rather than his own will.

That often seems to be charity which is rather carnality; for natural inclination, one's own will, the hope of reward, and the liking for comfort are rarely absent. But whoever has true and perfect charity seeks himself in nothing, but desires only the glory of God. He envies no one, because he loves no joy of his own, nor cares to rejoice in himself; but wishes, above all good things, to find felicity in God. Whoever has a spark of true charity feels at once that all earthly things are full Of vanity.

II.--Admonitions Leading to Inward Life

"The kingdom of God is within you," says the Lord. Turn yourself with your whole heart to the Lord, and leave this miserable world, and your soul shall find rest. Learn to despise outward things, and to give yourself to inward things, and you shall see the kingdom of God rise within you. For the kingdom of God is peace and joy in the Holy Spirit, and is not given to the impious. Christ shall come to you showing you His consolation, if you prepare within you a home fit for Him. All His glory and beauty are from within, and it is there that He delights Himself. He often visits the man of inward mind, with sweet colloquy, pleasant consolation, great peace, and most astounding familiarity.

If you know not how to contemplate high and celestial things, rest in the passion of Christ, and willingly dwell in His holy wounds. For if you devoutly have recourse to the wounds of Jesus you will feel great comfort introuble, care little for human contempt, and easily bear detracting words. For Christ, in the world, was despised by men, and in His greatest need was deserted, among insults, by His friends. Christ willed to suffer and to be despised, and shall you dare to complain of anything? Christ had enemies and detractors, and do you wish to have all friends and benefactors? Whence shall your patience be crowned if you have suffered no adversity? If you desire to suffer nothing contrary to you, how shall you be the friend of Christ?

He to whom all things taste as they really are, and not as they are spoken of or esteemed, is the truly wise man, taught by God rather than by men. Whoever knows how to walk from within, and to put little value on things without, needs not to find a place nor wait a time for his devout prayers. The man of inward mind quickly recollects himself, because he never spends himself wholly upon outward things.

First hold yourself in peace, and then you will be able to pacify others. The pacific man is of more service than the learned. But the passionate man turns even good to evil, easily believing evil. The peaceful man is good, and turns all things to good. The man who is well at peace is suspicious of nothing, but the discontented and turbulent is agitated by divers suspicions. He can neither himself be quiet, nor leave others in quiet. He often says what he ought not to say, and leaves undone what he ought to do. He thinks about what others ought to do, and neglects his own duty.

Man is raised from earthly matters by two wings--namely, simplicity and purity. Simplicity should be in his intention, and purity in his affection. Simplicity tends towards God, purity takes hold of Him.

Always to do well, and to hold oneself in small esteem, is the mark of a humble soul. To desire no consolation from any created thing is the sign of great purity and inward confidence. The man who seeks no witness forhimself from without has plainly committed himself altogether to God. For "not he who commends himself is approved," says blessed Paul, "but he whom God commends." To walk with God within, and to be held by no affection without, is the state of the inwardly-minded man.

Jesus has now many lovers of His celestial kingdom, but few bearers of His Cross. He has many who desire consolation, but few who desire tribulation. He finds many companions of His table, but few of His abstinence. All wish to rejoice with Him; few are willing to bear anything for Him.

In the Cross is safety; in the Cross is life; in the Cross is protection from enemies; in the Cross is the sweetness of heaven; in the Cross is strength of mind; in the Cross is the perfection of sanctity. There is no health for the soul nor hope of eternal life except in the Cross. Take up your cross, therefore, and follow Jesus.

If anything were better and more useful for the welfare of men than to suffer, Christ would have shown it both in His words and in His example. For He calls to the disciples who follow Him, and to all who desire to follow Him, and says: "If any

will come after Me, let him deny himself, and lift up his cross and follow Me."
When all has been read and studied, let this be our conclusion--"That through
many tribulations we must enter into the kingdom of God."

III.--Of Inward Consolation

I will hear what the Lord God may say in me. It is a blessed soul which hears the
Lord speaking in it, and receives the word of consolation from His lips. Speak,
Lord, for your servant hears.

"I have taught the prophets from the beginning," says the Lord, "and until now I
have not ceased to speak at all; but many are deaf and hard to My voice.Many
listen more willingly to the world than to God, and more easily follow the appetite
of the flesh than God's good pleasure. The world promises small and temporary
things, and is served with great eagerness; I promise supreme and eternal things,
but the hearts of mortals are torpid. Who serves and obeys Me in everything with
so great care as the world and its lords are served? Men run a long way for a trifling
reward, but for eternal life many scarcely lift a foot once from earth."

Lord God, you are all my good. And who am I that I should dare to speak to you?
I am the poorest and least of your servants, a wretched little worm, far more
miserable and contemptible than I know or dare to say, Yet remember me, Lord,
because I am nothing, I have nothing, and am worth nothing. Do not turn your
face from me; do not defer your coming; do not withdraw your consolation, lest
my soul become like a waterless land before you. Lord, teach me to do your will;
teach me to walk worthily and humbly in your presence; because you are my
wisdom, who truly know me, and knew me before the world was made and before
I was born in the world.

"Son, walk in My presence in truth, and seek Me always in the simplicity of your
heart. Whoever walks in My presence in truth will be kept safe from the assaults
of evil, and truth will liberate him from those who lead astray and from the
detractions of unjust men. If truth shall have liberated you, then you will be truly
free, and you will not care for the vain words of men."

It is true, Lord, I pray that it may be done with me as you say. Let your truth teach
me and guard me, and keep me to a salutary end. Let it liberate me from every
evil affection and inordinate love, and I shall walk with you in great liberty of heart.

"I will teach you," says Truth, "what things are right and pleasing in my Bight. Think
on your sins with great displeasure and sorrow, and never imagine yourself to be
anything because of your good works. You are really a sinner, liable to many
passions and entangled in them. Of yourself, you are always tending to
nothingness; you quickly slip, you are quickly overcome, you are quickly disturbed,
you quickly pass away. You have nothing in which you can glory, but much for
which you ought to hold yourself cheap; you are far more infirm than you are able
to understand.

"Some do not sincerely walk before me, but, led by a certain curiosity and arrogance, wish to know my secrets, and to understand the high things of God, neglecting themselves and their welfare. These often fall into great temptations and sins, when I resist them on account of their pride and curiosity. Fear the judgments of God; be exceedingly afraid of the anger of the Omnipotent. Do not discuss the works of the Highest, but scrutinise your iniquities, and see how gravely you have offended and how many good deeds you have neglected.

"There are others, enlightened in their minds and purged in their affections, who are always panting after eternal things and listen unwillingly to earthly things; these perceive what the spirit of truth says within them.

"Love is a great thing, altogether a great good, which alone makes light everything that is heavy, and carries evenly all that is uneven. For it bears the burden without being burdened, and makes sweet and tasteful everything that is bitter. The noble love of Jesus drives on to great deeds, and always excites to the desire of more perfect things. Love wills to rise upwards, and not to be held back by the lowest things. Nothing is sweeter than love, nothing is stronger, nothing higher or broader; nothing is more delightful or fuller in heaven or in earth; for love is born of God, and cannot rest except in God, above all created things."

IV.--Devout Exhortation to Holy Communion

The voice of Christ, "Come to Me all who labour and are burdened, and I will refresh you," says the Lord. "The bread which I will give you is My flesh for the life of the world. Receive and consume it; this is My body which will be delivered for you; do this in commemoration of Me. Whoever eats My flesh and drinks My blood remains in Me, and I in him. The words which I have spoken to you are spirit and life."

These are your words, Christ, Eternal Truth, although not given at one time nor written in one place. Because they are yours, and true, they are all to be received gratefully by me. They are yours, and you pronounced them; and they are mine also because you uttered them for my welfare. I gladly accept them from your lips, that they may be more closely buried in my heart. Words of such kindness, full of sweetness and love, arouse me. But my own sins frighten me, and my impure conscience repels me from taking hold of such great mysteries.

You bid me come to you trustfully if I would have part with you; and to receive the food of immortality if I wish to obtain eternal life and glory. "Come to Me," you say, "all who labour and are burdened, and I will refresh you." O sweet and friendly word in the ear of a sinner, that you, my Lord God, invite the destitute and poor to the communion of your most holy Body.

Lord, all things in heaven and in earth are yours. I desire to offer myself as a willing oblation, and to remain yours in perpetuity. Lord, in the simplicity of my heart I offer myself to you to-day to be for ever your servant--offer myself for obedience and for a sacrifice of eternal praise. Receive me with this holy offering of your precious Body, which I offer to you to-day in the presence of angels, assisting though unseen, that it may be for my welfare and for the welfare of all your people.

The voice of the beloved: "God does not deceive you; he is deceived who trusts too much to himself. God walks with the simple, reveals Himself to the humble, gives understanding to the feeble, opens His meaning to pure minds, and hides His grace from the inquisitive and proud. Human reason is weak and may be deceived, but true faith cannot be deceived.

"All reason and natural investigation ought to follow faith, and not precede it nor impair it. For faith and love excel here most of all, and work in hidden ways in, this most holy and transcendent sacrament. The eternal and immeasurable God of infinite power does great and inscrutable things in heaven and in earth, and there is no finding out of His wonderful works. If the works of God were such that they could easily be seized by human reason, they would not deserve to be called wonderful or ineffable."

THE KORAN

The Koran, the sacred book of Islam, and of more than a hundred millions of men, is the least original of all existing sacred books. Muslims agree in believing that it is from beginning to end, and word for word, inspired; and that it existed before the Creation on what is called the "Preserved Tablet." This tablet was brought by the Archangel Gabriel from the highest to the lowest heaven, whence it was dictated sura [chapter] by sura, verse by verse, and word by word, to the Prophet Muhammad. Its matter is, however, taken for the most part from the Old Testament, especially the narrative portions of the Pentateuch; from the New Testament; from the traditions of the ancient Arabs; and also from Zoroastrian and other scriptures or traditions. It is not likely that Muhammad used literary sources, except in a small measure. But there were Jews, Christians, Zoroastrians, and others in and around Arabia, and he must have learned from their lips the principal doctrines of their respective religions. Nevertheless, planless and fragmentary compilation though it be, the Koran, particularly in the earlier suras written at Mekka, has much of the grandeur and poetry of style and the passionate exaltation of a true prophet, the sincerity of whose zeal is unquestioned.

Introductory

The word "Koran," or "Quran," from a root *qara* = to read, means literally "what is to be read," *i.e.*, the written authority on all matters, religions, etc. It is the exact equivalent of the Rabbinical Hebrew word "Miqra" (from the Hebrew *qara* = to read). The idea involved in both the Arabic and Hebrew words is that what is so designated is the ultimate authority deciding all questions. The Rabbis of post-Biblical times (compare the Jewish Qabbalah) regarded the Old Testament as an encyclopaedia of universal knowledge. In the best-knownMuslim universities of modern times philosophy, science, and everything else are taught from the Koran, which is made in some way to contain implicitly the latest words of modern thought, invention, and discovery.

The Koran did not exist as a whole until after the Prophet Muhammad's death. It was then compiled by the order of Abu Bekr, the first Sunnite Caliph. Its contents were found written on palm leaves white stones, and other articles capable of being written on. The compilers depended, to a large extent, upon the memory of the prophet's first followers, but the Koran, as we now have it, existed without any appreciable divergence by the end of the first year, after Muhammad's death (A.D. 632).

This Muslim Bible has no scheme or plan because it is an almost haphazard compilation of unconnected discourses, uttered on various unexplained occasions, and dealing with many incidents and themes. There is practically no editing, and no attempt is made to explain when, or how, or why the various speeches were delivered.

The earliest native writers and commentators on the Koran arranged its suras in two main classes: (1) Those uttered at Mekka before the flight in A.D. 622; (2) those written at Medinah during the next ten years.

Most recent scholars follow the chronological arrangement proposed by the great Orientalist Nöldeke in 1860. Friedrich Schwally in his newly revised edition of Nöldeke's great work on the Koran follows his master in almost every detail. Rodwell's translation of the Koran, recently issued in "Everyman's Library,"arranges the suras chronologically according to Nöldeke'sscheme. In the summaries that follow, it is this chronological order that is adopted. In the Arabic editions followed by the well-known and valuable translations of Sale, E.H. Palmer (Clarendon Press, "Sacred Books of the East," vols. 6 and 9), and others, the principle adopted is to put the longest suras first and the shortest last.

The Mekkan suras are much more original than the Medinah ones, especially those of the first period--*i.e.*, those belonging to the first four years of Muhammad's prophetic mission, *e.g.*, suras 96, 74, etc. In these suras the style is grander, more passionate, and fuller of poetry. The prophet appears in a state of great mental exaltation, full of a zeal which no words can adequately express, and of a sincerity which few scholars have questioned.

The suras of the second period, the following two years of the prophet's mission (*e.g.*, suras 54, 37, etc.), have the same general character, but are less vehement. Still less vehement and more restrained are the suras of the third Mekkan period--*i.e.*, from the seventh year of the prophet's mission to his flight in A.D. 622 (*e.g.*, suras 32, 41, etc.). The style of the Medinah suras resembles that of the Mekkan revelations of the third period, only they are still more matter of fact and restrained, and are largely made up of appeals to Jews, Christians, and others to abandon their "unbelief," and to accept the prophet who had come to them with the true religion, a religion as old as Abraham, though forgotten for many ages.

The Koran differs from the Scriptures of the Old and New Testaments, including the Apocrypha, in that these latter are much-more varied, as emanating from many minds, and belonging to very different occasions. The Koran is, from beginning to end, the effusions (often very wild) of one man.

The present editor has kept before him the Arabic text of Maracci, Fluegel, and Redslob, and also severalOriental editions (Cairo, Constantinople, Calcutta, etc.). But, of course, the best known translations, and also the native commentaries (Baidhawi, etc.), have been consulted.

In the summaries which follow, numerals following the paragraphs indicate the number of the sura or suras in the Arabic text as well as in Sale's translation.

MEKKAN SURAS

I.--FIRST PERIOD (A.D. 613-617)

Muhammad's First Call to Read the Koran

In the name of the gracious and compassionate God.

Recite in the name of thy Lord, who created man and taught men to write, recite what God has revealed to thee His Prophet, and be not afraid. Consider not the opposition of Abu Gahl, who has threatened to put his foot on thy neck if thou dost worship Allah. (96.)

Denunciation of Abu Lahab

Abu Lahab's two hands shall perish, and he himself shall perish. His wealth shall not avail him, nor all that he has gained. He shall be burnt in the fiery flames of Hell, his wife carrying wood for fuel, with a cord of palm-tree fibres twisted round her neck. (III.)

Muhammad Commanded to Offer Sacrifices

We have given to thee, O Prophet, great wealth and abounding riches. Pray thou to Allah, and offer Him suitable sacrifices out of what He has bestowed upon thee. (108.)

[Compare with this paragraph the following, from sura 22 of the Medinah group:

We have ordained that ye offer sacrifices unto Allah, and that ye receive much benefit therefrom. When, therefore, ye slay your camels let the name of Allah be pronounced over them. Then eat of them and give to those who ask humbly, giving also to the poor and needy who ask not. Flesh and blood can never reach unto Allah (God), but your obedience and piety will reach unto Him.]

Believers and Unbelievers

We will make the path to happiness easy and safe to all such as fear Allah, and give alms, and believe the truth proclaimed by Allah's messenger. But we will make easy the path to distress and misery for all such as are niggardly, are bent on making riches, and deny the truth when it is proclaimed to them. When these last fall headlong into Hell, their wealth will avail them nothing. In the burning furnace they shall burn and broil. (92.)

The Duty of Exercising Charity

Verily, We (God) have created some men in such poverty and distress as to need the help of others. What does that braggart man mean when he says, "None shall prevail over me; I have and have scattered riches boundless"? Does he not know that there is a Divine eye that sees him? Have not We created him with a capacity of distinguishing between the two highways, that which descends towards evil, and that which ascends towards thegood? This niggardly man, however, makes no attempt to scale the heights. What is it to ascend the upward road? It is to free the prisoner, to feed the hungry, to defend the orphan who is akin, and the downtrodden poor. Besides this, it is enjoined that men believe in Allah and His Prophet; that they encourage each other to be steadfast in the faith, exercising mutual consideration and sympathy. All such as do these things shall be the people of the right hand. But all those who disbelieve Our signs shall be the companions of the left hand, over whom shall be a vault of fire.

Muhammad Commanded to Arise and Preach

O thou mantle-wrapped one, arise and warn the people, and magnify the Lord. The Day of Judgment will be a sad day for unbelievers. Leave thou thine enemy in Mine hands, and let Me visit upon him his well deserved punishment. For he has ridiculed the Koran; he has said: "This is nothing else than magic, they are the words of a man." I [God] will cast him into Hell, where he shall burn in torment. The fires of this Hell leave nothing unconsumed. It scorches men's flesh. We have appointed nineteen angels as guardians over Hell fire. But why nineteen? That believers may be sure of the veracity of this Book, and that unbelievers may have occasion for denying the divinity of the Koran, saying: "What means this number?" (74.)

The Koran Given to Muhammad

Verily, We have brought down to Muhammad the Koran on the Night of Power. This one Night of Power is better than a thousand months. On that night did Gabriel and the angels descend and reveal to Our Prophet all the words of the Koran. (97.)

Muhammad not Mad nor an Impostor

Believe thou not, O Messenger of Mine, when they say, "Thou art bereft of thy senses," when they charge thee with imposture. Thy Lord knoweth who are bereft of their senses, and who are the impostors. Warn thou those maligners of the awful judgment which awaits them. (68.)

God's Promise to Help Muhammad to Recite the Koran

We [Allah] shall enable thee to remember all the parts of the Koran, so that thou mayest recite them for the encouragement of those who believe and as a warning to all unbelievers. Nor shalt thou forget aught of this Revelation except what We please. All those who fear God will receive the prophet's warning, but all those who disbelieve shall be cast into terrible fire where they will neither live nor die. This doctrine which We command thee to preach is that taught in the ancient Books, the Books of Abraham and of Moses, who were faithful Muslims. (87.)

The Koran Inspired

By the falling star, your comrade Muhammad does not err, nor does he speak his own mind. What he utters has been revealed to him. The Koran is from God through Gabriel; it is not the work of man. Why worship ye goddesses like Allat and Al'Uzza and Manah?There are no goddesses (53.)

The Treatment of Women Believers

When believing women come to you as fugitives, leaving behind them unbelieving husbands, send them not back to the infidels, but test their faith, and if they are found true Muslims, pay back to their husbands the dowries which they have expended. Then may ye marry them, provided ye give them the accustomed dowries. (60.)

God's Unity

Say "He is but one God, the everlasting God who begets not, nor is begotten, and there is none like unto Him." (10.)

Formulæ of Exorcism

I flee for refuge to the Lord, that He may protect me against the evil things which He has created. Against night goblins when the night comes on, and from witches who bind by their magic knots, and from such as injure by the evil eye; I seek refuge with the Lord from charmers, from jinns [demons], and from evil men. (113.)

The Heaven of the Muslims

All who believe in Allah and His Prophet shall be admitted hereafter into delightful gardens [Paradise]. They shall repose for ever on couches decked with gold and precious stones, being supplied with abundance of luscious wine, fruits of the choicest variety, and the flesh of birds. They shall be accompanied by damsels of unsurpassed beauty, with large black, pearl-like eyes. (56.)

II.--SECOND PERIOD (A.D. 617-619)

Winds and Demons Subject to Solomon

And We made a strong wind subject to Solomon, so that it conveyed him whither he would. We also gave him the power of commanding demons, so that they dived into the sea to bring him pearls, and did everything else that he wished (21.)

The Miraculous Birth of Jesus

Remember Mary, who preserved her virginity, and into whom We breathed Our own spirit, so that when her son Isa [Jesus] was born, mother and son became a sign unto all mankind. (21.)

The Virgin Mary

After Mary, the Virgin, had begotten her son Isa [Jesus] she was found one day carrying the child in her arms when some pious men met her and rebuked her,saying: "O Mary, thou sister of Aaron, what is thisstrange thing thou hast done? Thy father Amram was an upright man, and thy mother was no harlot, as thou seemest to be." In answer to all this the infant child, not having previously lisped a syllable, said, "Verily, I am the servant of Allah, who has given me the Book of the Gospel, and appointed me to be His Prophet. He has made me blessed, and to be a blessing. Happy the day wherein I was born, and the day wherein I shall die, and the day whereon I shall be raised again." (19.)

Devils Sent by God to Make Men Sin

De ye not know that We [God] send devils against the unbelievers to move them, by their suggestions, to the sin of which these unbelievers become guilty? (19.)

Solomon's Army of Men, Birds, and Jinns (Demons)

Solomon was able to understand the speech of birds and to make them understand his speech. There gathered to him on a certain day his entire army of men, birds, and jinns in the Valley of Ants. The crowd was so great that one of the ants said to his fellows, "Get you at once into your ant-homes, or you will be trampled to death by one of these myriad feet."

The Queen of Sheba's Visit to Solomon

Solomon, one day reviewing his varied troops, missed among the birds the hoopoe, and asked whither this bird had gone, threatening all manner of punishments for his absence. Soon the missing bird came flying to the king, uttering the words, "I have just come from Sheba, where I have looked upon the most wonderful queen, sitting upon the most magnificent throne that I have ever set eyes on. But this queen and her subjects, unfortunately, worshipped not Allah, the true God, but the sun."

"I will test the truth of thy words!" replied the angry monarch. "Take thou this note of mine to the queen thou laudest so highly, bidding her come to my kingdom to acknowledge my authority."

Almost in a twinkling the hoopoe was back with the queen's answer consenting to visit Solomon and his dominions. Solomon, having received this answer, asked the nobles of his kingdom, "Which of you will bring me at once the Queen of Sheba's throne, to be here before she arrives?"

"I will!" said one of the wickedest of the jinns.

"And so will I, in a whiff!" answered a jinn that was well acquainted with the Scriptures.

In a very short time the throne was in Solomon's palace. "Alter ye it," said the king, "as much as ye may, to see whether she has any supernatural knowledge to identify it."

When the queen arrived, she was asked, "What throne is this?"

She replied, "It is mine--strangely mine." After she had witnessed the glory and wisdom of Solomon, she gave up her idols, and became the worshipper of Allah, the true God. (27.)

III.--THIRD PERIOD (A.D. 619-622)

Punishment for Violating the Sabbath

Ye know how We tested and proved those wicked people who dwelt in Elath on the Red Sea. On the Sabbath day We made the fish come right up to them, as if asking to be caught; but not so on other days. Those who yielded to the temptation, and thus violated the sanctity of the sacred day, We turned into apes as a punishment for their wrong-doing. (7.)

Mount Sinai Shaken Above the Israelites

When the Israelites doubted the authority of the Law which We had given them through Moses, Our servant, We caused Mount Sinai to rear itself above them as a covering, so that the people feared it was going to fall upon them. And We said to them, "Receive ye with reverence that Law which We have given you, and remember what is contained therein, taking heed thereto. (7.)

MEDINAH SURAS

Salvation for Others than Muslims

All such as believe in Allah and in the last day, and who do that which is right, whether they are Jews, Christians, Sabeans, or Muslims, shall have their reward from Allah, who will take away from them all fear and grief. (3.)

Muslims Only to be Saved

No one that follows any other religion than Islam will be accepted by God or saved from perishing in the life that is to come. (2.)

Abraham, Ishmael, Isaac, Jacob, and the Tribes of Israel all Muslims

Do ye Jews say that Abraham, Ishmael, Isaac, Jacob, and the tribes of Israel were Jews, or do ye Christians say that they were Christians? But God knows better, and has revealed to you the truth that all these were Muslims, followers of the religion of Islam. But God is cognisant of your unbelief, and will bring you to account. (2.)

The Qiblah Changed from Jerusalem to Mekka

Foolish men will say, "Why have they changed the Qiblah from Jerusalem to the Kaabah in Mekka?" Say to them, "God's is the east and the west, and He has commanded us to turn our face, when we pray, to the sacred mosque at Mekka." (2.)

Against Jews and Christians, Who Capriciously Choose and Reject What Divine Revelations They Please

Why, then, do ye believe part only of the Book, and deny that part which authenticates the mission of the Prophet of Allah? All those who are guilty of this sinshall have shame in this life, and on the Resurrection Day shall be driven into the most excrutiating torments. (2.)

The Mekka Temple Founded by Abraham

It was Abraham, our father, who first entered the Kaabah sanctuary at Mekka, and it is our bounden duty, if at all able, to visit this sacred house. (3.)

Jesus Predicts the Coming of Muhammad

Jesus, Mary's Son, said, "O Israelites, I am Allah's Apostle, sent to confirm the Law of the Old Testament, and to bring you good tidings of a great Apostle to come after me, whose name is Ahmad."

Muhammad the Last and Greatest of God's Messengers

In the former times We sent Our apostles with convincing arguments and all decisive miracles, and We gave them the Scriptures. We sent to men Noah, Abraham, and the prophets, but many believed not. Then We sent Our apostles, after whom came Jesus, Son of Mary. Then, last of all, came Our great apostle, Muhammad. O all ye believers, fear God and obey the words of Allah's messenger.

The Koran Consistent Throughout

Why do they not carefully and impartially consider the Koran? If it had not been wholly of God, unbelievers would have been able to find out contradictions. (4.)

Muhammad Contradicts the Fact of the Crucifixion of Christ

Christians say that Christ Jesus, Son of Mary, was slain. But He was not slain, nor crucified, but another was taken for Him. The true Isa [Jesus] was taken up by God unto Himself, not seeing death. (4.)

Muhammad Admits the Fact of the Crucifixion of Christ

And God said, "O Isa [Jesus], I will cause Thee to die, but I will take Thee up to Myself and deliver Thee from unbelievers!" (4.)

One God, Not Three Gods, According to the Scripture

O ye who have received the Scriptures, do not believe more than these sacred writings teach! Jesus, Son of Mary, was God's Apostle, His Word, a spirit proceeding from God. Do not say there are three gods--Allah, Isa, and Mary. There is but one God, and He can have no son. (4.)

Forbidden Food

Ye are forbidden to eat that which dies of itself, blood, swine's flesh, and that on which the name of any other god than Allah has been invoked; that which has beenstrangled, or killed by a blow, or by a fall, or what has been gored to death, and whatever has been sacrificed to idols. (5.)

Divination by Arrows Condemned

It is not allowed you to make division by casting lots with arrows.

Denial of the Divinity of Christ and the Trinity

Those are unbelievers who say that God is the Christ [lit., Messiah], Son of Mary. Nay, this Christ Himself said, "O Israelites, worship God, My Lord and yours!" He who associates with God any companion His equal shall be excluded from Paradise, and have his place in Hell fire. (5.)

Jesus Denies that He and His Mother were Gods

At the last day God will say unto Isa, "O Isa, Son of Mary, didst Thou say unto men, 'Take Me and My Mother for two Gods in addition to Allah'?" And He shall answer, "Praise be unto Thee. Thou knowest all things, and Thou knowest that I commanded men to worship Allah alone."

CARDINAL NEWMAN

Apologia Pro Vitâ Sua

That most remarkable ecclesiastic of the nineteenth century, John Henry Newman, born in London on February 21, 1801, was of Dutch extraction, but the name itself, at one time spelt "Newmann," suggests Hebrew origin. His mother came of a Huguenot family, long established in England as engravers and paper manufacturers. His early education he obtained at a school at Ealing, where he distinguished himself by diligence and good conduct, as also by a certain aloofness and shyness. The only important incident Newman connects with this period is his "conversion," an incident more certain to him "than that he had hands and feet." In 1820 he graduated at Trinity College, Oxford. The various phases of his religious career are amply set forth in his famous "Apologia pro Vitâ Sua" ("Apology for His Life"), afterwards called "A History of my Religious Opinions." The work was called out by an attack, in January, 1864, by Charles Kingsley, in a review of Froude's "History of England." Kingsley wrote: "Truth, for its own sake, had never been a virtue with the Roman clergy. Father Newman informs us that it need not, and, on the whole, ought not to be." Challenged to withdraw or substantiate this charge, Kingsley did neither, whereupon Newman, after much correspondence, wrote his "Apologia," which was published in bi-monthly parts. Newman died on August 11, 1890.

I.--History of My Religious Opinions to 1833

I was brought up to delight in the Bible, but I had no formed religious convictions till I was fifteen. Of course, I had a perfect knowledge of my Catechism. But when I was fifteen I fell under the influence of a definite creed, and believed that the inward conversion of which I was conscious, and of which I am still more certain than that I have hands and feet, would last into the next life, and that I was elected to eternal glory. This belief faded away at the age of twenty-one; but it had had some influence on my opinions, in isolating me from the objects which surrounded me, in confirming my mistrust of the reality of material phenomena, and in making me rest inthe thought of two, and two only, absolute and luminously self-evident beings, myself and my Creator. At the age of fifteen also I was deeply impressed by the works of Thomas Scott, by Law's "Serious Call," by Joseph Milner's "Church History," and by Newton, "On the Prophecies." Newton's book stained my imagination, till 1843, with the doctrine that the Pope was Antichrist. At this same time, the autumn of 1816, I realised that it would be the will of God that I should lead a single life, and this anticipation strengthened my feeling of separation from the visible world.

In 1822, at Oxford, I came under new influences. Dr. Hawkins, then vicar of St. Mary's, a man of most exact mind, led me to the doctrine of tradition, and taught me to anticipate that before many years there would be an attack made upon the books and the canon of Scripture. He gave me Summer's "Treatise on Apostolic Preaching," by which I was led to give up my remaining Calvinism, and to receive the doctrine of baptismal regeneration. I now read Butler's "Analogy," from which I learned two principles which underlie much of my teaching: first, that the idea of an analogy between the separate works of God leads to the conclusion that the less important system is sacramentally connected with the more momentous system; and secondly, Butler's doctrine that probability is the guide of life led me to the question of the logical cogency of faith.

I owe much to Dr. Whately, who taught me the existence of the Church as a substantive corporation, and fixed in me those anti-Erastian views of Church polity which characterized the Tractarian movement. That movement, unknown to ourselves, was taking form. Its true author, John Keble, had left Oxford for a country parish, but his "Christian Year" had waked a new music in the hearts of thousands. His creative mind repeated, in a new form, Butler's two principles: that material phenomena are the types and instruments of real things unseen;and that, in religious certitude, faith and love give to probability a force which it has not in itself.

Hurrell Froude, one of his pupils and a man of high genius, taught me to venerate the Church of Rome and to dislike the Reformation. About 1830 I set to work on "The Arians of the Fourth Century," and the broad philosophy of Clement and Origen, based on the mystical or sacramental principle, came like music to my inward ear.

Great events were now happening at home and abroad. There had been a revolution in France, and the reform agitation was going on around me as I wrote. The vital question was, how were we to keep the Church from being liberalised? I saw that reformation principles were powerless to rescue her. I ever kept before me that there was something greater than the Establishd Church, and that was the Church Catholic and Apostolic, of which she was but the local presence and the organ. She was nothing, unless she was this. I was now disengaged from college duties; my health had suffered from work; and in December, 1832, I joined Hurrell Froude and his father, who were going to the south of Europe. I went to various coasts of the Mediterranean. I saw nothing but what was external; of the hidden life of Catholics I knew nothing. England was in my thoughts solely, and the success of the liberal cause fretted me. The thought came upon me that deliverance is wrought not by the many but by the few, not by bodies but by persons.

I began to think that I had a mission. I reached England on July 9, and on July 14 Mr. Keble preached in the university pulpit on "National Apostasy." This day was the start of the religious movement of 1833.

II.--With the Tractarians

A movement had begun in opposition to the danger of liberalism which was threatening the religion of thenation. Mr. Keble, Hurrell Froude, Mr. William Palmer,Mr. Arthur Purceval, Mr. Hugh Rose, and other zealous, and able men had united their counsels. I had the exultation of health restored, a joyous energy which I never had before or since. And I had a supreme confidence in our cause; we were upholding that primitive Christianity which was delivered for all time by the early teachers of the Church. Owing to this supreme confidence, my behaviour had a mixture in it both of fierceness, and of sport, and on this account it gave offence to many.

The three propositions about which I was so confident were as follow: First was the principle of dogma; my battle was with liberalism--and by liberalism I mean the anti-dogmatic principle and its developments. I have changed in many things, but not in this; religion, as a mere sentiment, has been to me from childhood a dream and a mockery. Secondly, I was confident that there was a visible Church, with sacraments and rites which are the channels of invisible grace. Here, again, I have not changed. But, thirdly, I held a view of the Church of Rome which I have utterly renounced since.

The attack of liberalism upon the university and upon the old orthodoxy of England began in 1834. Thus, in a pamphlet by Dr. Hampden it was maintained that religion is distinct from theological opinion, that it is but a common prejudice to identify theological propositions with the simple religion of Christ; and so on. The tracts were widely read and discussed, but the counter-attack against liberalism was not a power until Dr. Pusey joined us. His great learning, his immense diligence, his simple devotion to the cause of religion, no less than his great influence in the university, at once gave us a position and a name. He taught us that there ought to be more sense of responsibility in the tracts and in the whole movement. Under his influence I wrote a work defining our relation to the Church of Rome, namely, "The Prophetical Office of the Church viewed relatively to Romanism and toPopular Protestantism." The subject of this volume,published in 1837, is the "Via Media." This was followed by my "Essay on Justification," and other works; and so I went on for years up to 1841. It was, in a human point of view, the happiest time of my life. We prospered and spread.

But the movement was to come into collision with the nation, and with the Church of the nation. In 1838 my bishop made some light animadversions on the tracts. But my tract on the Thirty-nine Articles, designed to show that the Articles do not oppose Catholic teaching, and but partially oppose Roman dogma, while they do oppose the dominant errors of Rome, brought down, in 1839, a storm of indignation throughout the country. I saw that my place in the movement was lost.

III.--A Theological Death-bed

In the long vacation of 1839 I began to study the history of the Monophysites, and was-absorbed in the doctrinal question. It was during this course of reading that for the first time a doubt came upon me of the tenableness of Anglicism, and by the end of August I was seriously alarmed. My stronghold was antiquity; yet here, in the fifth century, I found Christendom of the sixteenth and nineteenth centuries reflected.

The drama of religion and the combat of truth and error were ever one and the same; the principles of the Roman Church now were those of the Church then; the principles of heretics then were those of Protestants now; there was an awful similitude. Be my soul with the saints! In the same month the words of St. Augustine were pointed out to me, *"Securus judicat orbis terrarum";* they struck me with a power which I had never felt from any words before; the theory of the "Via Media" was absolutely pulverised.

In the summer of 1841, in retirement at Littlemore, I received three blows which broke me. First, in the historyof the Arians I found the same phenomena which I had found in the Monophysites: the pure Arians were the Protestants, the semi-Arians were the Anglicans, and Rome now was what it was then. Secondly, the bishops, one after another, began to charge against me in a formal, determinate movement. Third, it was proposed by Anglican authorities to establish an Anglican bishopric in Jerusalem--a step which amounted to a formal denial that the Anglican Church was a branch of the Catholic Church, and to a formal assertion that the Anglican was a Protestant Church. The Jerusalem bishopric brought me to the beginning of the end.

From the end of 1841 I was on my death-bed, as regards my membership of the Anglican Church, though at the time I became aware of it only by degrees. A death-bed has scarcely a history; it is a tedious decline, with seasons of rallying and seasons of falling back. My position at first was this: I had given up my place in the movement in the spring of 1841, but I could not give up my duties towards the many and various minds who had been brought into it by me; I expected gradually to fall back into lay communion; I never contemplated leaving the Church of England; I could not hold office in its service if I were not allowed to hold the Catholic sense of the Articles; I could not go to Rome while she suffered honours to be paid to the Blessed Virgin and the saints which I thought in my conscience to be incompatible with the supreme glory of the One, Infinite and Eternal; I desired a union with Rome under conditions, Church with Church; I called Littlemore my Torres Vedras, and thought that some day we might advance again within the Anglican Church; I kept back all persons who were disposed to go to Rome with all my might.

The "Via Media" was now an impossible idea; I abandoned that old ground, and took another. I said, "Much as Roman Catholics may denounce us at present as schismatical, they could not resist us if the Anglicancommunion had but that one note of the Church upon it--sanctity." I was pleased with my new view, but my friends were naturally offended at a novel line of argument which substituted a sort of methodistic self-contemplation for the plain and honest tokens of a divine mission in the Anglican Church.

In spite of my ingrained fears of Rome, in spite of my affection for Oxford and Oriel, yet I had a secret longing love of Rome, the Mother of English Christianity. It was the consciousness of this bias in myself which made me preach so earnestly against the danger of being swayed in religious inquiry by our sympathy rather than by our reason. I was in great perplexity, and hardly knew where I stood; I incurred the charge of weakness from some men, and of mysteriousness and underhand dealing from the majority. But I have never had any suspicion of my own honesty.

In July, 1844, I wrote to a friend: "I am far more certain, according to the fathers, that we *are* in a state of culpable separation than that developments do *not* exist under the Gospel, and that the Roman developments are not the true ones." I then saw that the principle of development was discernible from the first years of the Catholic teaching up to the present day. I came to the conclusion that there was no medium, in true philosophy, between atheism and Catholicity, and that a perfectly consistent mind must embrace either the one or the other. I saw that no valid reasons could be assigned for continuing in the Anglican Church, and that no Valid objections could be taken to joining the Roman.

In February, 1843, I had made a formal retraction of all the hard things which I had said against the Church of Rome, and in September I had resigned the living of St. Mary's, Littlemore included. I began my "Essay on the Development of Doctrine" in the beginning of 1845, and was hard at it till October. Before I got to the end, I resolved to be received into the Catholic Church.Father Dominic came to Littlemore on October 8, and did for me this charitable service. I left Oxford for good on February 23, 1846.

IV.--The Faith of a Catholic

From the time that I became a Catholic of course I have no further history of my religious opinions to narrate. I do not mean that I have given up thinking on theological subjects, but that I have had no variations to record, and have had no anxiety of heart whatever. I have been in perfect peace; I never have had one doubt.

Nor had I any trouble about receiving those additional articles which are not found in the Anglican creed. I am far from denying that every article of the Christian creed is beset with difficulties, and it is simple fact that I cannot answer those difficulties. But ten thousand difficulties do not make one doubt. Of all points of faith, the being of a God is encompassed with most difficulty, and yet borne in upon our minds with most power.

Starting, then, with the being of a God, which is as certain to me as my own existence, I look out of myself into the world of men, and there I see a sight which fills me with unspeakable distress. The world seems simply to give the lie to that great truth, of which my whole being is so full; I look into this living, busy world, and see no reflection of its Creator. To consider the world in its length and breadth, its various history; the progress of things, as if from unreasoning elements, not towards final causes; the greatness and littleness of man, his far-reaching aims, his short duration, the curtain hung over his futurity, the defeat of good, the prevalence and intensity of sin, the dreary, hopeless irreligion--all this is a vision to dizzy and appal, and inflicts upon the mind the sense of a profound mystery which is absolutely beyond human solution. What shall be said to this heart-piercing, reason-bewildering fact? I can only answer, that either there is no Creator, or this living society of men is in a true sense discarded from His presence.

And now, supposing it were the blessed will of the Creator to interfere in this anarchical condition of things, what would be the methods which might be necessarily or naturally involved in His purpose of mercy? What must be the face-to-face antagonist, by which to withstand and baffle the fierce energy and passion and the all-corroding, all-dissolving scepticism of the intellect in religious inquiries? There is nothing to surprise the mind, if He should think fit to introduce a power into the world, invested with the prerogative of infallibility in religious matters. Such a provision would be a direct, immediate, active, and prompt means of withstanding the difficulty; and when I find that this is the very claim of the Catholic Church, not only do I feel no difficulty in admitting the idea, but there is a fitness in it which recommends it to my mind.

I am defending myself from the charge that I, as a Catholic, not only make profession to hold doctrines which I cannot possibly believe in my heart, but that I also believe in a power on earth, which at its own will imposes upon men any new set of *credenda*, when it pleases, by a claim to infallibility; and that the necessary effect of such a condition of mind must be a degrading bondage, or a bitter inward rebellion relieving itself in secret infidelity, or the necessity of ignoring the whole subject of religion in a sort of disgust, and of mechanically saying everything that the Church says. But this is far from the result; it is far from borne out by the history of the conflict between infallibility and reason in the past, and the prospect in the future.

The energy of the human intellect thrives and is joyous, with a tough, elastic strength, under the terrible blows of the divinely fashioned weapon. Protestant writers consider that they have all the private judgment to themselves, and that we have the superincumbent oppression of authority. But this is not so; it is the vast Catholic body itself, and it only, which affords an arena for both combatants in that awful, never-dying duel. St. Paul says that his apostolical power is given him to edification, and not to destruction. There can be no better account of the infallibility of the Church. Its object is, and its effect also, not to enfeeble the freedom or vigour of human thought in religious speculation, but resist and control its extravagance.

I will go on in fairness to say what I think *is* the great trial to the reason when confronted with that august prerogative of the Catholic Church. The Church claims, not only to judge infallibly on religious questions, but to animadvert on opinions in secular matters which bear upon religion, on matters of philosophy, of science, of literature, of history, and it demands our submission to her claim. In this province, taken as a whole, it does not so much speak doctrinally, as enforce measures of discipline.

I will go on to say further, that, in spite of all the most hostile critics may urge about these verities of high ecclesiastics in time past, in the use of their power, I think that the event has shown, after all, that they were mainly in the right, and that those whom they were hard upon were mainly in the wrong. There is a time for everything, and many a man desires a reformation of an abuse, or the fuller development of a doctrine, or the adoption of a particular policy, but forgets to ask himself whether the right time for it is come.

There is only one other subject which I think it necessary to introduce here, as bearing upon the vague suspicions which are attached in this country to the Catholic priesthood. It is one of which my accusers have before now said much-- the charge of reserve and economy. I come to the direct question of truth, and of the truthfulness of Catholic priests generally in their dealings with the world, as bearing on the general question of their honesty, and of their internal belief in their religious professions. First, I will say that when I became a Catholic, nothing struck me more at once than the English outspoken manner of the priests. There was nothing of that smoothness or mannerism which is commonly imputed to them. Next, I was struck, when I had more opportunity of judging of the priests, by the simple faith in the Catholic creed and system, of which they always give evidence, and which they never seemed to feel in any sense at all to be a burden.

Vague charges against us are drawn from our books of moral theology. St. Alfonso Liguori, for instance, lays down that an equivocation is allowable in an extraordinary case. I avow at once that in this department of morality, I like the English rule of conduct better. Yet, great English authors, Jeremy Taylor, Milton, Paley, Johnson, distinctly say that under extraordinary circumstances it is allowable to tell a lie. Would anyone give ever so little weight to these statements, in forming an estimate of the veracity of the writers? And, in fact, it is notorious from St. Alfonso's life that he had one of the most scrupulous and anxious of consciences; and, further, he was originally in the law, and was betrayed on one occasion by accident into what seemed like a deceit, and this was the very occasion of his leaving the profession.

If Protestants wish to know what our real teaching is, let them look at the Catechism of the Council of Trent. Let me appeal also to the life of St. Philip Neri, founder of the Oratory: "As for liars, he could not endure them, and he was continually reminding his spiritual children to avoid them as they would a pestilence."

These are the principles on which I have acted before I was a Catholic, these are the principles which, I trust, will be my stay and guidance to the end.

THOMAS PAINE

The Age of Reason

In 1774, Thomas Paine, thirty-seven years of age, landed unknown and penniless in the American colonies. Born at Thetford, Norfolk, England, Jan. 29, 1737, of poor Quaker parents, he had tried many occupations, and had succeeded in none. Within two years he had become an intellectual leader of the American Revolution. Beginning his literary career with an attack on slavery, he continued it in 1776 by publishing his pamphlet "Common Sense," which gave an electric inspiration to the cause of separation and republicanism among the colonists. After serving the new commonwealth in office and with his pen, he went to France on an official mission in 1781; then returned to his native England, intent on furthering his views. In 1793 Paine wrote the first part of "The Age of Reason," which aroused a storm of indignation, but undaunted, he added a second and a third part to the work, consisting mostly of amplifications of some of the contentions advanced in the first part, in the writing of which Paine had no Bible to consult. The book, the first part of which was published in 1794, the second part in 1795, and the third in 1801, is an exposition of Deism on a purely scientific basis; the visible creation was everything to Paine in his reasonings, the religious hopes, fears and aspirations of men were nothing at all--this universal human phenomenon was curtly dismissed by him as a universal human delusion. Many of his comments on the Bible were rather crude anticipations of the modern Higher Criticism. But in dealing with the Bible, Paine showed the animus of a prosecuting counsel rather than the impartiality of a judge. His stormy life ended on July 8, 1809. (See also ECONOMICS, Vol. XIV.)

I.--Revealed Religion

It has been my intention, for several years past, to publish my thoughts upon religion. As several of my colleagues, and others of my fellow citizens of France, have given me the example of making their voluntary and individual profession of faith, I also will make mine; and I do this with all that sincerity and frankness with which the mind of man communicates with itself.

I believe in one God, and no more; and I hope forhappiness beyond this life.

I believe in the equality of man, and I believe that religious duties consist in doing justice, loving mercy, and endeavouring to make our fellow-creatures happy.

I do not believe in the creed professed by the Jewish Church, by the Roman Church, by the Greek Church, by the Turkish Church, by the Protestant Church, nor by any church that I know of. My own mind is my own church.

All national institutions of churches appear to me no other than human inventions set up to terrify and enslave mankind, and monopolise power and profit.

Each of those churches show certain books which they call "revelation," or the word of God. The Jews say that the word of God was given by God to Moses face to face; the Christians say that their word of God came by divine inspiration; and the Turks say their word of God (the Koran) was brought by an angel from heaven. Each of these churches accuses the other of unbelief; and, for my own part, I disbelieve them all.

As it is necessary to affix right ideas to words, I will, before I proceed further into the subject, offer some observations on the word revelation. Revelation, when applied to religion, means something communicated immediately from God to man.

No one will deny or dispute the power of the Almighty to make such a communication if he pleases. But admitting, for the sake of a case, that something has been revealed to a certain person, and not revealed to any other person, it is revelation to that person only.

When he tells it to a second person, a second to a third, a third to a fourth, and so on, it ceases to be a revelation to all those persons. It is a revelation to the first person only, and hearsay to every other; consequently they are not obliged to believe it, for they have only the word of the first person that it was made to him.

The world has been amused with the terms "revealedreligion," and the generality of priests apply this term to the books called the Old and New Testament. There is no man that believes in revealed religion stronger than I do; but it is not the reveries of the Old and New Testament that I dignify with that sacred title. That which is a revelation to me exists in something which no human mind can invent, no human hand can counterfeit or alter.

The word of God is the Creation we behold; and this word of God revealeth to man all that is necessary for him to know of his Creator.

Do we want to contemplate his power? We see it in the immensity of his creation.

Do we want to contemplate his wisdom? We see it in the unchangeable order by which the incomprehensible whole is governed.

Do we want to contemplate his munificence? We see it in the abundance with which he fills the earth.

Do we want to contemplate his mercy? We see it in his not withholding that abundance even from the unthankful.

Do we want to contemplate his will, so far as it respects man? The goodness he shows to all is a lesson for our conduct to each other.

In fine, do we want to know what God is? Search not the book called the Scripture, which any human hand might make, but the Scripture called the Creation.

II.--Theology and Religion

As to the Christian system of faith, it appears to me as a compound made up chiefly of manism with but little Deism, and is near to Atheism as twilight is to darkness.

That which is now called natural philosophy, embracing the whole circle of science, of which astronomy occupies the chief place, is the study of the works of God, and of the power and wisdom of God in his works,and is the true theology.

As to the theology that is now studied in its place, it is the study of human opinions and of human fancies concerning God. It is not the study of God Himself in the works that He has made, but in the works or writings that man has made; and it is not among the least of the mischiefs that the Christian system has done to the world that it has abandoned the original and beautiful system of theology, like a beautiful innocent, to distress and reproach, to make room for the bag of superstition.

It is an inconsistency, scarcely possible to be credited, that anything should exist under the name of a religion that held it to be irreligious to study and contemplate the structure of the universe that God had made. But the fact is too well established to be denied. The event that served more than any other to break the first link in the long chain of despotic ignorance is that known by the name of the Reformation by Luther. From that time, though it does not appear to have made part of the intention of Luther, or of these who are called Reformers, the sciences began to revive, and liberality, their natural associate, began to appear. This was the only public good the Reformation did; for with respect to religious good it might as well not have taken place. The mythology still continued the same; and the multiplicity of national popes grew out of the downfall of the Pope of Christendom.

The prejudice of unfounded belief often degenerates into the prejudice of custom, and becomes at last rank hypocrisy. When men from custom or fashion, or any worldly motive profess or pretend to believe what they do not believe, nor can give any reason for believing, they unship the helm of their morality, and, being no longer honest in their own minds, they feel no moral difficulty in being unjust to others. It is from the influence of this vice, hypocrisy, that we see so many church and meeting-going professors and pretenders toreligion so full of tricks and deceit in their dealings, and so loose in the performance of their engagements that they are not to be trusted further than the laws of the country will bind them. Morality has no hold on their minds, no restraint on their actions.

One set of preachers make salvation to consist in believing. They tell their congregations that if they believe in Christ their sins shall be forgiven. This, in the first place, is an encouragement to sin; in the next place, the doctrine these men preach cannot be true.

Another set of preachers tell their congregations that God predestined and selected from all eternity a certain number to be saved, and a certain number to be damned eternally. If this were true, the day of judgment is past; their preaching is in vain, and they had better work at some useful calling for their livelihood.

Nothing that is here said can apply, even with the most distant disrespect, to the real character of Jesus Christ. He was a virtuous and an amiable man. The morality that he preached and practised was of the most benevolent kind, and, though similar systems of morality had been preached by Confucius and by some of the Greek philosophers many years before, by the Quakers since, and by many good men in all ages, it has not been exceeded by any.

III.--The Bible

If we permit ourselves to conceive right ideas of things, we must necessarily affix the idea, not only of unchangeableness, but of the utter impossibility of any change taking place, by any means or accident whatever, in that which we would honour with the name of God; and therefore the word of God cannot exist in any written or human language.

The continually progressive change to which the meaning of words is subject, the want of an universal language which renders translation necessary, the errorsto which translations are again subject, the mistakes of copyists and printers, together with the possibility of wilful alteration, are of themselves evidences that human language, whether in speech or in print, cannot be the vehicle of the word of God. The word of God exists in something else.

It has been the practice of all Christian commentators on the Bible, and of all Christian priests and preachers, to impose the Bible on the world as a mass of truth, and as the word of God; they have disputed and wrangled, and have anathematised each other about the supposable meaning of particular parts and passages therein; one has said and insisted that such a passage meant such a thing; another, that it meant directly the contrary; and a third, that it meant neither the one nor the other, but something different from both; and this they have called understanding the Bible.

Now, instead of wasting their time, and heating themselves in fractious disputations about doctrinal points drawn from the Bible, these men ought to know, and if they do not it is civility to inform them, that the first thing to be understood is, whether there is sufficient authority for believing the Bible to be the word of God, or whether there is not.

I therefore pass on to an examination of the Books called the Old and the New Testament. The case historically appears to be as follows:

When the Church mythologists established their system, they collected all the writings they could find and managed them as they pleased. It is a matter altogether of uncertainty to us whether such of the writings as now appear under the name of the Old and the New Testament are in the same state in which these collectors say they found them; or whether they added, altered, abridged, or dressed them up.

Be this as it may, they decided by *vote* which of the books out of the collection they had made should be theword of God, and which should not. They rejected several; they voted others to be doubtful, such as the books called the Apocrypha; and those books which had a majority of votes they voted to be the word of God. Had they voted otherwise, all the people since calling themselves Christians, had believed otherwise; for the belief of the one comes from the vote of the other. Who the people were that did all this we know nothing of; they call themselves by the general name of the Church; and this is all we know of the matter.

There are matters in the Bible, said to be done by the express command of God, that are as shocking to humanity and to every idea we have of moral justice as anything done by Robespierre, by Carrier, by Joseph le Ben, in France; by the English Government in the East Indies; or by any other assassin in modern times. Are we sure that the Creator of man commissioned these things to be done? Are we sure that the books that tell us so were written by His authority? To read the Bible without horror, we must undo everything that is tender, sympathising, and benevolent in the heart of man. Speaking for myself, if I had no other evidence that the Bible is fabulous than the sacrifice I must make to believe it to be true, that alone would be sufficient to determine my choice.

But it can be shown by internal evidence that the Bible is not entitled to credit as the word of God. It can readily be proved that the first five books of the Bible, attributed to Moses, were not written by him nor in his time, but several hundred years afterwards. Moses could not have described his own death, nor mentioned that he was buried in a valley in the land of Moab. Similarly, the book of Joshua was not written by Joshua; it is manifest that Joshua could not write that Israel served the Lord not only in his days, but in the days of the elders that over-lived him. The book of Judges is anonymous on the face of it. The books of Samuelwere not written by Samuel, for they relate many things that did not happen till after his death.

The history in the two books of Kings, which is little more than a history of assassinations, treachery, and war, sometimes contradicts itself; and several of the most extraordinary matters related in Kings are not mentioned in the companion books of Chronicles. The book of Job has no internal evidence of being a Hebrew book; it appears to have been translated from another language into Hebrew; and it is the only book in the Bible that can be read without indignation or disgust. It is an error to call the Psalms the Psalms of David because historical evidence shows that some of them were not written until long after the time of David. The books of the prophets are wild, disorderly, and obscure compositions, the so-called prophecies in which do not refer to Jesus Christ, but to circumstances the Jewish nation was in at the time they were written or spoken.

I now go on to the book called the New Testament. Had it been the object of Jesus Christ to establish a new religion, he would undoubtedly have written the system himself, or procured it to be written in His lifetime. But there is no publication extant authenticated with his name. All the books called the New Testament were written after his death. He was a Jew by birth and profession, and he was the Son of God in like manner that every other person is; for the Creator is the Father of All.

The first four books--Matthew, Mark, Luke, and John--are altogether anecdotal. They relate events after they had taken place. They tell what Jesus Christ did and said, and what others did and said to him; and in several instances they relate the same event differently. Revelation, therefore, is out of the question with respect to these books. The presumption, moreover, is that they are written by other persons than these whose name they bear.

The book of Acts of the Apostles belongs also to theanecdotal part. All the rest of the New Testament, except the book of enigmas called the Revelation, are a collection of letters under the name of epistles, and the forgery of letters under the name of epistles. One thing, however, is certain, which is that out of the matters contained in these books, together with the assistance of some old stories, the Church has set up a system of religion very contradictory to the character of the person whose name it bears. It has set up a religion of pomp and reverence in pretended imitation of a person whose life was humility and poverty.

IV.--Mystery, Miracle, and Prophecy

I proceed to speak of the three principal means that have been employed in all ages and perhaps in all countries to impose upon mankind.

These three means are mystery, miracle, and prophecy. The two first are incompatible with true religion, and the third ought always to be suspected. With respect to mystery, everything we behold is, in one sense, a mystery to us. Our own existence is a mystery, the whole vegetable world is a mystery. We know not how it is that the seed we sow unfolds and multiplies itself.

The fact, however, as distinct from the operating cause, is not a mystery, because we see it; and we know also the means we are to use, which is no other than putting the seed in the ground. We know, therefore, as much as is necessary for us to know; and that part of the operation that we do not know, and which if we did we could not perform, the Creator takes upon Himself and performs it for us.

But though every created thing is in this sense a mystery, the word mystery cannot be applied to moral truth, any more than obscurity can be applied to light. The God in whom we believe is a God of moral truth, and not of mystery. Mystery is the antagonist of truth. It isa fog of human invention that obscures truth, and represents it in distortion.

Religion, therefore, being the belief of a God, and the practice of moral truth, cannot have connection with mystery. The belief of a God, so far from having anything of mystery in it, is of all beliefs the most easy, becauses it arises to us out of necessity. And the practice of moral truth, or, in other words, a practical imitation of the goodness of God, is no other than our acting towards each other as he acts benignly towards all.

When men, whether from policy or pious fraud, set up systems of religion incompatible with the word or works of God in the creation, they were under the necessity of inventing or adopting a word that should serve as a bar to all inquiries and speculations. The word "mystery" answered this purpose, and thus it has happened that religion, which in itself is without mystery, has been corrupted into a fog of mysteries.

As mystery answered all general purposes, "miracle" followed as an occasional auxiliary. Of all the modes of evidence that ever were invented to obtain belief to any system or opinion to which the name of religion has been given, that of miracle is the most inconsistent. For, in the first place, whenever recourse is had to show, for the purpose of procuring that belief, it implies a lameness or weakness in the doctrine that is preached. And, in the second place, it is degrading the Almighty into the character of a showman, playing tricks to amuse and make the people stare and wonder. It is also the most equivocal sort of evidence that can be set up; for the belief is not to depend upon the thing called a miracle, but upon the credit of the reporter who says that he saw it; and therefore the thing, were it true, would have no better chance of being believed than if it were a lie.

As mystery and miracle took charge of the past and the present, prophecy took charge of the future, and rounded the tenses of faith. The original meaning ofthe words "prophet" and "prophesying" has been changed, the Old Testament prophets were simply poets and musicians. It is owing to this change in the meaning of the words that the flights and metaphors of the Jewish poets, and phrases and expressions now rendered obscure by our not being acquainted with the local circumstances to which they applied at the time they were used, have been erected into prophecies, and made to bend explanations at the will and whimsical conceits of sectaries, expounders, and commentators. Everything unintelligible was prophetical.

V.--Deism

Fom the time I was capable of conceiving an idea, and acting upon it by reflection, I either doubted the truth of the Christian system or thought it to be a strange affair. It seems as if parents of the Christian profession were ashamed to tell their children anything about the principles of their religion. They sometimes instruct them in morals, and talk to them of the goodness of what they call Providence. But the Christian story of what they call God the Father putting his son to death, or employing people to do it--for that is the plain language of the story--cannot be told by a parent to a child; and to tell him it was done to make mankind happier and better is making the story still worse; and to tell him that all this is a mystery is only making an excuse for the incredibility of it.

How different is this from the pure and simple profession of deism! The true deist has but one Deity, and his religion consists in contemplating the power, wisdom, and benignity of the Deity in his works, and in endeavouring to imitate him in everything moral, scientific, and mechanical.

The religion that approaches the nearest of all others to true deism, in the moral and benign part thereof, isthat professed by the Quakers; but they have contracted themselves too much by leaving the works of God out of their system. Though I reverence their philanthropy, I cannot help smiling at the conceit, that if the taste of the Quaker could have been consulted at the creation what a silent and drab-coloured creation it would have been! Not a flower would have blossomed its gaieties, not a bird been permitted to sing.

Quitting these reflections, I proceed to other matters. Our ideas, not only of the almightiness of the Creator, but of His wisdom and His beneficence, become enlarged as we contemplate the extent and structure of the universe. The solitary idea of a solitary world rolling or at rest in the immense ocean of space gives place to the cheerful idea of a society of worlds, so happily contrived as to administer, even by their motion, instruction to man. We see our own earth filled with abundance, but we forget to consider how much of that abundance is owing to the scientific knowledge the vast machinery of the universe has unfolded.

But what are we to think of the Christian system of faith that forms itself upon the idea of only one world? Alas! what is this to the mighty ocean of space and the almighty power of the Creator? From whence, then, could arise the solitary and strange conceit that the Almighty, who had millions of worlds equally dependent on His protection, should quit the care of all the rest and come to die in our world, because they say one man and one woman had eaten an apple?

It has been by rejecting the evidence that the word or works of God in the creation affords to our senses, and the action of our reason upon that evidence, that so many wild and whimsical systems of faith, and of religion, have been fabricated and set up. There may be many systems of religion that so far from being morally bad are in many respects morally good; but there can be but one that is true, and that one necessarily must, as itever will, be in all things consistent with the ever-existing word of God that we behold in His works.

I shall close by giving a summary of the deistic belief:

First, that the creation we behold is the real word of God, in which we cannot be deceived. It proclaims His power, it demonstrates His wisdom, it manifests His goodness and beneficence.

Secondly, that the moral duty of man consists in imitating the moral goodness and beneficence of God manifested in the creation towards all His creatures. That seeing, as we daily do, the goodness of God to all men, it is an example calling upon all men to practise the same towards each other, and consequently that everything of persecution and revenge between man and man, and everything of cruelty to animals, is a violation of moral duty.

It is certain that, in one point, all nations of the earth and all religions agree. All believe in a God. The things in which they disagree are the redundancies annexed to that belief; and, therefore, if ever an universal religion should prevail, it will not be in believing anything new, but in getting rid of redundancies, and believing as man believed at first. But in the meantime let every man follow, as he has a right to do, the religion and the worship he prefers.

BLAISE PASCAL

Letters to a Provincial

Blaise Pascal, mathematician, theologian, and one of the greatest writers of French prose, was born on June 19, 1623, at Clermont-Ferrand, and died on August 19, 1662. His mother died in his fourth year, and the father, an eminent lawyer, took the boy with his two sisters to Paris. Pascal showed the most astonishing mathematical genius; he produced at the age of seventeen a profound work on conic sections, and devoted the following years to physical researches and to investigations in the higher mathematics. In 1654, Pascal, having experienced a remarkable vision, which he recorded on a parchment known as his "amulet," renounced the world and entered on the ascetic life, in close relations with the Jansenist community. Hence, in the interests of Arnauld, the Jansenist leader, Pascal issued the famous "Letters Written to a Provincial" ("Lettres Écrites par Louis de Montalte à un Provincial de ses Amis"), a series of eighteen tracts directed with the keenest and bitterest irony against the casuistry of the Jesuits. The "Letters" appeared during a period of fourteen months, the first being dated January 23, 1656, and the last March 24, 1657. They took the form of little pamphlets, each of eight or twelve quarto pages; they had a very large circulation, and created an immense impression throughout Catholic countries. They are open letters, intended really for the public and not for any individual.

I.--Lax Casuists

SIR,--I send you, as I promised, the chief outlines of the moral teaching of these good Jesuit fathers, these "men so eminent in doctrine and in wisdom, who are led by that divine wisdom which is more trustworthy than all philosophy." Possibly you think that I speak in jest. I speak seriously, or, rather, it is they who have spoken thus of themselves. I only copy their words where they write, "It is a society of men, or, rather, of angels, foretold by the prophet Isaiah." They claim to have changed the face of Christianity. We must believe it, since they have told us so; and, indeed, you will seehow far they have done so, when you have mastered their maxims.

I took care to be instructed by themselves and trusted to nothing which my friend had told me. I had been told such strange things that I could hardly believe them, until I was shown them in their own books; and then I could say nothing in their defence, except that these must be the principles of certain isolated Jesuits, and not those of the whole society. Indeed, I was able to say that I knew Jesuits who were as severe as these were lax.

It was on that occasion that the spirit of the society was explained to me, for it is not by any means known to every one. I was told as follows:

"You imagine that you are speaking in their favour when you say that there are among them fathers who are as obedient to the principles of the Gospel as others are distant from those principles, and you conclude therefore that these loose opinions do not characterise the whole society. That is true. But since the society admits of so licentious a doctrine within it, you must conclude that its spirit is not one of Christian severity."

"But what then," said I, "is the purpose of the whole institution? Is it that everyone should be free to say whatever he may happen to think?"

"That is not so," was the reply. "So great a society could not exist without discipline, and without one spirit governing and ruling all its movements."

The objects of the Jesuits is not to corrupt morals, but, on the other hand, they have not in view as their single object the reformation of morals, because they would find this a political disadvantage. Their principle is this: they have so high an opinion of themselves as to believe that it is advantageous, and even necessary, to the good of religion that their credit should extend everywhere and that they should govern all consciences. And as the severe maxims of the Gospel are suitable for governing certain temperaments, they make use of thesewhenever they serve their purpose. But since these same maxims do not at all suit the wishes of the generality of mankind, they usually put them aside so as to be able to please everyone.

Therefore, having to do with people of all sorts and conditions, and of diverse nationalities, they need casuists suited to all this diversity. From this principle you will easily see that if they had none but lax casuists they would defeat their chief purpose, which is to include the whole world. Truly pious people seek a more severe direction, but as there are not many who are truly pious the Jesuits do not need many strict directors to guide them. They have a few for the few who need them. On the other hand, the vast number of their lax casuists are at the service of the innumerable multitude who seek the broad and easy way.

It is by this obliging and accommodating conduct that they open their arms to all the world. Thus, if someone comes to them already determined to make restitution of goods which he has wrongly acquired, you need not fear that they will dissuade him. On the contrary, they will praise and confirm his holy resolution. But if another should come wishing to have absolution without making restitution, their position would be a difficult one, if they had not the means of giving him his desire. It is thus that they keep all their friends and defend themselves against their enemies. And if anyone accuses them of extreme laxity, they immediately bring forward their most austere directors, and certain books which they have written on the severity of the Christian law; and simple and uninquiring people are contented with these proofs.

They have proofs for all sorts of people, and make such ingenious replies to every question that when they find themselves in countries where a crucified God seems like madness, they suppress the scandal of the Cross and preach only Christ in glory. This they have done inIndia and China, where they even condone idolatry by a subtle device; they allow their people to carry with them hidden images of Christ, to which they should address the public worship ostensibly paid to their idols. This conduct led to their being forbidden under pain of excommunication to permit the adoration of idols, under any pretext, or to hide the mystery of the Cross from those whom they instruct in religion, and they have been forbidden to receive anyone in baptism until he has this knowledge, and are enjoined to erect in their churches the image of the crucifix.

Thus they have spread over the whole earth in the strength of their doctrine of "probable opinions," which is the fount and origin of all these irregularities. You may learn of this from themselves, for they take no pains to hide it, except that they cover their human and political prudence with the pretence of a divine and Christian prudence. They act as if the faith and the tradition which maintains it were not for ever invariable at all times and in all places, and as if nothing more were required, in order to remove the stains of guilt, than to corrupt the law of the Lord, instead of regarding that stainless and holy law as itself the instrument of conversion, and conforming human souls to its salutary precepts.

II.--The Doctrine of Intention

Sir,--I must now let you know what the good Jesuit father told me about the maxims of their casuists, with regard to the "point of honour" among gentlemen. "You know," said he, "that this point of honour is the dominating passion of men in that rank of life, and is constantly leading them into acts of violence which appear quite contrary to Christian piety. Indeed, we should have to exclude all of them from our confessionals, if our fathers had not in some degree relaxed the severity of religion and accommodated it to the weakness of men.But since they wished to remain attached to the Gospel by their duty towards God, and to men of the world by their charity towards their neighbour, they had to seek expedients by which they might make it possible for a man to maintain his honour in the ordinary way of the world without wounding his conscience. They had to preserve, at the same time, two things which are apparently so opposed to one another as piety and honour. But, however valuable their purpose might be, its execution was exceedingly difficult."

"I am surprised," I said, "that you find it difficult."

"Are you?" he replied. "Do you not know that on the one hand the law of the Gospel commands us never to render evil for evil, and to leave vengeance to God; and that on the other hand the laws of the world forbid that we should suffer injury without executing justice, even by the death of our enemies? Is it possible that two precepts should be more contrary to one another?"

"What I meant to say was, that after what I have seen of your fathers, I know that they can easily do things which are impossible to other men. I am quite ready to believe that they have discovered some means of reconciling these two precepts, and I beg of you to inform me what it is."

"You must know, then," he replied, "that this wonderful principle is our grand method of *directing the intention,* a principle of great importance in our moral system. You have already seen certain examples of it. Thus, when I explained to you how servants could carry with a clear conscience certain harmful messages, you must have seen that it was by diverting their intention from the evil of which they are the bearers and by turning it to the gain which they receive for their service. This is what we call 'directing the intention.' In the same way you have seen that those who give money in return for benefices would be guilty of simony unless they diverted their intention from the transaction. But I am going to show you this grand method in all its beauty in relation to homicide, which it justifies under a thousand circumstances."

"I am ready to believe," I said, "that your principle will permit everything, and that nothing will escape it."

"Not at all," he replied; "you are always running from one extreme to the other. We by no means permit everything. For instance, we never permit the formal intention of sin, for the mere sake of sinning, and we will have nothing to do with anyone who persists in seeking evil as an end in itself, for that is a devilish intention, in whatever age, sex, or rank it may be found. But so long as there is no such unhappy disposition as that, we try to put in practice our method of directing intention, which consists in proposing a lawful object as the end of one's actions. In so far as it is in our power, we turn away from forbidden things; but when we are unable to prevent the action, we at least try to purify the intention, and so correct the vice of the means by the purity of the end.

"That is how our fathers have been able to permit the acts of violence which are committed in the defence of honour. It is only necessary to turn away one's intention from the desire of vengeance, which is criminal, and to restrict it to the desire of defending one's honour, which is a lawful desire. It is thus that our fathers are able to fulfil their duties towards God and towards men alike. They please the world by permitting the actions, and they satisfy the Gospel by purifying the intentions. It is a method which was unknown to the ancients, and is entirely due to our fathers. Do you understand it now?"

"I understand it very well," I said. "You allow to men the external and material effect of the action, and you give to God the internal and spiritual movement of intention, and thus reconcile the human with the divine law. But though I understand your principle well enough, I should like to know what are its consequences.--I should like to know, for instance, all the cases in which your method permits one to kill. You have told me that whoever receives a blow may repay it with a sword-thrust without the guilt of vengeance, but you have not yet told me how far one may go."

"You can hardly make a mistake," said the father. "You may go as far as to kill the man. One of our authorities speaks: 'It is permitted to kill a man who has given a blow, even though he runs away, on the condition that it is not done through hatred or through vengeance, and that one's actions do not lead to murders which are excessive and harmful to the state.' The reason is, that one may thus run after one's honour as if after a stolen object. For though your honour is not exactly in the hands of your enemy as if it were something which he had picked up, you can yet recover it in the same way by giving a proof of greatness and of authority, and by thus acquiring human esteem. Indeed, he continues: 'Is it not true that he who has received a blow is considered disgraced until he has slain his enemy?'"

This appeared to me so horrible that I had difficulty in restraining myself. I felt that I had heard enough.

III.--The Charge of Raillery

Reverend Fathers,--I have read the letters which you have published in answer to some of mine on the subject of your moral principles; and I find that one of the principal points in your defence is that I have not spoken seriously enough of your maxims. You repeat this charge in all your writings, and you go so far as to say that I have turned holy things into ridicule.

This is a surprising and very unjust reproach; for where is a passage to be found in which I have treated holy things with raillery? It is true that I have spoken with little respect of the teachings of certain among you,but do you suppose that the imaginations of your authorsare to be taken as the verities of the faith? Is it impossible to laugh at passages of Escobar, and at the very fantastic and unchristian conclusions of others of your authors without being accused of ridiculing religion? Are you not afraid lest your reproaches should give me a new subject for ridicule, or lest it should be seen that when I make sport of your moral principles I am as far from laughing at holy things as the doctrine of your casuists is far from the holy teaching of the Evangel!

Truly, fathers, there is a great difference between laughing at religion, and laughing at those whose extravagant opinions are its profanation. It would be impious to be wanting in respect for the truths which the Spirit of God has revealed, but it would hardly be less impious that we should not show our contempt for the falsities which the human spirit has opposed to them.

I pray you to consider that just as Christian truth is worthy of love and of respect, the errors that are contrary to it deserve our contempt and hatred. For there are two qualities in the truths of our religion, a divine beauty which compels our love, and a holy majesty that demands our veneration; and there are two qualities in error, the impiety which makes it horrible, and the impertinence which renders it absurd.

Do not hope, therefore, to persuade the world that it is unworthy of Christians to deal with errors as absurdities, since this method has been common to the early fathers of the church, and is authorised by Holy Scriptures, by the example of the greatest saints, and even by that of God himself. For do we not see that God at the same time hates and despises sinners in such a degree that at the hour of their death, when their condition is at its saddest and most deplorable, the divine wisdom is said to unite mockery and laughter with the vengeance and fury which condemns them to perpetual torments.

Nay, it is worthy of our notice that in the first words which God spake to man after the fall the fathers of the church have discovered a tone of mockery, a stinging irony. After Adam had disobeyed, in the hope that the devil had given that he would then be made like a God, it appears from Scripture that God's punishment made him subject to death, and that after having reduced Adam to the miserable condition which his sin had deserved, God mocked him with words of piercing irony, saying: "There is the man who has become as one of us."

You see, therefore, that mockery is sometimes designed to turn men from their follies, and is then an act of righteousness. Thus Jeremiah says that the deeds of the foolish are worthy of laughter because of their vanity. And, again, St. Augustine says that the wise laugh at the foolish because they are wise, but in virtue not of their own wisdom, but of the divine wisdom which will mock at the death of the wicked.

What? Must we call in Scripture and tradition to prove that cutting down one's enemy from behind, and in an ambush is a treacherous murder? Or that giving a present of money to secure an ecclesiastical benefice is to purchase it? Of course, there are teachings which deserve our contempt, and can only be dealt with by mockery. Are you, fathers, to be permitted to teach that it is lawful to slay in order to avoid a blow and an affront, yet are we to be forbidden to refute publicly so grave an error? Are you to be at liberty to say that a judge may conscientiously retain a bribe given him to purchase injustice, yet may we never contradict you? Are you formally to pronounce that a man may be saved without ever having loved God, and yet close the mouths of those who would defend the truth of the faith, on the ground that their defence must wound fraternal charity by attacking you, and must grieve Christian modesty by laughing at your maxims?

IV.--The Sin of Simony

Reverend Fathers,--I was about to write to you concerning the accusations which you have so long brought against me, wherein you call me impious, buffoon, rogue, impostor, calumniator, swindler, heretic, disguised Calvinist, one possessed of a legion of devils. I wish the world to know why you speak thus, for I should be sorry that anyone should think thus of me; and I had already made up my mind to complain publicly of your calumnies and impostures when I saw your replies, wherein you bring the same charges against me. You have thus forced me to change my purpose. Yet I shall still carry it out in some degree, inasmuch as I hope that my defence will convict you of more real impostures which you have imputed to me. Truly, fathers, your position is more open to suspicion than mine, for it is very unlikely that I, being alone as I am, and without strength or human support against so powerful a society as yours, and being sustained only by truth and sincerity, should have exposed myself to the risk of losing all, by exposing myself to a conviction of imposture. But your position, fathers, is different; you can say of me what you please, and I can find no one to whom I may complain. Well, you have chosen your ground, and the war shall be made in your country and at your expense. Do not fear that I shall be tedious; there is something so diverting about your maxims that they never fail to rejoice the world.

Let me closely explain, for instance, your doctrine with regard to simony. Finding yourself in a dilemma between the canons of the church, which forbid with the severest penalties any trade in ecclesiastical benefices, and the avarice of so many people who promote this infamous traffic, you have followed your ordinary method, which is to give to men what they desire, and to offer to God nothing but words and appearances. For what do simonfacal persons demand, if not that they shall receive moneyin return for their benefices?

But that is precisely the transaction which you have cleared from the guilt of simony. Yet, since you cannot do away with the name of simony, and there must be some matter to which the name attaches, you have devised for that purpose an imaginary idea, which never enters the minds of simoniacs at all, and indeed would be quite useless to them. This is, that simony consists in valuing the money, considered in itself, as highly as the spiritual privilege, considered in itself. Who would ever dream of comparing things which are so disproportionate and of such different kinds? Yet, according to your authors, so long as a man does not entertain this metaphysical comparison, he may give his benefice to another, and may receive money in return, without incurring the guilt of simony. It is thus that you make game of religion in order to pander to human passions.

The abusive language which you utter against me will never clear up our differences, nor shall any of your threats restrain me from defending myself. You trust in your strength and impunity, but I believe that I possess truth and innocence. The war by which violence attempts to oppress the truth is a strange and a long one, for all the efforts of violence are unable to weaken truth, and serve only to make it more evident. On the other hand, all the light of truth can do nothing to arrest violence, but rather inflames it. When force combats force, the stronger destroys the weaker; when argument is opposed to argument, true and convincing reasoning confounds that which is based on vanity and lies; but violence and truth have, no power one over the other. That is not to say that these two things are equal. There is this extreme difference between them: the career of violence is limited by the divine order, which determines its effects to the glory of the truth which it attacks; but truth, on the other hand, exists externally, and triumphs at last over its enemies, because it is eternal and powerful as God Himself.

V.--Homicide

Let us now see, fathers, how you value that life of man, which is so jealously safeguarded by human justice. It appears from your novel laws that there is only one judge in a case of affront or injury, and that this judge is to be he who has received the offence. He is to be at the same time judge, plaintiff, and executioner. He demands the death of the offender, sentences him to death, and immediately executes the sentence; and so, without respect either for the body or for the soul of his brother, slays and imperils the salvation of him for whom Christ died. And all this is to be done to avoid a blow, a slander, an insulting word, or some other offence for which neither the law nor any authorised judge could assign the penalty of death.

Not only so, but even a priest is held to have contracted neither sin nor irregularity in this infliction of death without authority and against law. Can these be religious men and priests who speak in this way? Are they Christians or Turks--men or demons? Spread over the whole earth, according to St. Augustine, there are two peoples and two worlds--the world of the children of God, who form one body, of which Jesus Christ is king, and the world of the enemies of God, of whom the devil is king.

Now, Christ has founded honour on suffering; the devil has founded it on the refusal to suffer. Christ has taught those who receive a blow to offer the other cheek; but the devil has taught those who are in danger of a blow to kill the enemy who threatens them.

Consider, therefore, fathers, to which of these two kingdoms you belong. You have heard the language of the city of peace, which is called the mystical Jerusalem, and you have heard the language of the city of turmoil, which is called in the Scriptures the spiritual Sodom. Which of these two languages do you understand? According to St. Paul, those who belong to Christ act and speak on his principles; and, according to the words of Christ, those who are the children of the devil, who has been a murderer from the beginning of the world, follow his maxims. We listen, therefore, to the language of your teachers, and ask of them whether when a blow is threatened, we ought to suffer it rather than slay the offender, or whether we may kill him in order to escape the affront?

Lessius, Molina, Escobar, and other Jesuits say that it is lawful to kill the man who threatens a blow. Is that the language of Jesus Christ?

WILLIAM PENN

Some Fruits of Solitude

William Penn was born in London on October 14, 1644. In early life he joined the Quakers, and while still a young man underwent imprisonment for the expression of his religious views. For "A Sandy Foundation Shaken," an attack on the Athanasian Creed, he was in 1668 sent to the Tower, where he wrote, "No Cross, No Crown." Under James II., however, he was high in the favour of the court, and received a grant of the region afterwards known as Pennsylvania, whither he went with a number of his co-religionists in 1682. After his return to England, he suffered by the fall of James II., but under William III. was acquitted of treason, and spent his later years in retirement. He died at Ruscombe, in Berkshire, on July 30, 1718. "Some Fruits of Solitude, or the Maxims of William Penn," evidently the result of one of his sojourns in prison, was licensed in 1693. It was followed by "More Fruits of Solitude." The whole forms a collection of maxims which are shrewd, wise, and charitable, informed with a good courage for life, and a contempt for mean ends, if in their variety they do not always escape the touch of the commonplace. The book has become known as a favourite of R.L. Stevenson, who said of it that "there is not the man living--no, nor recently dead--that could put, with so lovely a spirit, so much honest, kind wisdom into words."

To the Reader

Reader, this Enchiridion I present thee which is the fruit of solitude; a school few care to learn in, though none instructs us better. Some parts of it are the result of serious reflection; others the flashings of lucid intervals. Writ for private satisfaction, and now published for an help to human conduct.

The author blesseth God for his retirement, and kisses that Gentle Hand which led him into it; for though it should prove barren to the world, it can never do so to him.

He has now had some time he could call his own; a property he was never so much master of before; inwhich he has taken a view of himself and the world; and observed wherein he hath hit and mist the mark; what might have been done, what mended, and what avoided in his human conduct; together with the omissions and excesses of others, as well societies and governments, as private families and persons. And he verily thinks, were he to live over his life again, he could not only, with God's grace, serve Him, but his neighbour and himself, better than he hath done, and have seven years of his time to spare. And yet perhaps he hath not been the worst or the idlest man in the world, nor is he the oldest. And this is the rather said, that it might quicken thee, reader, to lose none of the time that is yet thine.

There is nothing of which we are apt to be so lavish as of time, and about which we ought to be more solicitous; since without it we can do nothing in this world. Time is what we want most, but what, alas! we use worst; and for which God will certainly most strictly reckon with us, when time shall be no more.

The author does not pretend to deliver thee an exact piece; his business not being ostentation, but charity. 'Tis miscellaneous in the matter of it, and by no means artificial in the composure. But it contains hints that may serve thee for texts to preach to thyself upon, and which comprehend much of the course of human life. Since whatever be thy inclination or aversion, practice or duty, thou wilt find something not unsuitably said for thy direction and advantage. Accept and improve what deserves thy notice; the rest excuse, and place to account of good will to thee and the whole creation of God.

Ignorance

It is admirable to consider how many millions of people come into and go out of the world ignorant of themselves and of the world they have lived in. If one wentto see Windsor Castle or Hampton Court it would be strange not to observe and remember the situation, the building, the gardens, fountains, etc., that make up the beauty and pleasure of such a seat. And yet few people know themselves; no, not their own bodies, the houses of their minds, the most curious structure of the world, a living walking tabernacle: nor the world of which it was made, and out of which it is fed; which would be so much our benefit as well as our pleasure to know. We cannot doubt of this when we are told the Invisible things of God are brought to light by the things that are seen; and consequently we read our duty in them as often as we look upon them, to Him that is the Great and Wise Author of them, if we look as we should do.

The world is certainly a great and stately volume of natural things; and may not be improperly styled the hieroglyphics of a better. But, alas! how very few leaves of it do we really turn over! This ought to be the subject of the education of our youth, who at twenty, when they should be fit for business, know little or nothing of it.

Education

We are in pain to make them scholars, but not men; to talk rather than to know, which is true canting. The first thing obvious to children is what is sensible; and that we make no part of their rudiments.

We press their memory too soon, and puzzle, strain, and load them with words and rules; to know grammar and rhetoric, and a strange tongue or two, that it is ten to one may never be useful to them; leaving their natural genius to mechanical and physical, or natural knowledge uncultivated and neglected; which would be of exceeding use and pleasure to them through the whole course of their life.

To be sure, languages are not to be despised or neglected; but things are still to be preferred.

Children had rather be making of tools and instruments of play; shaping, drawing, framing, and building, etc., than getting some rules of propriety of speech by heart; and those also would follow with more judgment and less trouble and time.

It were happy if we studied nature more in natural things, and acted according to nature; whose rules are few, plain, and most reasonable.

Let us begin where she begins, go her pace, and close always where she ends, and we cannot miss of being good naturalists.

The creation would not be longer a riddle to us: the heavens, earth, and waters, with their respective, various, and numerous inhabitants: their productions, natures, seasons, sympathies, and antipathies; their use, benefit, and pleasure would be better understood by us: and an eternal wisdom, power, majesty, and goodness very conspicuous to us through those sensible and passing forms: the world wearing the mark of its Maker, whose stamp is everywhere visible, and the characters very legible to the children of wisdom.

And it would go a great way to caution and direct people in their use of the world that they were better studied and known in the creation of it.

For how could man find the confidence to abuse it, while they should find the Great Creator stare them in the face, in all and every part thereof?

Their ignorance makes them insensible and that insensibility hardy in misusing this noble creation, that has the stamp and voice of a Deity everywhere, and in everything to the observing.

It is pity, therefore, that books have not been composed for youth, by some curious and careful naturalists, and also mechanics, in the Latin tongue, to be used in schools, that they might learn things with words: things obvious and familiar to them, and which would make the tongue easier to be obtained by them.

Many able gardeners and husbandmen are yet ignorant of the reason of their calling; as most artificers are of the reason of their own rules that govern their excellent workmanship. But a naturalist and mechanick of this sort is master of the reason of both, and might be of the practice, too, if his industry kept pace with his speculation; which were very commendable, and without which he cannot be said to be a complete naturalist or mechanic.

Finally, if man be the index or epitome of the world, as philosophers tell us, we have only to read ourselves well to be learned in it. But because there is nothing we less regard than the characters of the Power that made us, which are so clearly written upon us and the world He has given us, and can best tell us what we are and should be, we are even strangers to our own genius; the glass in which we should see that true instructing and agreeable variety, which is to be observed in nature, to the admiration of that wisdom and adoration of that Power which made us all.

Frugality or Bounty

Frugality is good, if liberality be joined with it. The first is leaving off superfluous expenses; the last bestowing them to the benefit of others that need. The first without the last begins covetousness; the last without the first begins prodigality. Both together make an excellent temper. Happy the place wherever that is found.

Were it universal, we should be cured of two extremes, want and excess: and the one would supply the other, and so bring both nearer to a mean; the just degree of earthly happiness.

It is a reproach to religion and government to suffer so much poverty and excess.

Were the superfluities of a nation valued, and made a perpetual tax on benevolence, there were be more alms-housesthan poor, schools than scholars; and enough to spare for government besides.

Industry

Love labour; for if thou dost not want it for food thou mayest for physick. It is wholesome for thy body, and good for thy mind. It prevents the fruits of idleness, which many times come of having nothing to do, and lead too many to do what is worse than nothing.

A garden, an elaboratory, a work-house, improvements and breeding, are pleasant and profitable diversions to the idle and ingenious; for here they miss ill company, and converse with nature and art; whose variety are equally grateful and instructing; and preserve a good constitution of body and mind.

Knowledge

Knowledge is the treature, but judgment the treasurer of a wise man.

He that has more knowledge than judgment is made for another man's use more than his own.

It cannot be a good constitution, where the appetite is great and the digestion is weak.

There are some men like dictionaries; to be looked into upon occasions, but have no connection, and are little entertaining.

Less knowledge than judgment will always have the advantage over the injudicious knowing man.

A wise man makes what he learns his own, t'other shows he's but a copy, or a collection at most.

On the Government of Thoughts

Man being made a reasonable, and so a thinking creature, there is nothing more worthy of his being than the right direction and employment of his thoughts; sinceupon this depends both his usefulness to the publick and his own present and future benefit in all respects.

The consideration of this has often obliged me to lament the unhappiness of mankind, that through too great a mixture and confusion of thoughts have been hardly able to make a right or mature judgment of things.

Clear, therefore, thy head, and rally, and manage thy thoughts rightly, and thou wilt save time, and see and do thy business well; for thy judgment will be distinct, thy mind free, and the faculties strong and regular.

Always remember to bound thy thoughts to the present occasion.

Make not more business necessary than is so; and rather lessen than augment work for thyself.

Upon the whole matter employ thy thoughts as thy business requires, and let that have place according to merit and urgency, giving everything a review and due digestion, and thou wilt prevent many errors and vexations, as well as save much time to thyself in the course of thy life.

Friendship

Friendship is an union of spirits, a marriage of hearts, and the bond thereof virtue.

There can be no friendship where there is no freedom. Friendship loves a free air, and will not be penned up in strait and narrow enclosures. It will speak freely, and act so too; and take nothing ill where no ill is meant; nay, where it is 'twill easily forgive, and forget, too, upon small acknowledgements.

Friends are true twins in soul; they sympathise in everything, and have the same love and aversion.

One is not happy without the other, nor can either be miserable alone. As if they could change bodies, they take their turns in pain as well as in pleasure; relieving one another in their most adverse conditions.

What one enjoys the other cannot want. Like theprimitive Christians, they have all things in common, and no property but in one another.

They that love beyond the world cannot be separated by it.

Death cannot kill what never dies.

Nor can spirits ever be divided that love and live in the same divine principle, the root and record of their friendship.

If absence be not death, neither is theirs.

Death is but crossing the world, as friends do the seas; they live in one another still.

For they must needs be present that love and live in that which is omnipresent. In this divine glass they see face to face; and their converse is free, as well as pure.

This is the comfort of friends, that though they may be said to die yet their friendship and society are in the best sense ever present, because immortal.

Of Charity

Charity has various senses, but is excellent in all of them.

It imports, first, the commiseration of the poor and unhappy of mankind, and extends an helping hand to mend their condition.

Next, charity makes the best construction of things and persons; it makes the best of everything, forgives everybody, serves all, and hopes to the end.

It is an universal remedy against discord, an holy cement for mankind.

And, lastly, 'tis love to God and the brethren which raises the soul above all earthly considerations; and as it gives a taste of heaven upon earth, so 'tis heaven in the fulness of it hereafter to the truly charitable here.

This is the noblest sense charity has, after which all should press as being the more excellent way.

Would God this divine virtue were more implantedand diffused among mankind, the pretenders to Christianity especially; and then we should certainly mind piety more than controversy, and exercise love and compassion instead of censuring and persecuting one another in any manner whatsoever.

ERNEST RENAN

Life of Jesus

Ernest Renan, the most widely read writer of religious history in his day, was forty years old when the "Vie de Jésus," his most popular book, appeared as the first volume of a "History of the Origins of Christianity." He was born at Tréguier in Brittany, France, Feb. 27, 1823, a Breton through his father and a Gascon through his mother. Educated for the Church, under priestly tutelage, he specialised in the study of Oriental languages, with the result that he found it impossible to accept the traditional view of Christian and Jewish history. After holding an appointment in the Department of Manuscripts in the Bibliothèque Nationale, he became Professor of Hebrew in the Collège de France. At the age of 55 he was elected a member of the French Academy. His works include "A History of Semitic Languages," a "History of the Origins of Christianity," and a "History of the People of Israel," besides many volumes of essays and criticism, and several autobiographical books of great charm. Everybody read Renan, and disagreed with him. The orthodox rejected his opinions, and the unorthodox his sentiment. But his books marked an epoch in religious criticism. "The Life of Jesus" was the outcome of a visit to Palestine in pursuance of research studies of Phoenician civilisation. A feature is the importance given to scenic surroundings which he could so happily describe. Renan died on October 2, 1892, widely admired, honoured, and also condemned, and was buried in the Pantheon.

The Hour and the Man

The principal event in the history of the world is the revolution by which the noblest portions of humanity have forsaken the ancient religions of Paganism for a religion founded on the Divine Unity, the Trinity, and the Incarnation of the Son of God. Nearly a thousand years were required to achieve this conversion. The new religion itself took at least three hundred years in its formation. But the origin of the revolution is a historical event which happened in the reigns of Augustus and Tiberius. At that time there lived a manof supreme personality, who, by his bold originality, and by the love which he was able to inspire, became the object, and settled the direction, of the future faith of mankind.

The great empires which succeeded each other in Western Asia annihilated all the hopes of the Jewish race for a terrestial kingdom, and cast it back on religious dreams, which it cherished with a kind of sombre passion. The establishment of the Roman empire exalted men's imaginations, and the great era of peace on which the world was entering gave birth to illimitable hopes. This confused medley of dreams found at length an interpretation in the peerless man to whom the universal conscience has decreed the title of the Son of God, and that with justice, since he gave religion an impetus greater than that which any other man has been capable of giving--an impetus with which, in all probability, no further advance will be comparable.

Youth and Education

Jesus was born at Nazareth, a small town in Galilee, which before his time was not known to fame. The precise date of his birth is unknown. It took place in the reign of Augustus, probably some years before the year one of the era which all civilised peoples date from the day of his birth. Jesus came from the ranks of the common folk. His father, Joseph, and his mother, Mary, were people in humble circumstances, artisans living by their handiwork in the state, so usual in the East, which is neither ease nor poverty. The family was somewhat large. Jesus had brothers and sisters who seem to have been younger than he. They all remained obscure. The four men who were called his brothers, and among whom one at least, James, became of great importance in the early years of the development of Christianity, were his cousins-german. Thesisters of Jesus were married at Nazareth, and there he spent the early years of his youth.

The town must have presented the poverty-stricken aspect still characteristic of villages in the East. We see to-day the streets where Jesus played as a child in the stony paths or little lanes which separate the dwellings from each other. No doubt the house of Joseph much resembled these poor domiciles, lighted only by the doorway, serving at once as workshop, kitchen, and bedroom, and having for furniture a mat, some cushions on the ground, one or two clay pots, and a painted chest. But the surroundings are charming, and no place in the world could be so well adapted for dreams of perfect happiness. If we ascend to the plateau, swept by a perpetual breeze, above the highest houses, the landscape is magnificent. An enchanted circle, cradle of the Kingdom of God, was for years the horizon of Jesus, and indeed during his whole life he went but little beyond these, the familiar bounds of his childhood.

No doubt he learnt to read and write according to the Eastern method; but it is doubtful if he understood the Hebrew writings in their original tongue. His biographers make him cite translations in the Aramean language. Nevertheless, it would be a great error to imagine that Jesus was what we should call an ignorant man. Refinement of manners and acuteness of intellect have, in the East, nothing in common with what we call education. In all probability Jesus did not know Greek. His mother tongue was the Syrian dialect, mingled with Hebrew. No element of secular teaching reached him. He was ignorant of all beyond Judaism; his mind kept that free innocence which an extended and varied culture always weakens. Happily, he was also ignorant of the grotesque scholasticism which was taught at Jerusalem, and which was soon to constitute the Talmud. The reading of the books of the Old Testament made a deep impression on him, especially the book of Daniel, andthe religious poetry of the Psalms was in marvellous accordance with his lyrical soul, and all his life was his sustenance and support.

That he had no knowledge of the general state of the world is evident from every feature of his most authentic discourses, and he never conceived of aristocratic society, save as a young villager who sees the world through the prism of his simplicity. Although born at a time when the principles of positive science had already been proclaimed, he lived in entirely supernatural ideas. To him the marvellous was not the exceptional but the normal statf of things, since to him the whole course of things was the result of the free-will of the Deity. This led to a profound conception of the close relations of man with God.

Idyllic Surroundings

A mighty dream haunted the Jewish people for centuries, constantly renewing its youth. Judaea believed that she possessed divine promises of a boundless future. In combination with the belief in the Messiah and the doctrine of an approaching renewal of all things, the dogma of the resurrection had emerged and produced a great fermentation from one end of the Jewish world to the other. Jesus, as soon as he had any thought of his own, entered into the burning atmosphere created in Palestine by these ideas, and his soul was soon filled with them. A beautiful natural environment imprinted a charming and idyllic character on all the dreams of Galilee. During the months of March and April that green, shady, smiling land is a carpet of flowers of an incomparable variety of colours. The animals are small and extremely gentle--delicate and playful turtle-doves, blackbirds so light that they rest on a blade of grass without bending it, tufted larks which almost venture under the feet of the traveller, little river-tortoises with mild bright eyes, storks of gravely modest mien, which,casting aside all timidity, allow men to come quite near them, and indeed seem to invite his approach. In no country in the world do the mountains extend with more harmonious outlines, or inspire higher thought. Jesus seems to have had an especial love for them. The most important events of his divine career took place upon the mountains. This beautiful country in his time was filled with prosperity and gaiety. There Jesus lived and grew up. True, every year he knew the sweet solemnity of the pilgrimage to Jerusalem, and it is believed that early in life the wilderness had some influence on his development, but it was when he returned into his beloved Galilee that he once more found his Heavenly Father in the midst of green hills and clear fountains, and women and children who with joyous soul awaited the salvation of Israel.

A Character to Love

Jesus followed the trade of his father, which was that of a carpenter. In this there was nothing irksome or humiliating. The Jewish custom required that a man devoted to intellectual work should learn a handicraft. Jesus never married. His whole capacity for love was concentrated upon that which he felt was his heavenly vocation. He was no doubt more beloved than loving. Thus, as often happens in very lofty natures, tenderness of heart was in him transformed into an infinite sweetness, a vague poetry, a universal charm.

Through what stages did the ideas of Jesus progress during this obscure early period of his life? A high conception of the Divinity, the creation of his own great mind, was the guiding principle to which his power was due. God did not speak to him as to one outside of himself; God was in him; he felt himself with God, and from his own heart drew all he said of his Father. The highest consciousness of God which ever existed in theheart of man was that of Jesus; but he never once gave utterance to the sacrilegious idea that he was God. From the first he looked upon his relationship with God as that of a son with his father. Herein was his great originality; in this he had nothing in common with his race. Neither Jew nor Musselman has understood this sweet theology of love. The God of Jesus is our Father. He is the God of humanity. The Jesus who founded the true Kingdom of God, the kingdom of the humble and meek, was the Jesus of early life--of those chaste and simple days when the voice of his Father re-echoed within him in clearer tones. It was then, for some months, perhaps a year, that God truly dwelt on earth.

A Stimulating Acquaintance

An extraordinary man, whose position remains to some extent enigmatical, appeared about this time and unquestionably had some intercourse with Jesus. About the year 28 of our era there spread through the whole of Palestine the reputation of a certain John, a young ascetic, full of fervour and passion. The fundamental practice which characterised his sect was baptism; but baptism with John was only a sign to impress the minds of the people and to prepare them for some great movement. There can be no doubt he was possessed in the highest degree with hope for the coming of the Messiah. He was of the same age as Jesus, and the two young enthusiasts, full of the same hopes and the same hatreds, were able to lend each other mutual support, Jesus recognizing John as his superior, and timidly developing his own individual genius. John was soon cut short in his prophetic career, and cast into prison, from which, however, he still exercised a wide influence.

Jesus returned from the neighbourhood of the Dead Sea and the Jordan to Galilee, his true home, ripened by intercourse with a great man of very different nature,and having acquired full consciousness of his own originality. From that time he preached with greater power and made the multitude feel his authority. The persuasion that he was to make God reign upon earth took absolute possession of his spirit. He looked upon himself as the universal reformer. He aimed at founding the Kingdom of God, or, in other words, the Kingdom of the Soul. Jesus was, in some respects, an anarchist, for he had no idea of civil government. He never showed any desire to put himself in the place of the rich and mighty. The idea of being all-powerful by suffering and resignation, and of triumphing over force by purity of heart was his peculiar idea. The founders of the Kingdom of God are the simple--not the rich, not the learned, not the priests; but women, common folk, the humble, and the young. He now boldly announced "the good tidings of the Kingdom of God," and himself as that "Son of Man," whom Daniel in his vision had beheld as the divine herald of the last and supreme revelation.

Early Successes

The success of the new prophet's teaching was decisive. A group of men and women, all characterised by the same spirit of childish frankness and simple innocence, adhered to him, and said, "Thou art the Messiah." The centre of his operations was the little town of Capernaum, on the shore of the Lake of Genesareth. Jesus was much attached to the town and made it a second home. He had attempted to begin the work at Nazareth, but without success. The fact that his family, which was of humble rank, was known in the district lessened his authority too much; and it is moreover remarkable that his family were strongly opposed to him, and flatly declined to believe in his mission. In Capernaum he was much more favourably received, and it became"his own city." These good Galileans had never heard preaching so well adapted to their cheerful imaginations. They admired him, they encouraged him, they found that he spoke well, and that his reasons were convincing. The almost poetical harmony of his discourses won their affections. The authority of the young master increased day by day, and naturally the more that people believed in him the more he believed in himself. Four or five large villages, lying at half an hour's journey from one another, formed the little world of Jesus at this time. Sometimes, however, he wandered beyond his favourite region, once in the direction of Tyre and Sidon, a country which must have been marvellously prosperous at that time. But he returned always to his well-beloved shore of Genesareth. The motherland of his thoughts was there; there he found faith and love.

In this earthly paradise lived a population in perfect harmony with the land itself, active, honest, joyous, and tender of heart, and here Jesus became the centre of a little circle which adored him. In this friendly group he evidently had his favourites. Peter, for whom his affection was very deep, James, son of Zebedee, and John, his brother, formed a sort of privy council. Jesus owed his conquests to the infinite charm of his personality and speech. Everyone thought that he lived in a sphere higher than that of humanity. The aristocracy of the group was represented by a customs-officer, and by the wife of one of Herod's stewards. The rest were fishermen and common folk. Jesus lived with his disciples almost always in the open air, the faithful band leading a joyous wandering life, and gathering the inspirations of the Master in their first bloom. His preaching was soft and gentle, inspired with a feeling for nature and the perfume of the fields. It was above all in parable that the Master excelled. There was nothing in Judaism to give him a model for this delightful feature. He created it. In freeing man from what he called "the cares of this world" Jesus might go to excess and injure the essential conditions of human society; but he founded that spiritual exaltation which for centuries has filled souls with joy in the midst of this vale of tears. In our busy civilisation the memory of the free life of Galilee has been like perfume from another world, like the "dew of Hermon," which has kept drought and grossness from entirely invading the fields of God.

A Gospel for the Poor

Jesus very soon understood that the official world of his time would by no means lend its support to his kingdom. He took his resolution with extreme daring. Leaving the world, with its hard heart and narrow prejudices, on one side, he turned towards the simple. A vast rearrangement of classes was to take place. The Kingdom of God was made for children, and those like them; for the world's outcasts, victims of that social arrogance which repulses the good but humble man; for heretics and schismatics, publicans, Samaritans, and the pagans of Tyre and Sidon. That the reign of the poor is at hand was the doctrine of Jesus. This exaggerated taste for poverty could not last very long, but although it quickly passed, poverty remained an ideal from which true descendants of Jesus were never afterwards separated.

Like all great men, Jesus was fond of common folk, and felt at his ease with them. He particularly esteemed all those whom orthodox Judaism disdained. Love of the people, pity for their powerlessness, the feeling of the democratic leader who has the spirit of the multitude quick within him, reveal themselves at every instant in his acts and sayings. He had no external affection, and made no display of austerity. He did not shun pleasure; but went willingly to marriage feasts. Hisgentle gaiety found constant expression in amiable pleasantries. Thus he journeyed through Galilee in the midst of continual festivities. When he entered a house, it was considered a joy and a blessing. Children and women adored him. The children, indeed, were like a young guard about him, for the inauguration of his innocent kingship, and gave him little ovations. It was childhood, in fact, in its divine spontaneity, in its simple bewilderment of joy, that took possession of the earth.

How long did this intoxication last? We cannot tell. But whether it filled years or months, the dream was so beautiful that humanity has lived upon it ever since. Happy he to whom it has been granted to behold with his own eyes this divine blossoming, and to share, if but for a day, the incomparable illusion! But yet more happy, Jesus would tell us, shall he be who, by the uprightness of his will, and the poetry of his soul, shall be able to create anew in his own heart the true Kingdom of God!

The Priest in the Path

Nearly every year Jesus went to Jerusalem for the feast of the Passover. It was, it appears, in the year 31 that the most important of these visits took place. Jesus felt that to play a leading part he must leave Galilee and attack Judaism in its stronghold, Jerusalem. There the little Galilean community was far from feeling at home. Jerusalem was a city of pedantry, acrimony, disputation, hatreds, and pettiness of mind. Its fanaticism was extreme. All the religious discussions of the Jewish schools, all the canonical instruction, even the legal business and civil actions--in a word, all form of national activity, were concentrated in the temple. The Romans refrained from entering the sactuary; the surveillance of the Temple was in the hands of the Jews.It was in the Temple that Jesus spent his days during his sojourn at Jerusalem, and all that he saw aroused his aversion. These old Jewish institutions displeased him, and the necessity of conforming to them gave him pain. He who gave forgiveness to all men, provided they loved him, could find nothing congenial in vain disputations and obsolete sacrifices, and apparently he brought from Jerusalem one idea thenceforth rooted in his mind--that there was no understanding possible between him and the ancient Jewish religion. He no longer took his stand as a Jewish reformer, but as a destroyer of Judaism. In other words, Jesus is no longer a Jew. He is, in the highest degree, a revolutionary; he calls all men to a worship founded solely on the ground of their being children of God. Love of God, charity, and mutual forgiveness--in these consisted his whole law. Nothing could be less sacerdotal. It was on his return from Jerusalem, as he passed near Shechem, and when talking with a Samaritan woman, that Jesus gave utterance to the saying upon which will rest the edifice of eternal religion--Believe me, the hour cometh when neither in this mountain nor in Jerusalem shall ye worship the Father ... but the hour cometh, and now is, when the true worshippers shall worship the Father in spirit and in truth. On the day when he said these words he was truly Son of God.

Jesus returned to Galilee full of revolutionary ardour. His innocent aphorisms and beautiful moral precepts now culminated in a decided policy. The law is to be abolished, and it is he that will abolish it. The Messiah is come, and it is he that is the Messiah. The Kingdom of God is about to be revealed, and it is he that will reveal it. He knew well that he would be the victim of his own audacity, but it was by cries and the rending of hearts that the kingdom had to be established.

The proposition "Jesus is the Messiah" was followed by the proposition "Jesus is the Son of David," and, byan entirely spontaneous conspiracy, fictitious genealogies arose in the imaginations of his partisans, while he was still alive, to prove his royal descent. We cannot tell whether he knew anything of these legends. He never designated himself Son of David. That he ever dreamed of making himself pass for an incarnation of God is a matter about which no doubt can exist. Such an idea was entirely foreign to the Jewish mind. He believed himself to be more than an ordinary man, but separated by an infinite distance from God. He was the Son of God, but all men are, or may become so in divers degrees. Jesus apparently remained a stranger to the theological subtleties which were soon to fill the world with sterile disputations.

Time-worm Proofs

Two means of proof--miracles and the accomplishment of prophecies--could alone establish a supernatural mission in the opinion of the contemporaries of Jesus. He himself, but more especially his disciples, employed these two methods of demonstration in perfect good faith. For a long time Jesus had recognised himself in the sacred oracles of the prophets. As to miracles, they were considered at this epoch the indispensable mark of the divine, and the sign of the prophetic vocation. Jesus, therefore, was compelled either to renounce his mission or become a thaumaturgist. It must be remembered that not only did he believe in miracles, but he had not the least idea of an order of nature under the reign of law. On that point, his knowledge was in no way superior to that of his contemporaries. Indeed, one of his most deeply-rooted opinions was that by faith and prayer man had entire power over nature. Almost all the miracles Jesus believed he performed seem to have been miracles of healing. The kind of healing which he most often practised was exorcism, or the expulsionof demons. There can be no doubt that he had in his lifetime the reputation of possessing the greatest secrets of the art. There were many lunatics in Judaea wandering at large, and no doubt Jesus had great influence over these unhappy beings. Circumstances seem to indicate that he became a thaumaturgist late in life and against his own inclinations. He accepted miracles exacted by public opinion rather than performed them.

The New Kingdom of God

During the eighteen months between the return from the Passover of the year 31 and his journey to the feast of tabernacles in the year 32, all that was within Jesus developed with an ever-increasing degree of power and audacity. The fundamental idea of Jesus from his earliest days was the establishment of the Kingdom of God. This kingdom he appears to have understood in divers senses. At times it is the literal consummation of apocalyptic visions relating to the Messiah. At other times it is the spiritual kingdom, and the deliverance at hand is the deliverance of the soul. The revolution desired by Jesus in this last sense is the one which has really taken place. That the coming of the end of the world and the appearance of the Messiah in judgment was taken literally by the disciples, and at certain moments by the Master himself, appears absolutely clear. These formal declarations absorbed the minds of the Christian family for nearly seventy years. The world has not ended, as Jesus announced, and as his disciples believed it would end. But it has been renewed and in one sense renewed as Jesus desired. By the side of the false, cold, impossible idea of an ostentatious advent, he conceived the real City of God, the raising up of the weak, the love of the people, esteem for the poor, and the restoration of all that is humble and true and simple. This restoration he has depicted, as an incomparable artist, in touches which willlast for eternity. His Kingdom of God was doubtless the apocalypse which was soon to be unfolded in the heavens. But besides this, and probably above all, was the soul's kingdom, founded on freedom, and on the feeling of sonship which the good man knows in his rest on the bosom of his Father. This is what was destined to live. This is what has lived.

The Clash of Old and New

Throughout the first epoch of his career, it seems as though Jesus met with no serious opposition; but when he entered upon a path brilliant with public successes the first mutterings of the storm began to make themselves heard. He recognised only the religion of the heart, while the religion of the Pharisees almost exclusively consisted of observances. As his mission proceeded, his conflicts with official hypocrisy became incessant. His goal was in the future, not in the past. He was more than the reformer of an obsolete religion; he was the creator of the eternal religion of humanity. A hatred which death alone could satisfy was the consequence of these controversies. The war was to the death. Judaea drew him as by a charm; he wished to attempt one last effort to win the rebellious city, and seemed anxious to fulfil the proverb that a prophet ought not to die outside Jerusalem.

At the feast of tabernacles in the year 32, his relatives, always malevolent and sceptical, pressed him to go there. He set out on the journey unknown to every one and almost alone, and never again saw his beloved northern land.

In Jerusalem, Jesus was a stranger. There he felt a wall of resistance he could not penetrate. At every step he met with obstinate scepticism. The arrogance of the priests made the courts of the Temple disagreeable to him, and his criticisms naturally exasperated the sacerdotal caste. Imagine a reformer going, in our own time,to preach the overthrow of Islamism round the Mosque of Omar! His teaching in this new world was greatly modified; he had to become controversialist, jurist, theologian, though when alone with his disciples his gentle and irresistible genius inspired him with accents full of tenderness.

Approaching the Crisis

Jesus spent the autumn and part of the winter in Jerusalem. In the new year he undertook a journey to the banks of the Jordan, the district he had visited when he followed the school of John. After this pilgrimage he returned to Bethany, a place he especially loved, and where he knew a family whose friendship had a great charm for him. In impure and depressing Jerusalem, Jesus was no longer himself. His mission weighed him down, and he let himself be carried away by the torrent. The contrast between his ever-increasing exaltation and the indifference of the Jews became wider day by day. At the same time the public authorities began to be bitter against him. In February, or early in March, the council of the chief priests asked clearly the question "Can Jesus and Judaism exist together?" The High Priest was Joseph Kaiapha, but beside and behind him we always see another man, Hanan, his father-in-law. He had been High Priest, and in reality kept all the authority of the office. During fifty years the pontificate remained in his family almost without interruption. The family spirit was haughty, bold, and cruel. It was Hanan, his family, and the party he represented, who really put Jesus to death. After the death of Jesus was decided, he escaped for a short time by withdrawing to an obscure town, Ephron, and letting the storm pass over; but when the feast of the Passover drew nigh, he set out to see for the last time the unbelieving city. His followers all believed that the Kingdom of God was about to be realised there. As to Jesus, he grew confirmed in theconviction that he was about to die, but that his death would save the world.

During these last days a deep sadness appears to have filled the soul of Jesus, which was generally so joyous and serene. The enormous weight of the mission he had accepted bore cruelly upon him. All these inward troubles were evidently a sealed chapter to his disciples. His divine nature, however, soon gained the supremacy, and henceforth we behold him entirely himself and with his character unclouded. Each moment of this period is solemn, and counts more than whole ages in the history of humanity. A lofty feeling of love, of concord, of charity, and of mutual deference, animated the memories cherished of these last hours.

Victory Through Defeat

It was in the garden of Gethsemane that the guards of the Temple, supported by a detachment of Roman soldiers, executed the warrant of arrest. The course which the priests had determined to take against Jesus was in perfect conformity with the established law. The warrant of arrest probably came from Hanan, and before this powerful man Jesus was first brought for examination as to his doctrine. Jesus, with just pride, declined to enter into long explanations--he asked the ex-high priest to question those who had listened to him. Hanan then sent him to his son-in-law, Kaiapha, at whose house the Sanhedrim was assembled. It is probable that here, too, he kept silence. The sentence was already decided, and they only sought for pretexts. With one voice the assembly declared him guilty of a capital crime. The point now was to get Pilate to ratify the sentence. On being informed of the accusation, Pilate showed his annoyance at being mixed up in the matter, and called upon to play a cruel part for the sake of a law he detested. Perhaps the dignified and calm attitude of the accusedmade an impression upon him. To excite the suspicion of the Roman authorities, the charges now made were those of sedition and treason against the government. Nothing could be more unjust, for Jesus had always recognised the Roman government as the established power. Asked by Pilate if he really were the king of the Jews, Jesus, according to the fourth gospel, avowed his kingship, but uttered at the same time the profound saying, "My kingdom is not of this world." Of this lofty idealism Pilate understood nothing. No doubt Jesus impressed him as being a harmless dreamer. When, however, the people began to denounce Pilate's lack of zeal, in protecting an enemy of Caesar, he surrendered, throwing on the Jews the responsibility for what was about to take place. It was not Pilate who condemned Jesus. It was the old Jewish party; it was the Mosaic law. Intolerance is a Jewish characteristic. The Pentateuch has been the first code of religious terrorism in the world. It was, however, the chimerical "King of the Jews," not the heteradox dogmatist, who was punished, and the execution took the Roman form of crucifixion, carried out by Roman soldiers.

The horrors of that ignominious death were suffered by Jesus in all their atrocity. For a moment, according to certain narratives, his heart failed him; a cloud hid from him the face of his Father; he endured an agony of despair more acute a thousand times than all his torments. But his divine instinct again sustained him. In measure as the life of the body flickered out, his soul grew serene, and by degrees returned to its heavenly source. He regained the idea of his mission, in his death he saw the salvation of the world; the hideous spectacle spread at his feet melted from his sight, and profoundly united to his Father, he began upon the gibbet the divine life which he was to live in the heart of humanity through infinite years.

Rest now in thy glory, noble pioneer! Thy work isachieved, thy divinity established. At the price of a few hours of suffering, which have not even touched thy mighty soul, thou hast purchased the fullest immortality. For thousands of years the world will depend upon thee! A thousand times more alive, a thousand times more loved since thy death than during the days of thy pilgrimage here below, thou shalt become so truly the cornerstone of humanity that to tear thy name from this world were to shake it to its foundations.

Whatever the unexpected phenomena of the future, Jesus will never be surpassed. His worship will constantly renew its youth; the legend of his life will bring ceaseless tears; his sufferings will soften the best hearts; all the ages will proclaim that amongst the sons of men none has been born who is greater than Jesus.

EMANUEL SWEDENBORG

Heaven and Hell

Emanuel Swedenborg, author of a strange system of mystical theology, was of Swedish nationality and was born at Stockholm on January 29, 1688. He was educated at Upsala, and after travelling for several years in Western Europe was appointed to a post in the Swedish College of Mines. Thenceforth, until he was 55 years of age, Swedenborg pursued, with equal industry and ingenuity, the career of a man of science, doing valuable work in mathematics, astronomy, navigation, engineering, chemistry, and especially in mining and metallurgy. These inquiries were followed by studies in philosophy and anatomy and physiology. But about the year 1744 certain visions and other mystical experiences began to take hold of his mind, and three years later Swedenborg had come to regard himself as the medium of a new revelation of divine truth. His message, or theory, or vision, was first promulgated in the eight quarto volumes of the "Heavenly Arcana," published in London from 1749 to 1756, and this was followed by "Heaven and Hell," 1758, the work now before us, the full title of which is "Heaven and Its Wonders, the World of Spirits, and Hell: described by one who had heard and seen what he relates," and several other apocalyptic books, all of which were written in Latin. The main features of Swedenborg's theology were a strong emphasis on the divinity of Christ, the proclamation of the immediate advent of the "New Jerusalem," foretold by the seer of Patmos, and the conception of correspondences between the natural, spiritual, and mental worlds. His followers, known as Swedenborgians, or more properly as "The New Church signified by the New Jerusalem in the Revelation," are widely spread but not very numerous, in England and in the United States. Swedenborg died in London on March 29, 1772.

I.--Of Heaven

The first thing necessary to be known is, who is the God of heaven; for everything else depends on this. In the universal heaven, no other is acknowledged for its God, but the Lord Alone; they say there, as He Himself taught, that He is One with the Father; that the Father is in Him, and He in the Father; that whosoever seethHim, seeth the Father; and that everything holy proceeds from Him. I have often conversed with the angels on this subject, and they constantly declared that they are unable to divide the Divine Being into three, because they know and perceive that the Divine Being is one, and that He is One in the Lord.

The angels, taken collectively, are called heaven, because they compose it: but still it is the Divine Sphere proceeding from the Lord, which enters the angels by influx, and is by them received, which essentially constitutes it, both in general and in particular. The Divine Sphere proceeding from the Lord is the good of love and the truth of faith: in proportion, therefore, as the angels receive good and truth from the Lord, so far they are angels, and so far they are heaven.

As in heaven there are infinite varieties, and no society is exactly like another, nor indeed any angel, therefore heaven is divided in a general, in a specific, and in a particular manner. It is divided, in general, into two kingdoms, specifically, into three heavens, and in particular, into innumerable societies.

There are angels who receive the Divine Sphere proceeding from the Lord more and less interiorly. They who receive it more interiorly are called celestial angels; but they who receive it less interiorly are called spiritual angels. Hence, heaven is divided into two kingdoms, one of which is called the Celestial Kingdom, and the other, the Spiritual Kingdom.

The angels of each heaven do not dwell all together in one place, but are divided into larger and smaller societies, according to the difference of the good of love and faith in which they are grounded; those who are grounded in similar good forming one society. There is an infinite variety of kinds of good in the heavens; and every angel is such in quality as is the good belonging to him.

That heaven, viewed collectively, is in form as oneman, is a mystery which is not yet known to the world: but it is well known in the heavens; for the knowledge of this mystery, with the particular and most particular circumstances relating to it, is the chief article of the intelligence of the angels; since many other things depend upon it, which, without a knowledge of this as their common centre, could not possibly enter distinctly and clearly into their ideas. As they know that all the heavens together with their societies are in form as one man, they also call heaven THE GRAND AND DIVINE MAN; divine, because the Divine Sphere of the Lord constitutes heaven.

From my experience, which I have enjoyed for many years, I can affirm that angels are in every respect men; that they have faces, eyes, ears, a body, arms, hands, and that they see, hear, and converse with each other; in short they are deficient in nothing that belongs to a man except that they are not super-invested with a material body.

Their habitations are exactly like our houses on earth, but more beautiful. They contain chambers, with-drawing-rooms, and bed-chambers, in great numbers, and are encompassed with gardens and flower-beds. Where the angels live together in societies the habitations are contiguous, and arranged in the form of a city, with streets, squares, and churches. It has also been granted to me to walk through them, and to look about on all sides, and occasionally to enter the houses. This occurred to me when wide awake, my interior sight being open at the time.

That it is by derelation from the Lord's Divine Humanity that heaven, both in whole and in parts, is in form as a man, follows as a conclusion from all that has been advanced.

There is a correspondence between all things belonging to heaven and all things belonging to man. It is unknown at this day what correspondence is. This ignoranceis owing to various causes; the chief of which is, that man has removed himself from heaven, through cherishing the love of self and of the world. For he that supremely loves himself and the world cares only for worldly things, because they soothe the external senses and are agreeable to his natural disposition; but has no concern about spiritual things, because these only soothe the internal senses and are agreeable to the internal or rational mind. These, therefore, they cast aside, saying that they are too high for man's comprehension. Not so did the ancients. With them the science of correspondences was the chief of all sciences: by means of its discoveries, also, they imbibed intelligence and wisdom, and such of them as belonged to the church had by it communication with heaven; for the science of correspondences is the science of angels.

It shall first be stated what correspondence is. The whole natural world corresponds to the spiritual world; and not only the natural world collectively, but also in its individual parts: wherefore every object in the natural world, existing from something in the spiritual world, is called its correspondent. The natural world exists and subsists from the spiritual world, just as the effect exists from the efficient cause.

Since man is both a heaven and a world in miniature, he has belonging to him both a spiritual world and a natural world. The interiors, which belong to his mind, and have relation to his understanding and will, constitute his spiritual world; but his exteriors, which belong to his body, and have reference to its senses and actions, constitute his natural world.

The nature of correspondence may be seen from the face of man. In a countenance which has not been taught to dissemble, all the affections of the mind display themselves vividly, in a natural form, as in their type; whence the face is called the index of the mind. Thus man's spiritual world shows itself in its natural world. Allthings, therefore, which take effect in the body, whether in the countenance, the speech, or the gestures, are called correspondences.

The angels rejoice that it has pleased the Lord to reveal many particulars to mankind. They desire me to state from their lips, that there does not exist, in the universal heaven, a single angel who was created such from the first, nor any devil in hell who was created an angel of light and afterwards cast down thither; but that all the inhabitants, both of heaven and of hell, are derived from the human race; the inhabitants of heaven being those who had lived in heavenly love and faith, and those of hell who had lived in infernal love and faith.

II--Of the World of Spirits

The world of spirits is not heaven nor yet hell, but is a place or state intermediate between the two. Thither man goes after death; and having completed the period of his stay there, according to his life in the world he is either elevated into heaven or cast into hell.

The world of spirits contains a great number of inhabitants, because it is the region in which all first assemble, and where all are examined and are prepared for their final abode. Their stay there is not limited to any fixed period: some do but just enter it, and are presently either taken up to heaven or cast down to hell: some remain there only a few weeks; and some for several years, but never more than thirty. The varieties in the length of their stay depend upon the correspondence, or noncorrespondence between their interiors and their exteriors.

As men enter the world of spirits, they are distinguished by the Lord into classes. The wicked are immediately connected by invisible bonds with the society of hell, and the good, in a similar way, with the society of heaven, but notwithstanding these bonds, they meet andconverse together. I saw a father conversing with his six sons, all of whom he recognised; but as they were different in disposition, resulting from their course of life in the world, after a short time they were parted.

The spirit of a man, when first he enters the world of spirits, is similar in countenance and in the tone of his voice to what he was in the world. The reason is, because he is then in the state of his exteriors and his interiors are not yet laid open. This is the first state of man after death. But afterwards his countenance is changed; being rendered similar to his governing affection or love, which is that in which the interiors belonging to his mind had been grounded while in the world, and which had reigned in his spirit while this was in the body. For the face of a man's spirit differs exceedingly from that of his body; the face of his body being derived from his parents, but that of his spirit from his affection, of which it is the image.

That his own life remains with everyone after death is known to every Christian from the Word. Everyone, also, who thinks under the influence of good and of real truth, has no other idea than that he who has lived well will go to heaven, and he who has lived ill will go to hell.

But by deeds and works are not merely meant deeds and works as they appear in their external form, but as they appear internally. Everyone knows, that every deed or work proceeds from the will and thought of the doer; for otherwise they would be mere motions, such as are performed by automatons and images. The deed or work, then, viewed in itself, is nothing but an effect, which derives its soul and life from the will and thought from which it is performed; and so completely is this the case that the deed or work is the will and thought in their effect, and is, consequently, the will and thought in their external form. It hence follows, that such as are, in quality, the will and thought which produce the deed or work, such, also, is the deed or work itself; and thatif the thought and will are good the deeds or works are good; and if the thought and will are evil the deeds and works are evil, notwithstanding in their external form they appear like the former.

To sum up the truths concerning man's state after death, I will say, first: that man, after death, is his own love, or his own will; secondly: that, in quality, man remains to eternity, such as he is with respect to his will or governing love; thirdly: that the man whose love is celestial and spiritual goes to heaven, but that the man whose love is corporeal and worldly, destitute of such as is celestial and spiritual, goes to hell; fourthly: that faith does not remain with man, if not grounded in heavenly love; fifthly: that what remains with man is love in act, consequently his life.

III.--Of Hell

When treating above respecting heaven, it has everywhere been shown, that the Lord is the God of heaven, and thus that the whole government of the heavens is that of the Lord. Now as the relation which heaven bears to hell, and that which hell bears to heaven, is such as exists between two opposites, which mutually act against each other, and the result of whose action and reaction is a state of equilibrium, in which all things may subsist, therefore, in order that all and everything should be maintained in equilibrium, it is necessary that he who governs the one should also govern the other. For unless the same ruler were to restrain the assaults made by the hells, and to keep down the insanities which rage in them, the equilibrium would be destroyed, and with it the whole universe.

It is this spiritual equilibrium that causes man to enjoy freedom in thinking and willing. For whatever a man thinks and wills has reference either to evil and the falsity proceeding from it, or to good and the truthwhich comes from that source: consequently, when he is placed in that equilibrium he enjoys the liberty of either, admitting and receiving evil and its falsity from hell, or good in its truth from heaven. Every man is maintained in this equilibrium by the Lord, because he governs both--heaven as well as hell.

Hell, like heaven, is divided into societies; and every society in heaven has a society opposite to it in hell; which is provided for the preservation of the equilibrium.

It is by influence from hell that man does evil, and by influence from the Lord that he does good. But as man believes that whatever he does, he does from himself, the consequence is that the evil which he does adheres to him as his own. It hence follows that the cause of his own evil lies with man, and not at all with the Lord. Evil as existing with man is hell, as existing with him: for whether you say evil or hell, amounts to the same thing. Now since the cause of his own evil lies with man himself, it follows that it is he who casts himself into hell, and not the Lord; and so far is the Lord from leading man into hell, that he delivers from hell, so far as the man does not will and loves to abide in his own evil. But the whole of man's will and love remains with him after death: whoever wills and loves evil in the world, wills and loves the same evil in the other life; and he then no longer suffers himself to be withdrawn from it. It hence results, that the man who is immersed in evil is connected by invisible bonds with hell: he is also actually there as to his spirit; and, after death, he desires nothing more earnestly than to be where his evil is.

From an inspection of the monstrous forms belonging to the spirits in the hells, it was made evident to me that they all, in general, are forms of self-love and the love of the world, and that the evils, of which in particular they are the forms, derive their origin from those two loves. It has also been told me from heaven, andproved to me by much experimental evidence, that those two loves--self-love and the love of the world--reign in the hells and also constitute them; whereas love to the Lord and love towards the neighbour reign in the heavens and also constitute them: and that the two former loves, which are the loves of hell, and the two latter, which are the loves of heaven, are diametrically opposite to each other.

As by the fire of hell is to be understood all the lust of doing evil flowing from self-love, by the same is also meant torment, such as exists in the hells. For the lust flowing from that love is, in those who are inflamed by it, the lust of doing injury to all who do not honour, respect, and pay court to them; and in proportion to the anger which they thence conceive against such individuals, and to the hatred and revenge inspired by such anger, is their lust of committing outrages against them. Now when such a lust rages in everyone in a society, and they have no external bond to keep them under restraint, such as the fear of the law, and of the loss of character, of honour, of gain, and of the like, everyone under the influence of his own evil attracts another and, so far as he is strong enough, subjugates him, subjects the rest to his own authority, and exercises ferocious outrages with delight upon all who do not submit to him. All the hells are societies of this description: on which account, every spirit, and every society, cherishes hatred in his heart against every other, and, under the influence of such hatred, breaks out into savage outrages against him, as far as he is able to inflict them. These outrages, and the torments so occasioned, are also meant by hell fire; for they are the effects of the lusts which there prevail.

In order that man may be in a state of liberty, as necessary to his being reformed, he is connected, as to his spirit, with heaven and with hell: for spirits from hell, and angels from heaven, are attendant on every man. By the spirits from hell, man is held in his evil; but by theAngels from heaven, he is held in good by the Lord.

Thus he is preserved in spiritual equilibrium, that is, in freedom or liberty.

The particulars which have been delivered in this work respecting heaven, the world of spirits, and hell, will appear obscure to those who take no pleasure in acquiring a knowledge of spiritual truths; but they will appear clear to those who take pleasure in that acquirement; and especially those who cherish an affection of truth for its own sake,--that is, who love truth because it is truth. For everything that is loved enters with light into the ideas of the mind: and this is eminently the case, when that which is loved is truth: for all truth dwells in light.

THE TALMUD

The word "Talmud," from the Hebrew verb *lamad*, equalling "to learn," denotes literally "what-is-learning." Then it comes to mean "instruction," "teaching," "doctrine." What is usually called the Talmud consists of two parts: 1. The Mishnah (literally, "tradition" and then "traditional doctrine") a code of Jewish laws, civil, criminal, religious, and so forth; based ostensibly on the Pentateuch, expounding, applying, and developing the laws contained in the so-called five books of Moses. 2. The Gemara, a word which means literally "completion," or "supplement," *i.e.*, in reference to the Mishnah. Some, however, explain the word as meaning "teaching." The word is used technically to denote the expansion, exposition, and illustration of the Mishnah which is found in the Talmud. Strictly speaking, the word "Talmud" denotes the Gemara only, but in its ordinary sense the word denotes the Mishnah together with its completion in the Gemara. In the Talmud itself, as usually printed, the section of the Mishnah to be commented on and illustrated is followed by the Gemara in which the opinions of the great Rabbi are stated and discussed.

As in the case of the Mishnah, so, also, the Talmud has six principal divisions: these will be followed in the subsequent epitomes and need not, therefore, be given here. There are two versions or forms of the Talmud: 1. The Babylonian, or that due to the studies and discussions of the Jewish doctors in the various Hebrew colleges of Babylon (Sura, Pumbaditha, and so forth): in this the Gemara is some ten times as large as the Mishnah. When we speak of the Talmud it is that of Babylon which is always meant. Its language is Eastern Aramaic. 2. The Palestinian Talmud, compiled and edited by the heads of the Hebrew schools in Palestine, Tiberius, Sepphoris, and so forth. Its language is Western Aramaic, and its final editor is said to be Rabbi Ashe, who died A.D. 427. This is often erroneously called the Jerusalem Talmud. In its present form it is only about one-fourth as large as the Babylonian Talmud. The latter discusses nearly every section of the Mishnah, whereas the Palestine Talmud passes by a large proportion of the Mishnah without note or comment. That is, however, because much of this latter Talmud has been lost, for, in the time of Maimonides (died at Cairo A.D. 1204) the Gemara of the Jerusalem Talmud discussed nearly every part of the Mishnah. The Mishnah is usually said to have been completed by Rabbi Jehudah Hannasi, or the Prince (Hannasi), called simply "Rabbi" by way of preeminence, who died in A.D. 210 in his sixtieth year. But there are parts of the Mishnah which are older, and parts also at least a century later than the death of that great scholar. There is no absolute proof that the Mishnah was committed to writing until some time after the completion of the Palestinian (about A.D. 400) or even of the Babylonian (about A.D. 500) Talmud, for, in neither Gemara is there any reference to a written Mishnah, nor is a written form of the Mishnah implied anywhere. The preservation of this wonderful code of Jewish laws was due to memory alone, men being appointed in the various synagogues to learn the Mishnaic sections and to recite them whenever it was necessary. Extracts will be given below from the Mishnah and also from the Gemara, the letters M and G preceding paragraphs indicating which of the two is summarised.

Division I.--Called Seeds

[This part deals first of all with prayer, and then most of all with the various tithes and donations which are due to the priests, Levites, and the poor, from the products of the land.]

SECTION I. TREATISE ON BLESSINGS *(Berakot)*. The time for reading or reciting the Shemang. (1).

M. At what time in the evening may shemang be read? From the time when the priests, having cleansed themselves, enter the sanctuary to partake of the offering (2)(*i.e.,* when the stars come out) until the end of the first watch (about 10 p.m.). So says Rabbi Eliezar, but otherwise men extend the time until midnight. Rabbi Gameliel makes the time reach even to the dawn of the following day. It happened once that his sons returned home at midnight without having read the shemang. On asking their father if it was too late he replied that the obligation to perform the duties of each day is valid until the first light of morning shows itself.

The morning Shemang.

M. From what time may the morning shemang be read? From the moment when there is light enough to distinguish between purple-blue and white. Rabbi Eliezar says "between purple-blue and leek-green" (which areharder to distinguish) (3). Up to when may the morning shemang be read? Until the sun has risen. Rabbi Jose says "until the end of the third hour after sunrise, for it is the custom of kings' sons to rise in the third hour of the day. Yet a good act, such as shemang is, never loses its virtue whenever it is performed."

The attitude in which the shemang should be read.

M. The (strict) School of Shammai say men ought to bow in reading the evening shemang, but to stand upright when saying shemang in the morning, their scripture warrant being Deut. vi, 7, "when thou liest down and when thou risest up." But according to (the more liberal) School of Hillel, people must be allowed to read the shemang in whatever attitude they choose, referring to the words in the same passage: "When thou sittest in thy house and when thou walkest in the way." Why then the words "when thou liest down and when thou risest up?" Because these are the acts that men perform when the shemang would be usually read. Rabbi Tarphon said that once when journeying of an evening, he stooped in order to read the shemang, with the result that his goods were almost taken from him by unsuspected robbers. He was told that he would have deserved it, had he been actually robbed, for not having followed the decision of the Hillel School. The

Gemara on the above Mishnahs gives the opinions of a large number of Rabbis, reporting also discussions in which they took part.

The benedictions before and after the Shemang.

M. Two benedictions (4) are to be said before the morning shemang, and one after it.

When the Shemang is rightly read.

M. He who reads the shemang without hearing his own voice has yet discharged his duty if only his heart has gone with the reading.

Persons not to read the Shemang:

Women, slaves, and minors are not commanded to read the Shemang, or to wear phylacteries. They are, however, expected to recite the eighteen benedictions, the grace after meat, and also to see that the Mezuza is attached to the doorpost. (5).

G. Where are we taught that the Shechinah rests upon *one* who studies the law? In Exodus xx, 24, where it is written: "In all places where I record my name I will come unto *thee*, and I will bless *thee*." The Palestine Talmud paraphrases thus: "In every place in which ye shall memorialise My holy name, My word shall be revealed unto *you*, and shall bless *you*." Hear, O Israel, Jehovah our God, even Jehovah is one. Deut. vi, 4. Whoever prolongs the utterance of the word *one* (Heb. *ekhad*), his days and years shall be prolonged.

Once, the Rabbis say, the Roman government decreed that no Israelite should be allowed to study the Law. Immediately after, Rabbi Agiba was found teaching the Law to crowds of people who had gathered around him. Some one passing by asked him "Fearest thou not the Roman government?" To which he said, "I will answer by a parable: A fox was once walking by a river side when he saw the fish rushing distractedly hither and thither. On asking them the cause of all their perturbation, they replied: 'We are afraid of the nets which wicked men are ever setting to catch us.' 'Why, then,' said the fox, 'do you not leave that dangerous element and try the dry land with me?' 'Surely,' replied the fish, 'thou art in this most foolish and unfoxlike, for if it is dangerous for us to dwell in this, our native element, how much more would it be if we left it for the dry land?' So," continued Agiba,"all those who study the Law have the Divine Promise,"Deut. xxx, 20: "He is thy life and the length of thy days."

Division II--Feasts (Mongëd)

[contains directions for observing the festivals, including the Sabbath. The aim in all is professedly to make explicit what is implicit in the Pentateuch. But many late ideas and customs are brought into this division, of which the Pentateuch knows nothing. Even the feast of Purim mentioned here it quite unmencioned in the Pentateuch.]

1. TREATISE ON THE SABBATH. Law regarding transfer of goods on the Sabbath.

M. It is commanded in Exodus xvi, 29, that no man go out of his place on the Sabbath day. This implies that no one is to take goods from his own premises to those of another.(6). What, however, constitutes one's own premises? *(Reshut).* There are many cases to be considered. Suppose a beggar stand outside and the master of the house inside. If the first reaches his hand through a window or door to the second, or takes something out of the hand of the latter, the beggar is guilty, but the master is absolved. If, on the other hand, the master puts his hand outside the house, and places something in the beggar's hands, he is guilty, but the beggar is absolved.

[There are in all four cases treating of the man inside and four of the man outside.]

G. Rabbi Mathra said to Abazi, "There are eight or even ten cases of transfer." Rab questioned Rabbi, "Suppose one from the outside were laden in the house with food, fruit, etc. How stands the law? Is the removal of his body tantamount to the removal of a thing from its place?" "Yes," said Rabbi; "this is not like the case of removing the hand, because the latter was not at rest, while in the former, the body, before and after removal, was entirely at rest." "Suppose," said one Rabbi to another, "that a person has put bread into an oven and it is not done by the time the Sabbath begins. May he take it out before it is spoiled?" "He may lawfully do so if he put it there, believing it would be fully baked before the Sabbath arrived."

Acts forbidden on Sabbath eve.

M. Just before the time of Sabbath evening prayer (7), a man is not allowed to sit to a barber, to enter a bath, a tanyard, to sit to a meal, or to begin to act as judge in a Law Court. He must first of all perform his devotions. But supposing that one has commenced any one of these acts, then let them be finished.

G. A man begins the act of haircutting when the barber's cloth is spread over him. Bathing has begun if the outer coat has been pulled off. A man has commenced to tan if his working apron has been tied around him. A meal begins when the hands are washed or (as some say) when the girdle has been removed. The process of judging has begun when the judges have donned their professional robes, or (as some have it) directly the litigants begin pleading.

The Jew and a non-Jew.

M. The school of Shammai forbids a Jew to sell anything to a non-Jew on the Sabbath eve, or to help him with a load unless the Jew can reach some neighbouring village before the Sabbath fully sets in. The School of Hillel, however, allows it.

Miscellaneous prohibitions.

M. A tailor must not go out on the Sabbath eve with his needle, lest he forget it and carry it during the Sabbath. Nor must the professional writer (scribe) go out with his writing reed on the Sabbath eve. According to the School of Shammai it is unlawful on the Sabbatheve to deliver skins to a heathen tanner, or clothes to be washed to a non-Jewish laundress, unless there be time enough for them to be got quite ready before the Sabbath begins. But the School of Hillel allowed perfect freedom in the matter. Rabbi Simeon ben Gemaliel says, "it was the custom in my parental home to hand over to the non-Jewish laundress things to be washed, three days before the Sabbath." It is forbidden to fry meat, onions, or eggs, on the Sabbath eve, unless they can be completely cooked before the Sabbath begins. Bread must not be put into the oven, nor cakes on the coal, unless there is time before the Sabbath comes in for the surface to become encrusted.

Concerning the Sabbath lamp. (8).

M. Wherewith may one light the Sabbath lamp? Not with wicks made with cedar moss, or raw flax, or silk fibre, or weeds growing in water, or ship moss. Nor shall pitch, wax, cottonseed oil, or oil of rejected offerings, or oil from sheeptail fat, be used for these lamps.

G. The Rabbis allowed the aforementioned ingredients to be used for the Sabbath fires, though not for the Sabbath lamps. Why are wicks made of the above materials prohibited? Because they give but a flickering light. The oily substances mentioned are forbidden because they do not adhere to the wick.

About extinguishing the Sabbath lamp.

M. He who extinguishes the Sabbath lamp for fear of non-Jews or robbers or of evil spirits, or in order that the sick may sleep, is free from guilt. But if the object is merely to save expense the lamp extinguisher stands condemned.

Three things to say on the Sabbath eve.

M. I. Have ye tithed the food to be eaten on the

Sabbath? 2. Have ye made the *erub*? 3. Light ye theSabbath lamp.

Man's two Sabbath angels.

G. As he returns home from the Synagogue on the Sabbath eve, every man is accompanied by two angels, one good, the other evil. If, on coming home, the man finds the lamp lit, the tables spread, and everything in order, the good angel says, "May the coming Sabbath be as this present one." To which the evil angel is compelled reluctantly to respond "Amen." But if everything be in disorder the bad angel says, "May the coming Sabbath be as the present one." To which the good angel is obliged reluctantly to respond, "Amen."

The overturning of Mount Sinai. (9).

G. When the Israelites refused to believe the words of Moses after he had returned from the mountain, the Holy One, blessed be He, inverted the mountain above them like a top, and said unto them, "If ye receive the Law, well, but if not, your graves shall be here."

Lucky and unlucky birthdays.

G. Rabbi Simon ben Levi said that whoever is born on the first day of the week (Sunday) will be either thoroughly good or thoroughly bad, because on that day light and darkness were created. If on the second day of the week, he will be stingy, because the waters were divided on that day. If on the third day, he will be rich and prosperous, because on that day abundant vegetation was created. If on the fourth day, he will be wise and happy, because on that day the luminaries were fixed. If on the fifth day, he will be good-natured, because fishes and fowls were then created, and these are fed by God alone. If on the sixth day, he will be likely to give himself to good works, because that is the Sabbath preparation day. If, however, he be born on the Sabbath, he will also die on the Sabbath, as a punishment for hisdesecration of that sacred day by his birth.

2. TREATISE ON THE PASSOVER (*Pesakhin*). No. 3 in order.

M. On the eve of the fourteenth Nisan, search must be made for leaven by the light of a lamp (10).

G. What means the Hebrew word *or?* (Translated above "on the eve of"). Rabbi Huna says it means, "when the day begins to dawn": but according to Rabbi Jehuda it means "at night," but in Genesis xliv, 3, and 2nd Sam. xxiii, 4, the verb means "to get day, to dawn," so that Rabbi Huna is right. Abazi said that no student should enter upon his studies just before the dawn of the fourteenth Nizan, lest he forget to search for leaven.

G. To Amorain (11) propose the following question: "Suppose a man let a house to another, telling him that he had removed all leaven but subsequently it was found that some leaven had been left. Is the agreement to take the house binding?" Abazi said, "Yes, it is, for it is better that each householder sees for himself that all leaven has been removed. Before beginning the search for leaven a blessing must be said, as, indeed, before any religious act is performed."

By the light of the lamp.

G. The light of the sun or of the moon or of a flame of fire may not be used in searching for leaven, as the Rabbis say is taught in Zephaniah i, 12 (I will search Jerusalem with lights), and Prov. xx, 27 (Man's soul is Jehovah's lamp searching the inner chambers of the body.)

3. TREATISE ON NEW YEAR'S DAY (*Rosh Hashshanah*). No. 8 in order.

G. The generation before the flood was punished with boiling water. (12).

4. TREATISE ON THE ROLL (13) *(Megillah)*. No. 10in order.

M. The Megillah *(i.e.,* Esther) is sometimes read on the 11th, 12th, 13th, 14th, or 15th of the month Adar, not earlier nor later (for details see the Mishnah and Gemara).

G. Rabbi Jehuda says on the authority of Samuel, that the book of Esther does not defile the hands (14), *i.e.,* that this book was not given by the inspiration of God. Samuel, however, explained that Esther was dictated by the Spirit of God, but only to be orally repeated, and not to be written.

G. When a scroll of the Law has become through age unfit for use it is to be buried in an earthen vessel, as is said in Jeremiah xxii, 14, "And put them in an earthen vessel, that they may continue many days." A scroll of the Law ought never to be sold unless the object be to enable the seller to study the Law better, or to take himself a wife. Rabbi Simon ben Gemaliel said "whoever sells a scroll of the Law, or a daughter, though he does it because he has nothing to eat, will have no good from the purchase money."

5. TREATISE DEALING WITH THE LAWS ABOUT FESTIVAL OFFERINGS. *(Khagiga).* No. 12 in order.

Those under an obligation to offer the burnt offerings during the three *great* annual Feasts.

M. Everyone is under an obligation to offer the burnt offering except the following: A deaf man, a fool, a child, one of doubtful sex, one of double sex, a woman, a slave, a lame man, a blind man, a sick man.

What is meant by a child? One not able to ride upon his father's shoulders in order to go up from Jerusalem to the Temple. So say the School of Shammai, but the Hillel School define child, "One unable to take hold of his father's hand to go from Jerusalem to the Temple."

G. What does the expression "everyone" include?

Him who is half a slave and half free and also him whois lame on the first day and well on the second day, as well as the man who is blind in one eye, except the deaf man, a fool, and à child, and so forth. A deaf man is like a fool and a child, for he is not responsible for his actions any more than they are.

THE WORD TOHU RIGHTLY TRANSLATED "VOID" IN GENESIS i. 2.

G. Tohu is a green line (Heb. Qav or Qaw) which surrounds the entire world, and from which darkness proceeds. (15).

THE SEVEN HEAVENS (16).

G. Resh Lagish used to say, "There are seven heavens, named as follows: 1. Vilon (equals Velum, a curtain). 2. Ragiang. 3. Sheklagim. 4. Zebul. 5. Mangon. 6. Makon. 7. Ngarabot."

SATAN AND HIS COMPANIONS ENDEAVOURING TO STEAL A HEARING OF GOD'S WORDS.

G. Satan and his fellow-fallen angels are in the habit of listening from behind a curtain to the words which God speaks to the angels in heaven (17).

III.--Women (Nashim)

[This division deals with betrothals, marriage, divorce, and the like. One treatise discusses vows.]

1. TREATISE ON WIDOWS UNDER AN OBLIGATION TO UNDERGO THE LEVIRITE MARRIAGE *(Yebamot)*. No. I in order (18).

M. A childless widow is under an obligation to marry the eldest unmarried brother of her deceased husband. If that brother-in-law refuses to marry her, she is allowed in the presence of the nation's leaders to loose his shoe from his foot, to spit in his face, and to say to him,"Thus shall be done to the man who will not build up his brother's house." (see Deut. xxii, 9).

The following classes of women are released from the necessity of marrying any brother-in-law: 1. The illegitimate daughter of the brother. 2. Her daughter. 3. The daughter of his illegitimate son. 4. His wife's daughter. 5. Her son's daughter. 6. Her daughter's daughter. 7. His mother-in-law. 8. The mother of his mother-in-law. 9. The mother of his father-in-law, and so forth.

2. TREATISE ON VOWS (*Nedarim*). No. 3 in order.

The Scriptures Given as a Punishment for Men's Sin.

G. If the Israelites had not been guilty of sin they would never have required more Scripture than the Pentateuch and the Book of Joshua. The last is indispensable as it records the way in which the land was divided among the Israelites. The other Scriptures (the Prophets and the Writing) because in much wisdom there is grief. (Eccles. i, 18).

3. TREATISE ON BETROTHALS (*Qidushin*). No. 7 in order.

The Families Who went up from Babylon to Jerusalem.

M. Ten kinds of families left Babylon for Palestine after the edict of Cyrus went forth in B.C. 538 permitting the nation to return. These were as follows: 1. Priests. 2. Levites. 3. Israelites. 4. Degraded Priests (lit. profaned ones). 5. Proselytes (19). 6. Freedmen. 7. Bastards. 8. Netinim. 9. Those of unknown lineage. 10. Foundlings. The three first are allowed to intermarry: the last six may also intermarry. All those whose mother is known but not their father are said to be of unknown lineage. A foundling is one picked up in the streets whose parents are both unknown.

The Evil of Idolatry. *G.* The worship of idols is so grave a sin that he who renounces or disavows it does as much as if he confessed his belief in the whole law.

Sons More Desirable than Daughters.

G. The world cannot exist without males and females, yet blessed is he whose children are boys, and unlucky he whose children are girls. Cf. Baba Bathra, p. 113, col. I:--"Whoever does not leave a son to be heir, God will heap wrath upon him."

IV.--Concerning Penalties (Nezikin)

[In this division the principal part of the civil and criminal court of the Hebrews is included. See especially the treatise "Sanhedrin."]

1. TREATISE CALLED LIT. Chap. I, or THE FIRST GATE. (20)(Heb. *Baba Qama.*)

Damages to be made good by those responsible for them.

M. There are four principal causes of damage to life and property. I. The Ox. 2. The Uncovered Pit. 3. The Man who sets fire to anything. 4. The Fire which starts of its own accord through neglect.

Whenever damage is done in any of these four ways the one that is responsible for it must make the loss good.

G. The Rabbis teach that there are many specific forms of the above four kinds of injuries, *i.e.,* the ox can do an injury with his horns, his teeth, or his feet.

Accident through falling over a jug or barrel.

M. If anyone places a jug on a public road and another person stumbles over it and breaks it, the latter is not liable for the breakage. But if he is injured by the fall, the owner of the barrel is liable for the damage.

G. The Mishnah uses "jug" in the first clause and "barrel" in the second. Rabbi Papa said that the same thing is meant in both cases.

On breaking a jug full of water on a public road.

M. If a jug full of water breaks on a public road and its contents cause a person to slip, or if in any way one is injured by the pieces, he who carries the jug is liable for any injury. Rabbi Jehuda, however, says he is only liable if he breaks it intentionally.

2. TREATISE CALLED THE MIDDLE CHAPTER (Heb. *Baba Metsia*). 2nd in order.

G. It was Elijah's custom to frequent the Rabbi's council chamber. On one occasion, being later than usual, Rabbi asked him to explain his delay. Elijah answered as follows: "It is my business to wake up Abraham, Isaac, and Jacob one after the other, to wash each one's hand, and to wait until each one has said his prayers and returned to rest." "But," said Rabbi, "why don't they all rise at the same time?" "Because," was Elijah's reply, "if they all three prayed at once, their united prayers would precipitate the advent of the Messiah before its appointed time."

"Then," said Rabbi, "have we amongst us such praying people?" Elijah said there were, mentioning Rabbi Khizah and his sons. Rabbi then proclaimed a fast, which Rabbi Khizah and his sons came to observe. When repeating the 18 benedictions (21) they were about to say "Thou restorest life to the dead" when the world was convulsed and it was asked in Heaven who revealed to them the secret. Elijah was then beaten sixty times with a rod of fire. He afterwards came down like a fiery bear and scattered the congregation.

3. TREATISE CALLED THE LAST CHAPTER *(Baba Bathra)*. No. 3 in order.

G. The members of the Great Synagogue who wrote the Book of Ezekiel, the Books of the twelve minorprophets, the Book of Daniel, and the Book of Ezra (22).

4. TREATISE CALLED SANHEDRIN. NO. 4 in order. [It treats at length of the institution of the municipal and provincial courts called Sanhedrin from a Greek word, and also of the great Sanhedrin, or *Bethdin*, at Jerusalem.]

Jewish Courts and their Constitution.

G. [The Sanhedrin was composed of 71 members. If an Israelite had a point of law to decide, he first proposed it to the Court which met in his own city. If they failed to decide the matter, it was submitted to the judgment of the Court of the next city. If the Justices of the immediate district failed to come to a decision, the case was laid before the Court which met at the entrance of the Temple area. In the event of their failing to decide, they appealed to the Court which met at the entrance to the ante-court. Failure in this Court was followed by an appeal to the Supreme Court of 71, where the matter was finally disposed of by a majority of votes.

The Sanhedrin sat in a semicircle in order that the members might be able to see one another. There were two notaries, one on the right and the other on the left, to count the "Ayes" and "Noes" in all cases of voting.]

The authorship of the BOOK OF EZRA.

G. [The Book of Ezra was written by Nehemiah. He does not attach his name to it because he gave too much attention to his own merits, as it is written (Neh. v, 19) "Think upon me, my God, for good, according to all that I have done for my people."

5. TREATISE ON IDOLATRY *(Aboda Zara)*. No. 8 in order.

M. It is forbidden to have any dealings with non-Jewsfor three days before they hold their unholy festivals (23). One must not lend them any money, for that could be useful to them in preparing for the festival. Nor must one borrow from them, for they would gain thereby and be more able, out of the interest, to meet the expenses of their coming feasts. Similarly, one must not pay them any money, even though due, nor in return must payment be received.

Rabbi Jehuda, however, maintains that payment should be allowed because that is a displeasure and a disadvantage to those who pay.

M. When there is an idol in the city one may go to that city, providing that the road does not lead to the idol alone. Jews are not allowed to sell to non-Jews any of the following things, because they can be used for purposes of heathen worship:--Fir cones, white figs, or their stems, frankincense, and a white cock. A white cock may, however, be sold if one of its claws has been cut off, since non-Jews do not sacrifice an animal when an organ is lacking.

THE BOOK OF YASHAR (see 2nd Sam. i, 18).

G. What is meant by the Book of Yashar? Rabbi Khyiah bar Abba on the authority of Rabbi Jokhanan says "It is the book of Abraham, Isaac and Jacob, they being called righteous *(yesharim),* and concerning whom it is written, Numb, xxiii, 10, 'Let me die the death of the righteous'" *(yesharim).*

6. TREATISE CALLED "SENTENCES OF THE FATHERS" (Heb. *Pirga Abot).* No. 9 in order.

[This treatise, on which no Gemara has been handed down, contains moral precepts, aphorisms, and so forth, of the elder Tannain. It has been often translated, an excellent rendering by the late Dr. Charles Taylor having been published by the Cambridge Press.]

The Two Tables of the Law. *M.* The two Tables of the Law, handed to Moses on Mount Sinai, were created, along with nine other things, at the time when the world was made, and at sunset, before the first Sabbath began.

V.--Sacred Things, Sacrifices, Measurements of the Temple, etc.

1. TREATISE ON THE MEASUREMENTS OF THE TEMPLE *(Middot).* 10th in order.

Extent of the Temple Area.

M. The Temple Mount was 500 cubits square. The space was largest on the south, next largest on the east, the third largest being on the north, and the least, westward. All who entered this area did so on the south side, going round and passing on to the left.

VI.--Legal Purifications, Laws of Clean and Unclean, Etc. (Teharot)

1. TREATISE ON PRESERVING THE HANDS FROM CEREMONIAL UNCLEANNESS. *(Jadaim).*

The Aramaic passages in Ezra and Daniel make the hands unclean (25). But Aramaic written in Hebrew characters and Hebrew written in Aramaic (Syriac) characters, or in the primitive Hebrew characters (much like the Phoenician) do not make the hands unclean. Scriptures, though the matter is the same, never make the hands unclean unless the characters or letters, in which they are written, are the square Assyrian letters introduced by Ezra, the second Moses.

ZOROASTRIANISM

Zend Avesta

Zoroastrianism, or, more correctly, Zarathustraism, is derived from Zoroaster, or, more strictly, Zarathustra, the founder of the religion. Modern scholarship inclines to the belief that this great religious leader was born in West Media about B.C. 600, and carried on his great work in Bactria. The religion with which his name is connected is really a reformed and spiritualised kind of that Magism which prevailed in Media and contiguous countries. The priests, who are called "Atharvans," fire-priests, in the Avesta (compare the same name in Hinduism, the Atharvan Veda, etc.) are identical with the Magi, priests of the religion which Zarathustra (Zoroaster) found in his original and adopted home. According to some, the founder of Zarathustrianism lived at a very much earlier time, and there are great scholars (Tiele, Darmesteter, Edouard Meyer) who wholly deny the historicity of such a character. No doubt, in later years, there gathered around Zarathustra an immense number of fictitious and silly legends, as was the case with Buddha, Jesus, and even Muhammad; but that each one of these religious teachers lived and wrought is beyond the reach of reasonable doubt.

Introductory

This is the Bible of the Zarathustrians and of their modern representatives, the Parsees, who flourish for the most part in Bombay. The title "Zend Avesta" is an anomaly, for "Zend" is not the name of a language at all, but means "commentary," the word "Avesta" connoting the original text on which the commentary is written. The original title denotes Avesta and Zend, which is a correct description, for what is now known as the Zend Avesta is really a combination of text (Avesta) and commentary (Zend), just as the Jewish Talmud is a combination of Mishnah (text) and Gemara (commentary, or, literally, completion). The word "Avesta" denotes (perhaps literally) knowledge, beingcognate with the Sanscrit word "Veda." But A.V.W. Jackson derives it from a form *Upasta*, denoting "the original text." Darmesteter makes the word Old Persian, denoting "law."

The existing Avesta is more like a prayer book than a Bible, for it is as a liturgical work that it took on its present form, and as such that it is now generally used, though the part called "Vendidad" includes a large number of laws for religious ceremonies and the like.

What is known to modern scholars as the Avesta is, however, only a portion of the original work, the latter having been largely lost through the conquests over Persia of Alexander the Great, and especially owing to the more thorough subjugation of the Sassanid Persians by the Muslims in A.D. 632. The latter were much more bigoted and uncompromising in their treatment of other religions and their literatures than were Alexander the Great and his successors. The original Avesta, as described in Pahlavi text which have come down to us, contain twenty-one Nasks or books. These existed, in a more or less incomplete state, down to the ninth century of our era, to which century the Pahlavi work "Dindard" belongs.

The Avesta which exists to-day may be divided thus:--

I. The strictly canonical parts, including the following, which will be more fully described in connection with the summaries.

1. Yasnas, including the Gathas.
2. Vispereds.
3. Vendidads.

II. The Apocryphal Avesta usually called the Khorda Avesta, or the short Avesta. This is much less esteemed than the Avesta proper. It comprises,

1. Yashts (invocation).
2. Minor Prayers.

The language of the Avesta can be correctly describedonly as Avestan, for no other literature in the same language exists. It resembles the Pahlavi, or Ancient Persian, but it is identical with no language. The Zend, or commentary, is written in the Pahlavi language.

The present writer wishes to express his obligation to the translation of the Avesta by Spiegel (in German); Hang in his "Essays on Sacred Language, Writing, and Religion of the Parsees "; and also to those by Darmesteter and L.H. Mills in the "Sacred Books of the East," volumes iv, xxiii, xxxiii. On the question whether or not the Achaemenian kings of Persia, Cyrus I., and so forth, were Zarathustrians, see "Century Bible,"--Ezra--Nehemiah--Esther.

I.--Yasnas, or Sacrificial Prayers and Songs

[This section of the Avesta constitutes the principal liturgical text-book of the great Yasna ceremony, which is made up chiefly of the preparation and offering of the Parahoma (the juice of the homa or soma plant mixed with milk and aromatic ingredients). There are seventy-two chapters in the Yasnas, though they contain a good number of repetitions. It is in this main part of the Avesta that the five metrical Gathas are to be found, these being the oldest and by far the most important of the Avesta.]

CHAPTER I. THE PROCLAMATION OF SALVATION. I (Zarathustra) make known to Ahura-Mazda the Great God, that I am about to offer him my prayers and sacrifices. (Yasnas.) He is the greatest and best, the most powerful and wise. I pay homage, also, to the bountiful immortals (the Amensha-Spentas), the guardians of the world. And to the body of the sacred cow and its soul; (i) to Ahura (Jupiter), Mithra the sun, to the star Sirius; and to the Fravashis (guardian angels of the saints). If I have offended thee, oh thou greatest one, Ahura-Mazda, or if I have diminished ought of the sacrifices(Yasnas) due to thee, forgive me, O forgive me, thou unerring one. I declare myself to be a Mazdaist, a Zarathustrian, a sworn foe to the Daevas (2) and a worshipper of Ahura-Mazda.

CHAPTER 4. We present as offerings, pure thoughts, kind words, beneficent works, the Homa (Soma) flesh-offerings, zaothras (3), the holy veresma (4), suitable prayers, Gatha hymns, and mathra (the Vedic mantra) sacred songs--these all we present as sacrifices to Ahura-Mazda, the holy Srosh (5), to the bountiful immortals, to the Fravashis, and souls of the pure, and also to the sacred fire of Ahura-Mazda.

CHAPTER 8. I offer to thee, O Ahura-Mazda, sacrifices of all kinds. Mayest thou, O all-powerful, all-wise one, rule over thy creatures, over all waters and trees, all empires and dominions, causing fertility, happiness, and universal justice to abound in the world. In all conflicts between light and darkness, between the good and the bad, let the right prevail, O thou king of righteousness. I, Zarathustra, urge heads of families, chiefs of clans, and rulers of states, to follow the true religion, that revealed by Ahura-Mazda and proclaimed by his prophet Zarathustra.

CHAPTERS 9 AND 10. [In some manuscripts these chapters are designated Homa-Yashts, because they celebrate the praises of Homa and have the form of Yashts. In these chapters Homa is personified, as, also, in the Vedas, is the Sanscrit Soma. In the period before the separation of the Iranians and Indians the worship of the Homa plant (the god of inspiration, etc.) bulked largely. It died out, however, among the Iranians at an early period, perhaps owing to its prevalence among their Indian rivals, who traced to it that very courage with which they contended against the Iranians. The present chapters belong to the period of the revival of the Homa cult among the Mazdaists or Zarathustrians. This comparatively late date is confirmed by the vocabulary and styleof the chapters.]

When Zarathustra was engaged in singing the Dathas and attending the sacred fire, Homa appeared before him in resplendently supernatural guise and explained "I am Homa, whom thou shouldst worship as the sages and prophets of old have done." "Tell me," replied Zarathustra, "who was it that first worshipped thee by extracting thy juice from the plant?" "The first," said Homa, "was Vivan-Ghvant whose reward was the birth of his august and renowned son, Yima, (6) the king, in whose reign there was neither death, nor scorching heat, nor benumbing cold, but when fulness of life, perfection of happiness, and unfailing justice prevailed. The second to worship me," said Homa, "was Athwya, the blessed one, and to him as a reward was born Thraetaona, who slew the three-mouthed, three-tailed, six-eyed, thousand-scaled dragon that wrought such dire havoc in the world. The third to worship me was Thrita, to whom, in recompense, were born two sons of illustrious name, one great as ruler of men, and the other a brave warrior who slew the man-and-horse-swallowing dragon. The fourth was thine own distinguished father, Pourushasha, and the reward that he received was to have thee, O great prophet of men, for his son." On hearing which Zarathustra immediately set about walking around the sacred fire singing lustily the praises of the god Homa, whom his father had worshipped. "It is Homa," sang the prophet, "that gives men knowledge of things new and old. Even men buried under a weight of book-lore receive from him inspiration and perception of truth that no books can impart. It is Homa that gives kind and wealthy husbands to unwed maidens; that fills the sky with clouds and refreshes the ground with life-giving showers, causing the plants to grow on the lofty mountains on whose brow thine own sacred plant (asclepias) flourishes."

CHAPTER 12. [Profession of faith on the part of the new convert, uttered by the ancient Iranians on their givingup the worship of Daevas and the nomad life, and on their being received into the religious community established by Zarathustra.]

Now cease I to be a Daeva worshipper and make profession of the religion of Ahura-Mazda, proclaimed by Zarathustra. I ascribe all good things everywhere to Ahura-Mazda, the true, shining and holy one. I will never more molest Mazdaists. I will forsake the Daevas, the false and wicked originators of all the mischief in the universe. I forsake also all Daeva like beings, witches, wizards, and the like. I belong to the Mazdaist religion, and will support it to my dying day. There is no joy of virtue but has come from Ahura-Mazda.

CHAPTER 19. The importance and value of the Ahuna-Vairya prayer, said Zarathustra to Ahura-Mazda "O holiest and best of beings, what words taughtest thou me before the world was, or human life began its history?" "It was," responded the supreme being, "the Ahuna-Vairya prayer. Whoever, O Zarathustra, recites this prayer or intones it, or even whispers it under his breath, I will carry him safely across the bridge which leads to paradise. But whoever cuts this prayer short by a half, a third, a fourth, or by any quantity, his soul shall I keep out of paradise and it shall wander in sorrow for ever."

CHAPTER 22. ADORATION OF THE FRAVASHIS (GUARDIAN ANGELS OF THE SAINTS). I will praise the Fravashis, who have existed from time immemorial. Those of the houses, villages, and provinces, who preserve order in the heavens above, on the earth, and in the waters. I praise the Fravashis of Ahura-Mazda, the Fravashis of the bountiful immortals, and those of Zarathustra and of the Holy Counsellors. All good Yazads (7) deserve homage and sacrifice.

CHAPTER 35. AHURA-MAZDA AND THE IMMORTALS ADORED AND SUPPLICATED. We adore thee, O thou great God, Ahura-Mazda, and also the bountiful immortals.We laud all good thoughts and words and deeds that have been, are, or will be. It is our duty to live the good life, for that is best for both worlds. Thine, O lofty spirit, is the kingdom, thine the power, and thine the glory. Thy righteous rule surpasses every other rule; thy praise all other praise; thy hymns are the loftiest and best.

CHAPTER 57. IN HONOUR OF SROSH. We pay homage to thee, Srosh, the obedient and blessed one, the first of creatures to worship Ahura-Mazda, the Creator. Thou didst also worship the bountiful immortals, and wast the first to brandish the veresma and to sing the Gathas. Thou didst slay the all-destroying demon, and thou protectest the world and its denizens. Thou sleepest not, nor slumberest day or night. Thou teachest men the true religion--that of Ahura-Mazda.

The Five Gathas

[*Gatha* means "song," and is the same word as the Sanscrit *Gita* (Cf. p. 61 Bhagavad-Gita). These five gathas include yasnas 28-34, 43-46, 47-50, and 51-53. In metre, vocabulary, and matter, the gathas prove themselves to be the oldest part of the Avesta. The doctrines taught are likewise purer and more rational. Note the following:--I. There is one supreme good deity, Ahura-Mazda, the conception of whom is so lofty that, in order to save his character, a spirit of evil (Ahriman) has been invented. To the supreme good spirit are ascribed six attributes which are often personified. In the later parts of the Avesta these attributes are made independent persons (the bountiful immortals, or the Amesha Spentas). But in the Gathas they form with Ahura-Mazda a unity much resembling the Sabellian trinity. 2. The doctrine of reward and punishment that is taught in the Gathas is subjective, *i.e.*, it makes a man's reward and punishment consist in change of character, disposition,etc.

It is a strange coincidence that the highest form of Indian and Iranian belief is to be found in the earliest literature of these religions, *i.e.*, the Vedas and the Gathas. This does not agree with the opinion that most prevails, that in religions there is ever progress from lower to higher forms.

In these Gathas there is a unity of thought and feeling suggesting strongly unity of authorship. There is general agreement that the one author to whom at least the great bulk of the Gathas is due is Zarathustra himself. Roth, L.H. Mills, and other scholars date the Gathas as they would the Vedas, somewhere between B.C. 1200 and 1500, and they therefore fix upon the same date for the work of Zarathustra himself. Other Avestan scholars (A.V.W. Jackson, etc.) fix the date of Zarathustra's life, and therefore of the Gathas, some time near B.C. 600. If the latter opinion is held, it is probable that the substance of the Gathas is much older than the form which they take in the Avesta.]

GATHA I, Yasnas 28-34, 29, which is earlier than 28.

THE CALL OF ZARATHUSTRA. The afflicted people cry out aloud to thee, O Ahura-Mazda, and also to the Asha, the author of the divine order. Why were we made to be exposed to the attacks of suffering and of sin? The divine one asked Asha "Hast thou appointed a guardian over this people to defend them from evil?" Said Asha: "There is no man in this world that has to bear his lot of suffering and to resist moral adversaries, but the great Creator knows all about his life, and demands from him all that he is capable of. No man can choose anyone who is able to secure justice and happiness in the world." "But I," said Ahura-Mazda, "have chosen one for this great task, it is Zarathustra, the prophet and priest." On hearing of his divine appointment, Zarathustra prayed to his god, saying, "Do thou, O all-wise one, aid me, directingmy thoughts, choosing for me my words, and guiding my steps, for without thee I can do nothing."

28. ZARATHUSTRA'S PRAYER FOR HELP. Teach me, O loftiest one, thy ways, and encourage me by thy promises to observe thy ceremonies. When shall I become acquainted with thine own pure mind, and know what is truly good? When shall I realise thee in my own soul, and have fellowship with thee without the mediation of man or angels? I do not ask for riches, or booty, or worldly prosperity, but for righteousness.

GRATITUDE FOR BLESSINGS ALREADY RECEIVED. Thou hast granted my requests, and given me the boon which I asked for. May I never offend thee, nor be ungrateful! Supply my lot with what thou knowest to be best, and not with what I desire. Make thou clear to me the laws which govern thy kingdom, that I may be a safe guide to others.

30. THE CREED WHICH ZARATHUSTRA IS TO PREACH. I announce to all who desire to know, the true doctrine about the Creation. Let all that listen give heed and shape their ways according to this teaching:--There were at the beginning two spirits and nothing more--a better principle and a worse. This pair existed independently each of the other. The good spirit (Ahura-Mazda) made all that he created perfect and just, like himself, but the evil spirit (Ahriman) created things that were evil. Why have the Daevas-worshippers perverted the truth and gone astray from the right path? Because the creator of evil has taken possession of them. All such as make their thoughts, words, and deeds conform to the will of the good spirit have an eternal reward, and their salvation has already begun. But such as yield to the evil impulses prompted by Ahriman shall abide eternally in woe and misery.

31. THE TWO PARTIES. Many there are who hiss at this teaching of mine, and will have none of it, but the people of Ahura give heed thereto. O supreme spirit ofgood, grant me by the sacred fire and the holy ritual some sign that will convince and convert men, so that all may be brought to thee and be made to abandon their Daevas. O ye bountiful immortals, will ye give me prophetic knowledge that I may lead men aside from the error of their ways; what punishment shall be his who strives to set up in our midst a king belonging to the Daeva party?

GATHA 2. 43-46.

[This part of the Avesta gives a fuller and correcter view of the work and teaching of Zarathustra than any other.]

43. The Theophany of Ahura-Mazda to Zarathustra. I saw Ahura-Mazda on high and he made known to me his truth, that I may tell it to men.

44. A PRAYER FOR KNOWLEDGE. Speak thou truly to me, O Ahura-Mazda, and not falsely as the Daevas do to their worshippers. How came this present world to be, and to be supported, if not through thee? Who made the sun and moon and stars, and the waters and the winds and the trees, who, if not thou? Reveal thou to me, O great one, the inner truth of things.

O ye crowds of men, when will ye call evil, evil, and good, good, instead of the contrary? Have the Daevas ever supplied good rulers?

II.--Vispereds

[The word Vispered means "all the lords," and this section is so called because it contains invocations to all the lords or gods. It consists almost entirely of extracts from other parts of the Avesta, especially from the Yasnas. What is not found elsewhere has no special value and need not be summarised.]

III.--*Vendidads* (lit. "laws against demons")

[This is not strictly a liturgical work, but a priestly code describing the various purifications, penalties and expiations by which faults of various kinds are atoned for, or their consequences annulled. The existing Vendidads agree almost exactly with Nask (19) of the original Avesta, the only part of the Avesta in which one of the Nasks has been completely preserved. The Vendidads are divided into twenty-two Fargads, or sections.]

FARGAD 3. THE SANCTITY OF AGRICULTURE. The earth should be cultivated, 1. that it may bring forth food for man and beast, 2. because it promotes human piety. "How is it, O great creator," asks Zarathustra, "that religion is to be spread?" "By cultivating barley," was the answer, "for he who cultivates barley, cultivates purity. When barley is threshed or ground, and when flour is produced, devils whistle, whine, and waste away, knowing full well that man's idleness is their only opportunity." (Cf. compare Dr. Watts' line "Satan finds some mischief still, for idle hands to do.")

FARGAD 4. CIVIL AND CRIMINAL LAW. Whoever refuses to restore property to one to whom he knows it belongs by right, is a thief. Every day and night that he keeps this property he is guilty of theft. "How many kinds of property are there?" asked Zarathustra. "These six," was the answer. "1. That made by mere words. 2. That made by striking hands. 3. That made by depositing a sheep as security. 4, 5, 6. Those cases in which the security is respectively an ox, a man's value, and the value of a full field." Then there follow details of penalties for violating these several contracts:--*e.g.*, for breaking the first--300 stripes of the rod, and so forth.

FARGADS 5-18, give the laws for the treatment of dead bodies. The two determining principles are--1. That a dead body is impure. 2. The elements earth, fire, andwater, are absolutely pure and sacred. Bodies are not, therefore, to be buried, or they would pollute the earth; nor are they to be burnt, or they would pollute fire, nor thrown into water of any kind. They must be carried up to a lofty mountain, placed on stones, or iron plates, and exposed to dogs and vultures. Impurity from contact with a dead body, etc., is removed by pure water (Cf. the water of baptism). Then there follow laws prescribing the counter-charms to be used against evil spirits; the methods by which the sacred fire must be made and used, and so forth.

FARGAD 19, treats of the fate of the soul after death.

The Aprocryphal or Khorda Avesta

[The Yashts resemble closely the prayers of the Yasnas and the Vispereds, differing only in this, that each one of the twenty-four extant is devoted to the traits of a single deity, or at least of one class of divine beings (the bountiful immortals, and so forth). The usual word in the Yashts for the superhuman beings at rest is Yazads.]

YASHT I. The names of Ahura-Mazda and their efficacy.

Asked Zarathustra, "What, O Most High, are the most effective counter-charms (mantras) against evil spirits?" He received for answer that the pronunciation of the twenty different names of Ahura-Mazda are the best and strongest spells. These are the following:--1. The Revealer. 2. The Herd-giver, etc., etc. The twentieth and last is Mazda, the All-knowing One.

Philosophy

ARISTOTLE

The Ethics of Aristotle

Aristotle was born at Stagira, a Greek colony on the Macedonian frontier, in 384 B.C., when Plato was forty-three, fifteen years after the death of Socrates. Going to Athens, he became one of Plato's pupils in philosophy at the age of twenty. In 342 he became tutor to the future Alexander the Great, and some years later opened, again at Athens, his own school, whose disciples were called the Peripatetics. He died in 322 B.C. His works laid the systematic foundations of every science known in his time. His various treatises on logic were comprised in the "Organon"; he dealt with psychology and metaphysics; with rhetoric and the principles of literary criticism. He also systematised the natural sciences; and the two works here given, "the Ethics" and "Politics," have profoundly influenced ethical and political thought from his own day to ours. In particular, his classification of the virtues, and his doctrine that virtue lies in a "mean," have dominated a vast amount of moral speculation. The treatises as we know them are so crabbed and condensed in style as to give the impression that they are to a large extent not the finished works, but notes and summaries.

I.--The End of Life and the Meaning of Virtue

Every art and science, every action, has for its end some good, whether this be a form of activity or an actual product. The ends of minor arts are only means to the ends of superior arts. If there is one supreme end, this is The Good, inquiry into which belongs to the supreme Social Science [for which the Greek term is Politics]. The name given to this supreme good, the attainment of which is the object of Politics, is Happiness, good living, or welfare.

But Happiness itself is variously defined; some identify it with Pleasure, others with Honour--the first a degrading, and the second an inadequate view. Platonists find it in an abstract Idea of Good, a Universal which precludes particulars. There is a great deal to be said against this doctrine, even as a question of logic or metaphysic; but apart from that, the theory is out of court, for the all sufficient reason that its practical value is *nil*-knowledge of the great Universal Good in the abstract is of no practical use whatever in everyday life, which is a fundamental point for us.

If, then, there is a supreme dominating Good to be aimed at, what are the essential characteristics it must display? The Good of all Goods, the Best, must be complete in itself, a consummation. Whatsoever is a means to some end beyond fails so far of completeness; when we say that our end must be "complete," it follows that it must always be an end, never a means. It is not merely one amongst others of which it is the best, but the one in which all the others are summed up. It is of itself quite sufficient for the individual, and that not merely in isolation, but as a member of society--which it is his nature to be.

Let us then define Happiness as Man's *Work*--the performance of his function as man. Everything has some specific function, the performance of which is its Good, and man, too, must have a specific function. Now, this cannot be the kind of life which he shares with the vegetable or with the brute creation, therefore it must be the active life of his distinctive--*i.q.,* his rational--part, exercised in accordance with the virtue or virtues which perfect it, and in his life as a whole, not merely at moments.

Testing our conclusions by the judgments of common experience, we gather support from them. Goods external, and goods of the body, are reckoned inferior to goods of the soul, which is recognised as the seat of activities. The identification of happiness with virtue, however, necessitates the distinction between active virtue and virtuousness. As conducing to active virtue, the other kinds of goods are elements in happiness. We must assume it to be not something granted to us, outside our own control, but attainable by effort and education.

Virtues are of two kinds: of the intellect, acquired by study; and moral, acquired by practice. The moral virtues are not implanted by nature, but we have the capacity for them by nature, and achieve them by practice, as by practice we acquire excellence in the arts, or control over our passions. Education, then, is of the utmost importance, since the state or habit of virtue is the outcome of virtue in act.

The manner, the "how" of action, must be in accord with Right Reason, whereof we shall speak elsewhere. Here we must recognise that we are not laying down universal propositions, but general rules which are modified by circumstances. Our activities must lie in a mean between the two extremes of excess and defect, and this applies both to the process of generating virtue, and to its manifestation. The virtues are concerned with pleasure and pain, because these act as inducements or opposing influences; Beauty, Advantage, and Pleasure being the three standing inducements, and Pleasure entering into both the others; so that in one aspect Virtue is the Best action in respect to pleasure.

But it does not lie in the mere act; the act must be born of knowledge and of choice done for its own sake, and persistently--the first, knowledge, being the least important; to make it the most important is a speculative error.

Now, there are three modes of mind: feeling or passion, faculty, and habit. We do not praise or blame passion in itself, or the faculty; therefore virtue can lie in neither, but must be found in habit or condition. The virtuous habit or condition is what enables that whereof it is the virtue to perform its function, which, in the case of man, is the activity of the soul, preserving always a middle course between excess and deficiency, by choice.

In another sense, however, we must remember that there are qualities in themselves wrong, and that virtue may be presented as not something intermediate, but a consummation. But when we name each of these virtues--Courage, Temperance, Liberality, etc.; the social virtues, or good manners; the virtues concerned with the passions--we can name the corresponding excess or deficiency. Justice and the intellectual virtues demand a separate analysis.

Each virtue stands in opposition to each of the extremes, and each of these to the other extreme, though in some cases the virtue may be more antagonistic to one extreme than to the other, as courage to cowardice more than to rashness. In individual cases, it is difficult to avoid being deflected towards one or other of the extremes.

Before proceeding with this analysis, we must examine the question of choice. To be praiseworthy, an act must be voluntary. An act is not voluntary if it is the outcome of external compulsion. Where there is a margin of choice, an act must still, on the whole, be regarded as voluntary, though done "against our will." Of properly involuntary acts, we must distinguish between the unintentional and the unwilling, meaning by the latter, in effect, what the agent would not have done if he had known.

Choice is not the same thing as a voluntary act; nor is it desire, or emotion, or exactly "wish," since we may wish for, but cannot make choice of, the unattainable. Nor is it Deliberation--rather, it is the act of decision following deliberation. If man has the power to say yes, he has equally the power to say no, and is master of his own action. If we make a wrong choice through ignorance for which we are ourselves responsible, the ignorance itself is culpable, and cannot excuse the wrong choice; and so, when the choice is the outcomeof a judgment disordered by bad habits, men cannot escape by saying they were made so--they made themselves so. To say they "could not help" doing wrong things is only an evasion.

II.--The Moral Virtues Examined

Virtues, then, are habits, issuing in acts corresponding to those by which the habit was established, directed by Right Reason, every such act being voluntary, and the whole process a voluntary process.

We may now turn to the analysis of the several virtues.

Courage has to do with fear. Not all kinds; for there are some things we ought to fear, such as dishonour and pauperism, the fear of which is compatible with dauntless courage, while the coward may not fear them. Fearlessness of what is in our control, and endurance of what is not, for the sake of true honour, constitute the courageous habit. Its excess is rashness or foolhardiness, the deficiency cowardice. Akin to it, but still spurious, is the courage of which the motive is not Honour but honours or reputation. Spurious also is the courage which arises from the knowledge that the danger is infinitesimal; so is that which is born of blind anger, or of elated self-confidence, or of mere unconsciousness of danger. True Courage lies in resisting a temptation to pleasure or to escaping pain, and, above all, death, for Honour's sake. The exercise of a virtue may be very far from pleasant, except, of course, in so far as the end for which it was exercised is achieved.

Temperance is concerned with pleasures of the senses; mainly of touch, in a much less degree of taste; but not of sight, hearing, or smell, except indirectly. Of carnal pleasures, some are common to all, some have an individual application. Temperance lies in beingcontent to do without them, and desiring them only so far as they conduce to health and comfort. The characteristic of intemperance is that it has to do with pleasures only, not with pains. Hence, it is more purely voluntary than cowardice, as being less influenced by perturbing outward circumstances as concerns the particular case, though not the habit.

Liberality is concerned with money matters, and lies between extravagance and meanness. Really it means the right treatment of money, both in spending and receiving it--the former rather than the latter. A man is not really liberal who lavishes money for baser purposes, or takes it whence he should not, or fails to take due care of his property. The liberal man tends to err in the direction of lavishness. Extravagance is curable, but is frequently accompanied by carelessness as to the objects on which the money is spent and the sources from which it is obtained. The habit of meanness is apt to be ineradicable, and is displayed both in the acquisition and in the hoarding of money.

Munificence is a virtue concerned only with expenditure on a large scale, and it implies liberality. It lies between vulgar ostentation and niggardliness. It is possible only for the wealthy, and is concerned mainly with public works, but also with private occasions of ceremony. The error of vulgar ostentation is misdirection of expenditure, not excess. Niggardliness abstains from a proper expenditure.

Magnanimity is the virtue of the aristocrat; its excess is self-glorification, its deficiency self-depreciation. The magnanimous man will bate nothing of his claim to honour, power and wealth, not as caring greatly for them, but as demanding what he knows to be his due. This character involves the possession of the virtues; the man must act in the grand manner and on the grand scale. He knows his own superiority, does not conceal it, and acts up to it. Self-glorification overrates itsown capacities; self-depreciation underrates them and shuns its responsibilities, being the more reprehensible of the two.

There is a nameless virtue which stands to magnanimity in the same relation as that of liberality to munificence; these being concerned with honours, as those with money. The excess is ambition, the deficiency is the lack of it; but here terminology fails us.

Good temper is a mean between ill-temper--whether of the irascible, the sulky, or the cantankerous kind--and something for which we have no name (poor-spiritedness). Friendliness comes between the excessive desire to please and boorishness. It is a social virtue which might be defined as goodwill *plus* tact.

Sincerity [there is no English term quite corresponding to the Greek] is the quality opposed on the one side to boastfulness, and on the other to mock-modesty; it is displayed by the man who acknowledges, but who never exaggerates his own merits. In the social display of wit and humour, there is a marked mean between the buffoon and the dullard or prig. Shame is a term implying a feeling rather than a habit; like fear, it has a physical effect, producing blushes, and seems, in fact, to be fear of disrepute. To the young, it is a safeguard against vice; the virtuous man need never feel it; to be unable to feel it implies the habit of vice. Continence is not properly in the category of moral virtues.

III.--Justice

We come now to Justice. A specific habit differs from a specific faculty or science, as each of the latter covers opposites, *e.g.*, the science of health is also the science of sickness; whereas the habit of Justice does not cover but is opposed to the habit of Injustice. Justice itself is a term used in various senses; and the senses in which injustice is used vary correspondingly.Confusion is apt to arise from these varying senses not being distinguished. Injustice includes law-breaking, grasping and unfairness. Grasping is taking too much of what is good only; unfairness is concerned with both what is good and what is injurious. But in the legal sense, whatever law lays down is assumed to be just. Law, however, covers the whole field of virtuous action as it affects our neighbours, so that in this general sense justice is an inclusive term equivalent to righteousness. We, however, must confine ourselves to the specific sense of the terms.

Grasping is, in fact, included in unfairness, which is the real opposite of specific justice; it includes law-breaking only so far as the law is broken for the sake of gain. The justice with which we are concerned has two branches: Distributive, of honours and the like among citizens by the State, and of private property by contract and agreement; and Corrective, the remedying of unfair distribution. There are always two parties, and justice is the mean between the unfairness which favours A and the unfairness which favours B. Distributive justice takes into consideration the merits of the parties; corrective justice is concerned only with restoring a balance which has been disturbed. The distribution is a question not of equality, but of right proportion; and this applies to retribution, which is recognised as one of its aspects, *e.g.*, the retribution for an officer striking a private and for a private striking an officer. Proportional requital is the economic basis of society, arrived at by the existence of a comparatively unfluctuating currency which provides a criterion.

In the State, as such, justice is obtained from the law and its administrators; justice is the virtue of the magistrate. Since he has nothing to gain or lose himself, it has been supposed that justice is "another's good," not our own. In the family, justice does not come in, the whole household being, in a sense, parts of the *paterfamilias*; and as you cannot be unjust to yourself, you cannot be unjust to your household.

In the State, what is just is fixed partly by the nature of things, partly by law or convention.

As to individual acts, injury may arise from a miscalculation, or from an incalculable accident; it becomes a wrong when it was intentional but not premeditated, an injustice when premeditated. An act *prima facie* unjust is not so if done with the free consent of the person injured. It is the agent of distribution, not the recipient, who is unjust (when they are different persons); and similarly, the agent, not the instrument. And even the agent of unjust distribution is not really unjust unless he was really actuated by motives of personal gain.

The performance of a particular act is easy. To perform it rightly as the outcome of a right habit, is not; nor is it easy to be confident as to what is right in the particular case. The man who is just, having the habit, does not find it easy to act unjustly.

What we must call equity may be opposed to justice, but only in the legal sense of that term. It is justice freed from the errors incidental to the particular case, for which the law cannot provide. Injustice, again, is found in self-injury or suicide; which the law penalises, not because the individual thereby treats himself unjustly, but because he does an injustice to the community. It is only by metaphor that a man may be called unjust to himself, an expression which means that the relation between one part of him and another part of him is analogous to the unjust relation between persons.

IV.--Wisdom, Prudence and Continence

The ensuing discussion of intellectual virtue requires some remarks on the soul. We distinguish in the rational part, that which knows, concerned, with the unchanging; and that which reasons, concerned with thechanging. Our intellects and our propensions--not our sense-perceptions, which are shared with animals-- guide our actions and our apprehension of truth. Attraction and repulsion, in correspondence with affirmation and denial, combine to form right choice; the practical--as opposed to the pure--reason having an external object, and being a motive power.

There are five modes of attaining truth: (1) Concerning things unalterable, defined as demonstrative science; (2) concerning the making of things changeable, art; (3) concerning the doing--not making--of things changeable, prudence; (4) intuitive reason, the basis of demonstrative science; (5) wisdom, the union of intuitive reason and science.

Wisdom and prudence are the two virtues of the intellect. Wisdom implies intuitive reason, which grasps undemonstrable first principles; it is concerned with the interests not of the moment, the individual, or the locality. Whereas prudence is concerned precisely with these; it is essentially practical. Wisdom cannot be identified with statesmanship; which, again, is not the same as prudence--which applies to the self, and to the family, as well as to the State; it differs from wisdom as requiring experience.

Wisdom, knowledge of the ultimate bases, is equally without practical bearing for those who have acquired a right habit and for those who have not; just as a knowledge of medical theory is of no use to the average man. But being an activity of the soul, *ipso facto*, it conduces to happiness. The general conclusion is that what we have called "prudence" shows the means to the end which the moral virtues aim at. It is not a moral virtue, but the moral virtues accord with it. Both are necessary to the achievement of goodness.

We come now to a second group of qualities, concerned with conduct. We have dealt with the virtues and their opposing vices. We pass by the infra-humanand the supra-human bestiality and holiness; but have still to deal with Continence and its contrasted qualities, which are concerned with the passions.

In the popular view, continence, self-control, is adherence to our formed judgment. Incontinence is yielding to passion where we know it to be wrong, and may be indulged in the pursuit of vengeance, honour, or gain. A number of *prima facie* contradictions are started out of the popular views. We find that a man does not act against complete knowledge or knowledge of which he is fully conscious. The knowledge may, so to speak, be there, but is in abeyance, a condition which is palpably exemplified in a drunken man. Now, incontinence is concerned with pleasures, which are necessary--as for sustenance of life--and unnecessary but, *per se*, desirable, as honour. Incontinence is a term applied only by analogy in the case of the latter; its proper concern--as with the moral vice, which we call intemperance--is with the former. It implies, however, violent desire, which intemperance does not. We have examples of such desires in a morbid or diseased form, species of mania; but here again the term incontinence is only applied by analogy. Its legitimate application, in short, is restricted to the normal.

Incontinence in respect of anger is not so bad as in respect of desire. It is often constitutional, it is in itself painful, and it is not wanton, being in all three points unlike the other. What we spoke of as bestiality is more horrible than vice or incontinence, as being inhuman; but it does less harm. Incontinence means transgressing the ordinary standards in respect of pleasure and pain. Such transgression, when of set purpose, and not followed by repentance--consequently, incurable--is the moral vice of intemperance; which, being characterised by the absence of violent desire, is worse than incontinence. The latter is open, and is curable. The confusion between the two is due to their issuingin like acts; the passionate impulse is temporary; it is not a formed habit of wrong choice.

Continence is acting on conviction in resistance to passion; not merely sticking to any and every opinion, which is really rather more like incontinence. The other extreme, of actual apathy, is rare. Continence differs from temperance, as implying resistance to strong desires; whereas temperance implies that such desires are not active. Prudence--but not the acuteness which is sometimes confused with prudence--is incompatible with incontinence, which is least curable when the outcome of weakness.

Here it becomes necessary to make some inquiry as to Pleasure and Pain. Some maintain that pleasure is never good, some that it is partly good and partly not; some that it is good, but not the best But it cannot be bad *per se*, since it may be defined as the unimpeded activity of a formed faculty. Pleasure, as such, is not a hindrance to any activity, but its fulfilment; *e.g.,* the pleasure of speculative inquiry does not hinder it. As a matter of fact, everyone does pursue pleasure; the denial that it is good results from thinking of it as meaning only bodily pleasures. And even they are not evil, but only the excessive pursuit of them. As to pleasure being fleeting, that is only because circumstances vary. The pleasure of the unchanging would be permanent.

V.--Friendship

A quality rendered as "Friendship"--though the Greek and English terms are not identical in content--now comes under examination. It is a relation to some other person or persons without which life is hardly worth living. Some account for it on the principle of "like to like," others on the opposite theory. Now, lovableness comes of goodness, or pleasantness, or usefulness. Love is not bestowed on the inanimate, and itmust be mutual; it is to be distinguished from goodwill or devotion, which need not be reciprocated.

Genuine friendship must be based on goodness; what rests on pleasantness (as with the young), or on utility (as with the old), is only to be recognised conventionally as friendship. In perfection it cannot subsist without perfect mutual knowledge, and only between the good; hence it is not possible for anyone to have many real friends. Of the conventional forms, that which is born of intellectual sympathy is more enduring than what springs from sexual attraction; while what comes of utility is quite accidental. The former may develop into genuine friendship if there be virtue in both parties. Companionship is a necessary condition, in any case.

Variants of friendship, however, may subsist between unequals, as between parents and children, princes and subjects, men and women, where there is a difference in the character of the affection of the two parties. A certain degree of inequality-- though we cannot lay down the limitation--makes "friendship" a misnomer. One would not desire the actual apotheosis of a friend, because that would take him out of reach; it would end friendship. Friendship lies rather in the active loving than in being loved, though most people are more anxious to be loved than to love.

Every form of social community--typified in the State--involves relationships into which friendship enters. The relationships in the family correspond to those in states; monarch to subjects as father to children, tyrant to subjects as master to slaves; autocratic rule to that of the husband, oligarchic rule to that of the wife; what we call Timocracy to the fraternal relation, and Democracy to the entirely unregulated household. In some kinds of association, friendship takes the form of *esprit de corps*. It may be seen that quarrels arise most readily in those friendships between equals which are based uponinterest, and in friendships between unequals.

Friendship is a kind of exchange--equal between equals, and proportional between unequals; a repayment. This suggests various questions as to priority of claim-- *e.g.,* between paying your father's ransom and repaying a loan, both being in a sort the repayment of a debt. No fixed law can be laid down--*i.e.,* it cannot be said that one obligation at all times and in all circumstances overrides all others.

The dissolution of friendship is warranted when one party has become depraved, since he has changed from being the person who was the object of friendship. But he should not be given up while there is hope of restoring his character. Again, if one develops a great superiority, friendship proper cannot persist--at least, in its first form. Our relations with a friend are much like those with our own selves; the true friend is a sort of *alter ego.* Friendship is not to be identified with goodwill, though the latter is a condition precedent; we may feel goodwill, but not friendship, towards a person we have never seen or spoken to. Unanimity of feeling--not as to facts, but as to ends and means--is a sort of equivalent to friendship in the body politic. The reason why conferring a benefit creates more affection than receiving it seems to be that the benefactor feels himself the maker of the other; we all incline to love what we produced--as parents their children, or the artist his own creations.

Self-love is wrong in a sense--the usual sense in which the term is used, of giving priority to oneself in the acquisition of material pleasures. But the seeking of the noblest things for oneself is really self-love, and may involve giving others, especially friends, the priority in respect of desirable things--even to resigning to another the opportunity of doing a noble deed. In this higher sense, self-love is praiseworthy.

The good man is self-sufficing, but friends are desirable,if not actually necessary to him, as giving scope for the exercise of beneficent activities, not as conferring benefits upon him. Besides, man's highest activities must be exercised not in isolation, but as a member of society, and such life lacks completeness if without friends. Finally, friendship attains its completest realisation where comradeship is complete; that is to say, in a common life.

VI.--Conclusion

We must revert once more to the question of Pleasure and Pain. To say that pleasure is not good is absurd; he who does so stultifies himself by his own acts. Eudoxus thought it was *the* good, his opinion being the weightier because of his temperateness.

It is desired for its own sake; its opposite is admittedly undesirable. But since it may be added to other good things, it cannot be *the* good: though to say that what every one desires is not good at all is folly. That it is not "a quality," or that it is "indeterminate," are irrelevant arguments, both statements applying to what are admittedly among "goods." The doctrine that it is a process, again, will not hold water. Pleasure is a thing complete; whereas a process is complete at no moment unless it be that of its termination. It is the completion of its appropriate activity; not in the sense that a habit makes the activity complete, but as its accompaniment and complement. Continuous it is not, just as the activity is not. It is not the complete life, but is inseparable from it. Pleasures, however, differ specifically and in value, as do the qualities with whose activities they are associated. The pleasures proper to men are those associated with the activities proper to man as man, those shared with other animals being so only in a less degree.

It remains to recapitulate the sum of our conclusionsregarding Happiness. It is not a habit, but lies in the habitual activities--desirable in and for themselves not as means--exercised deliberately, excluding mere amusement. Man's highest faculty being intelligence, its activity is his highest happiness--contemplation--constant, sufficient, and sought not as a means, but as an end.

This kind of happiness belongs to the gods also. Exclusively human, but below the other, is the fulfilment of the moral life, conditioned by human society, and more affected by environments and material wants. For contemplative activity, the barest material needs suffice. But this does not of itself induce the moral life, being apart from conduct. To induce morality, not only knowledge, but the right habit of action--which does not follow from knowledge and may be implanted without it-- is absolutely necessary. Compulsion may successfully establish the habit where argument might fail. Compulsion, therefore, is the proper course for the State to take.

MARCUS AURELIUS

His Discourses with Himself

Marcus Aurelius Antoninus, Roman emperor and Stoic philosopher, was born on April 20, 121 A.D. Having been adopted by Antoninus Pius, whose daughter Faustina he married, he succeeded him as emperor in 161, but freely shared the imperial throne with Lucius Verus, who also had been adopted by Pius. Marcus Aurelius reigned until his death, on March 17, 180, in almost uninterrupted conflict with rebellious provinces, and often heavily burdened with the internal troubles of Rome. But the serenity of this august mind, and his constancy to wisdom, virtue and religion, were never shaken. For magnanimity, fidelity, resignation, fortitude and mercy, he stands unrivalled by any other figure of the pagan world. Nor did that world produce any other book which, like his, remains as an unfailing companion to every generation of the modern age. The charm of these fragmentary meditations depends greatly on their convincing candour; there is not a trace of the cant and exaggeration that so taint the moralisings of lesser men. It depends also on their iron stoicism; there are here no doubtful comforts, no rosy illusions. But it depends chiefly on the admirable and lovable human character which is revealed in them. They were written in Greek, and were probably jotted down at odd moments under the most various circumstances. Tradition says that they were intended for the guidance of his son.

Book I

The example of my grandfather Verus taught me to be candid and to control my temper. By the memory of my father's character I learned to be modest and manly. My mother taught me regard for religion, to be generous and open-handed, and neither to do an ill turn to anyone nor even to think of it. She bred me also to a plain and inexpensive way of living. I owe it to my grandfather that I had not a public education, but had good masters at home. From my tutor I learned not to identify myself with popular sporting interests, but to work hard, endure fatigue, and not to meddle with other people's affairs. Diognetus taught me tobear freedom and plain dealing in others, and gave me a taste for philosophy. Rusticus first set me to improve my character, and prevented me from running after the vanity of the Sophists, and from concerning myself with rhetorical and poetic conceits, or with the affectations of a dandy. He taught me to read an author carefully, and gave me a copy of Epictetus. Apollonius showed me how to give my mind its due freedom, to disregard everything that was not true and reasonable, and to maintain an equable temper under the most trying circumstances. Sextus taught me good humour, to be obliging, and to bear with the ignorant and thoughtless. From Maximus I learned to command myself, and to put through business efficiently, without drudging or complaint. From my adoptive father I learned a smooth and inoffensive temper, and a greatness proof against vanity and the impressions of pomp and power; I learned that it was the part of a prince to check flattery, to have his exchequer well furnished, to be frugal in his expenses, not to worship the gods to superstition, but to be reserved, vigilant and well poised.

I thank the gods that my grandfathers, parents, sister, preceptors, relatives, friends and domestics were almost all persons of probity, and that I never happened to disoblige any of them. By the goodness of the gods I was not provoked to expose my infirmities. I owe it to them also that my wife is so deferential, affectionate and frugal; and that when I had a mind to look into philosophy I did not spend too much time in reading or logic-chopping. All these points could never have been guarded without a protection from above.

Book II

Put yourself in mind, every morning, that before night you will meet with some meddlesome, ungrateful and abusive fellow, with some envious or unsociable churl.Remember that their perversity proceeds from ignorance of good and evil; and that since it has fallen to my share to understand the natural beauty of a good action and the deformity of an ill one; since I am satisfied that the disobliging person is of kin to me, our minds being both extracted from the Deity; since no man can do me a real injury because no man can force me to misbehave myself; I cannot therefore hate or be angry with one of my own nature and family. For we are all made for mutual assistance, no less than the parts of the body are for the service of the whole; whence it follows that clashing and opposition are utterly unnatural. This being of mine consists of body, breath, and that part which governs. Put away your books and face the matter itself. As for your body, value it no more than if you were just expiring; it is nothing but a little blood and bones. Your breath is but a little air pumped in and out. But the third part is your mind. Here make a stand. Consider that you are an old man, and do not let this noble part of you languish in slavery any longer. Let it not be overborne with selfish passions; let it not quarrel with fate, or be uneasy at the present, or afraid of the future. Providence shines clearly through the work of the gods. Let these reflections satisfy you, and make them your rule to live by. As for books, cease to be eager for them, that you may die in good humour, heartily thanking the gods for what you have had.

Remember that you are a man and a Roman, and let your actions be done with dignity, gravity, humanity, freedom and justice; let every action be done as though it were your last. Have neither insincerity nor self-love. Man has to gain but few points in order to live a happy and godlike life. And what, after all, is there to be afraid of in death? If the gods exist, you can suffer no harm; and if they do not exist, or take no care of us mortals, a world without gods or Providence is not worth a man's while to live in. But the being of thegods, and their concern in human affairs, is beyond dispute; and they have put it in every man's power not to fall into any calamity properly so called. Living and dying, honour and infamy, pleasure and pain, riches and poverty--all these are common to the virtuous and the depraved, and are therefore intrinsically neither good nor evil. We live but for a moment; our being is in a perpetual flux, our faculties are dim, our bodies tend ever to corruption; the soul is an eddy, fortune is not to be guessed at, and posthumous fame is oblivion. To what, then, may we trust? Why, to nothing but philosophy. This is, to keep the interior divinity from injury and disgrace, and superior to pleasure and pain, and to acquiesce in one's appointed lot.

Book III

Observe that the least things and effects in Nature are not without charm and beauty, as the little cracks in the crust of a loaf, though not intended by the baker, are agreeable and invite the appetite. Thus figs, when they are ripest, open and gape; and olives, when they are near decaying, are peculiarly attractive. The bending of an ear of corn, the frown of a lion, the foam of a boar, and many other like things, if you take them singly, are far from beautiful; but seen in their natural relations are characteristic and effective. So if a man have but inclination and thought to examine the product of the universe, he will find that the most unpromising appearances have their own appropriate charm.

Do not spend your thoughts upon other people, nor pry into the talk, fancies and projects of another, nor guess at what he is about, or why he is doing it. Think upon nothing but what you could willingly tell about, so that if your soul were laid open there would appear nothing but what was sincere, good-natured, and public-spirited.A man thus qualified is a sort of priest and minister of the gods, and makes a right use of the divinity within him. Be cheerful; depend not at all on foreign supports, nor beg your happiness of another; don't throw away your legs to stand upon crutches.

If, in the whole compass of human life, you find anything preferable to justice and truth, temperance and fortitude, or to a mind self-satisfied with its own rational conduct and entirely resigned to fate, then turn to it as to your supreme happiness. But if there be nothing more valuable than the divinity within you, if all things are trifles in comparison with this, then don't divide your allegiance. Let your choice run all one way, and be resolute for that which is best. As for other speculations, throw them once for all out of your hand.

Book IV

It is the custom of people to go to unfrequented places and to the seashore and to the hills for retirement; and you yourself have often wished this solitude. But, after all, this is only a vulgar fancy, for it is in your power to withdraw into yourself whenever you have a mind to it. One's own heart is a place the most free from crowd and noise in the world if only one's thoughts are serene and the mind well ordered. Make, therefore, frequent use of this retirement, therein to refresh your virtue. And to this end be always provided with a few short, uncontested notions, to keep your understanding true. Do not forget to retire to this solitude of yours; let there be no straining or struggling in the matter, but move at ease.

If understanding be common to us all, then reason, its cause, must be common, too. And so also must the reason which governs conduct by commands and prohibitions be common to us all. Mankind is thereforeunder one common law, and so are fellow-citizens; and the whole world is but one commonwealth, for there is no other society in which mankind can be incorporated.

Do not suppose that you are hurt, and your complaint will cease.

If a man affronts you, do not defer to his opinion, or think just as he would have you do. No; look upon things as reality presents them. When incense is thrown upon the altar, one grain usually falls before another; but it matters not.

Adhere to the principles of wisdom, and those who now take you for a monkey or a beast will make a god of you in a week.

A thing is neither better nor worse for being praised. Do virtues stand in need of a good word, or are they the worse for a bad one? An emerald will shine none the less though its worth be not spoken of.

Whatever is agreeable to You, O Universe, is so to me, too. Your operations are never mistimed. Whatever Your seasons bring is fruit for me, O Nature. From You all things proceed, subsist in You, and return to You. The poet said, "Dear City of Cecrops"; shall we not say, "Dear City of God"?

The greater part of what we say and do is unnecessary; and if this were only retrenched we should have more leisure and less disturbance. This applies to our thoughts also, for impertinence of thought leads to unnecessary action.

Mankind are poor, transitory things: one day in life, and the next turned to mummy or ashes. Therefore manage this minute wisely, and part with it cheerfully; and like a ripe fruit, when you drop, make your acknowledgments to the tree that bore you.

Book V

When you feel unwilling to rise early in the morning, make this short speech to yourself: "I am getting up now to do the business of a man; and am I out of humour for going about that I was made for, and for the sake of which I was sent into the world? Was I then designed for nothing but to doze beneath the counterpane?" Surely action is the end of your being. Look upon the plants and birds, the ants, spiders and bees, and you will see that they are all exerting their nature, and busy in their station. Shall not a man act like a man?

Be not ashamed of any action which is in accordance with Nature, and never be misled by the fear of censure or reproach. Where honesty prompts you to say or do anything, let not the opinion of others hold you back. Go forward by the straight path, pursuing your own and the common interest.

Some men, when they do you a kindness, ask for the payment of gratitude; others, more modest, remember the favour and look upon you as their debtor. But there are yet other benefactors who forget their good deeds; and these are like the vine, which is satisfied by being fruitful in its kind, and bears a bunch of grapes without expecting any thanks for it. A truly kind man never talks of a good turn that he has done, but does another as soon as he can, just like a vine that bears again the next season.

We commonly say that Aesculapius has prescribed riding for one patient, walking for another, a cold bath for a third. In the same way we may say that the nature of the Universe has ordered this or that person a disease, loss of limbs or estate, or some such other calamity. For as, in the first case, the word "prescribed" means a direction for the health of the patient, so, in the latter, it means an application suitable for hisconstitution and destiny.

Be not uneasy, discouraged or out of humour, because practice falls short of precept in some particulars. If you happen to be vanquished, come on again, and be glad if most of what you do is worthy of a man.

We ought to live with the gods. This is done by being contented with the appointments of Providence, and by obeying the orders of that divinity which is God's deputy; and this divine authority is no more nor less than that soul and reason which every man carries within him.

Book VI

The best way of revenge is not to imitate the injury. Be always doing something serviceable to mankind; and let this constant generosity be your only pleasure, not forgetting a due regard to God.

The world is either an aggregation of atoms, or it is a unity ruled by Law and Providence. If the first, what should I stay for, where Nature is a chaos and things are blindly jumbled together? But if there is a Providence, then I adore the great Governor of the world, and am at ease and cheerful in the prospect of protection.

Suppose you had a stepmother and a mother at the same time; though you would pay regard to the first, your converse would be principally with the latter. Let the court and philosophy represent these two relations to me.

If an antagonist in the circus tears our flesh with his nails, or tilts against us with his head, we do not cry out foul play, nor are we offended, nor do we suspect him afterwards as a dangerous person. Let us act thus in the other instances of life. When we receive a blow, let us think that we are but at a trial of skill, and depart without malice or ill-will.

It is enough to do my duty; as for other things, I will not be disturbed about them.

The vast continents of Europe and of Asia are but corners of the creation; the ocean is but a drop, and Mount Athos but a grain in respect of the universe; and the present instant of time is but a point to the extent of eternity.

When you have a mind to divert your fancy, try to consider the good qualities of your acquaintance--such as the enterprising vigour of this man, the modesty of another, the liberality of a third, and so on. Let this practice be always at hand.

Book VII

What is wickedness? It is nothing new. When you are in danger of being shocked, consider that the sight is nothing but what you have frequently seen already. All ages and histories, towns and families, are full of the same stories; there is nothing new to be met with, but all things are common and quickly over.

Nature works up the matter of the universe like wax; now it is a horse; soon afterwards you will find it melted down and run into the figure of a tree; then it is a man; and so on. Only for a brief time is it fixed in any species.

Antisthenes said: "It is the fate of princes to be ill spoken of for their good deeds."

Consider the course of the stars as if you were driving through the sky and kept them company. Such contemplations as these scour off the rust contracted by conversing here below.

Rational creatures are designed for the advantage of each other. A sociable temper is that for which human nature was principally intended.

It is a saying of Plato's that no one misses the truth by his own goodwill. The same may be said of honesty, sobriety, good nature, and the like. Remember this, forit will help to sweeten your temper.

Though the gods are immortal, and have had their patience tried through so many ages, yet they not only bear with a wicked world, but even provide liberally for it. And are you tired with evil men already, though you are one of those unhappy mortals yourself?

Book VIII

Every man has three relations to acquit himself in: his body is one, God is another, and his neighbours are the third. Have you seen a hand or a foot cut off and removed from the body? Just such a thing is the man who is discontented with destiny or cuts himself off by selfishness from the interest of mankind. But here is the fortunate aspect of the case--it lies in his power to set the limb on again. Consider the peculiar bounty of God to man in this privilege: He has set him above the necessity of breaking off from Nature and Providence at all; but supposing this misfortune to have occurred, it is in man's power to rejoin the body, and grow together again, and recover the advantage of being the same member that he was at first.

Do not take your whole life into your head at a time, nor burden yourself with the weight of the future, nor form an image of all probable misfortunes. Neither what is past nor what is to come need afflict you, for you have only to deal with the present; and this is strangely lessened if you take it singly and by itself. Chide your fancy, therefore, if it offers to grow faint under so slender a trial.

Throw me into what climate or state you please, for all that I will keep my soul content. Is any misadventure big enough to ruffle my peace, or to make my mind mean, craving and servile? What is there that can justify such disorders?

Be not heavy in business, nor disturbed in conversation, nor rambling in thought. Do not burden yourself with too much employment. Do men curse you? This cannot prevent you from keeping a wise, temperate, and upright mind. If a man standing by a lovely spring should rail at it, the water is none the worse for his foul language; and if he throw in dirt it will quickly disappear, and the fountain will be as wholesome as ever. How are you to keep your springs always running, and never stagnate into a pool? You must persevere in the virtues of freedom, sincerity, moderation, and good nature.

Book IX

Do not drudge like a galley-slave, nor do business in a laborious manner, as if you wish to be pitied or wondered at.

As virtue and vice consist in action, and not in the impressions of the senses, so it is not what they feel, but what they do, which makes mankind either happy or miserable.

This man prays that he may gain such a woman; but do you rather pray that you may have no such inclination. Another invokes the gods to set him free from some troublesome circumstance; but let it be your petition that your mind may not be set upon such a wish. A third is devout in order to prevent the loss of his son; but I would have you pray rather against the fear of losing him. Let this be the rule for your devotions, and watch the event.

Book X

O my soul, are you ever to be rightly good, sincere, and uniform, and made more visible to yourself than the body that hangs about you? Are you ever likely to relish good nature and general kindness as you ought? Will you ever be fully satisfied, rise above wanting and wishing, and never desire to obtain your pleasure out of anything foreign, either living or inanimate? Are you ever likely to be so happily qualified as to converse with the gods and men in such a manner as neither to complain of them nor to be condemned by them?

Put it out of the power of all men to give you a bad name, and if anyone reports you not to be an honest or a good man let your practice give him the lie. This is quite feasible; for who can hinder you from being just and sincere?

There is no one so happy in his family and friends but that some of them, when they see him going, will rejoice at a good riddance. Let him be a person of never so much probity and prudence, yet someone will say at his grave: "Well, our man of order and gravity is gone; we shall be no more troubled with his discipline." This is the best treatment a good man must expect.

Book XI

What a brave soul it is that is always ready to depart from the body, and is unconcerned as to whether she will be extinguished, scattered, or removed! But she must be prepared upon reasonable grounds, and not out of mere obstinacy like the Christians; her fortitude must have nothing of noise or of tragic ostentation, but must be grave and seemly.

How fulsome and hollow does that man seem who cries: "I'm resolved to deal sincerely with you!" Hark you, friend, what need of all this flourish? Let your actions speak. Your face ought to vouch for you. I would have virtue look out of the eye no less apparently than love does. A man of integrity and good nature can never be concealed, for his character is wrought into his countenance.

Gentleness and good humour are invincible, provided they are of the right stamp and without hypocrisy. This is the way to disarm the most outrageous person--to continue kind and unmoved under ill usage, and to strike in at the right opportunity with advice. But let all be done out of mere love and kindness.

Book XII

I have often wondered how it is that everyone should love himself best, and yet value his neighbour's opinion of him more than his own. If any man should be ordered to turn his inside outwards, and publish every thought and fancy as fast as they come into his head, he would not submit to so much as a day of this discipline. Thus it is that we dread our neighbour's judgment more than our own.

What a mighty privilege man is born to, since it is in his power not to do anything but what God Almighty approves, and to be satisfied with all the distributions of Providence!

Reflect upon those who have made the most glorious figure or have met with the greatest misfortunes. Where are they all now? They are vanished like a little smoke. The prize is insignificant, and the play not worth the candle. It is much more becoming to a philosopher to stand clear of affectation, to be honest and moderate upon all occasions, and to follow cheerfully wherever the gods lead on, remembering that nothing is more scandalous than a man who is proud of his humility.

Listen, friend! You have been a burgher of this great city. What matter though you have lived in it fewer years or more? If you have kept the laws of the corporation, the length or shortness of the time makes no difference. Where is the hardship, then, if Nature, that planted you here, orders your removal? You cannot say you are sent off by an unjust tyrant No! You quit the stage as fairly as a player does who has his discharge from the master of the revels. "But I have only gone through three acts, and not held out to the end of the fifth!" True; but in life three acts may complete the play. He is the only judge of completeness who first ordered your entrance and now your exit; you are accountable for neither the one nor the other. Retire therefore, in serenity, as He who dismisses you is serene.

FRANCIS BACON

The Advancement of Learning

Francis Bacon, English philosopher and Chancellor, was born on January 22, 1561, the son of Lord Keeper Bacon, was sent to Trinity College, Cambridge, in 1573, and entered Gray's Inn in 1576. He had already become profoundly dissatisfied at Cambridge with the Aristotelian philosophy, and the conception of a humble and methodical study of Nature had early become the dominant passion of his life. Bacon became a member of parliament in 1584, and nine years later distinguished himself by coming forward as the champion of the privileges of the House of Commons against the Lords. The "Essays" were published in 1597. Bacon was knighted in 1603, on the accession of James I. In October, 1605, he published the "Advancement of Learning," a work designed to interest the king in the new philosophy, of which book we here give a summary. This review of the existing state of knowledge was intended to be made, later, into the first part of the "Instauratio Magna" under the title of "Partitiones Scientiarum." For this purpose Bacon was constantly revising it, and eventually he had it translated into Latin, and it was so published, greatly enlarged, in 1623, under the title of "De Dignitate et Augmentis Scientiarum." The summit of his career was reached in 1621, when he became Viscount St. Albans. His fall, on a charge of corruptions in the Court of Chancery, took place in the following March, and from this period until his death, on April 9, 1626, he devoted himself to his philosophical and literary works.

First Book

Let us weigh the dignity of knowledge in the balance with other things. In its archetype it is the Divine wisdom, or sapience, manifested in the creation. In the celestial hierarchy the supposed Dionysius of Athens places the angels of knowledge and illumination before those of office and domination. Then, the first material form that was created was light, which corresponds in corporal things to knowledge in incorporai. The day wherein God contemplated His own works was blessed above the days wherein He accomplished them. Man's first employment in Paradise consisted of the two chief parts of knowledge, the view of creatures, and the imposition of names. In the age before the Flood, Scripture honours the names of the inventors of music and of works in metal. Moses was accomplished in all the learning of the Egyptians. The book of Job is pregnant with natural philosophy. In Solomon, the gift of wisdom and learning is preferred before all other earthly and temporal felicity.

Our Saviour first showed His power to subdue ignorance by His conference with the doctors, before He showed His power to subdue Nature by miracles; and the coming of the Holy Spirit was chiefly figured in the gift of tongues, which are the vehicles of knowledge. St. Paul, most learned of the apostles, had his pen most used in the New Testament. Many of the ancient fathers of the Church were excellently read in all the learning of the heathen; and that heathen learning was preserved, amid Scythian and Saracen invasions, in the sacred bosom of the Church. And in our own day, when God has called the Roman Church to account for degenerate manners and obnoxious doctrines. He has also ordained a renovation of all other knowledges; and, on the other side, the Jesuits, by quickening the state of learning, have done notable service to the Roman See. Wherefore two principal services are performed to religion by human learning: first, the contemplation of God's works is an effectual inducement to the exaltation of His glory; and, secondly, true learning is a singular preservative against unbelief and error.

To pass now to human proofs of the dignity of learning, we find that among the heathen the inventors of new arts, such as Ceres, Bacchus, and Apollo, were consecrated among the gods themselves by apotheosis. The fable of Orpheus, wherein quarrelsome beasts stood sociably listening to the harp, aptly described the nature of men among whom peace is maintained so long as they give ear to precepts, laws, and religion. It has been said that people would then be happy, when kings were philosophers, or philosophers kings; and history shows that the best times have ever been under learned princes.

As for the services of knowledge to private virtue, it takes away all levity, temerity, and insolence by copious suggestion of all doubts and difficulties, and acquainting the mind to balance reasons on both sides. It takes away vain admiration of anything, which is the root of all weakness. No man can marvel at the play of puppets that goes behind the curtain. And certainly, if a man meditate much upon the universal frame of Nature, the earth with men upon it (the divineness of souls except) will not seem much other than an ant-hill, where some ants carry corn, and some carry their young, and some go empty, and all to and fro a little heap of dust. But especially learning disposes the mind to be capable of growth and reformation. For the unlearned man knows not what it is to descend into himself or to call himself to account, nor the pleasure of feeling himself each day a better man than he was the day before; he is like an ill mower, that mows on still and never whets his scythe. Knowledge crowns man's nature with power. It even gives fortune to particular persons; and it is hard to say whether arms or learning have advanced greater numbers. As for the pleasure and delight thereof, in knowledge there is no satiety. "It is a pleasure incomparable," says Lucretius, "for the mind of man to be settled, landed, and fortified in the certainty of truth; and from thence to descry the errors and perturbations of other men."

Lastly, by learning man excels man in that wherein man excels beasts. The great dignity of knowledge lies in immortality or continuance, and the monuments of learning are more durable than the monuments of power. Have not the verses of Homer continued twenty-five hundred years or more, without the loss of a syllable or letter, during which time infinite palaces, temples, castles, cities, have been decayed and demolished?

If the invention of the ship was thought so noble, which carries riches and commodities from place to place, and consociates the most remote regions in participation of their fruits, how much more are letters to be magnified? Popular and mistaken judgments will continue as they have ever been, but so will that also continue whereupon learning has ever relied, and which fails not.

"Wisdom is justified of her children."

Second Book

The parts of human learning have reference to the three parts of man's understanding--history to his memory, poetry to his imagination, and philosophy to his reason. Divine learning receives the same distribution, so that theology consisteth of history of the Church; of parables, which are divine poetry; and of holy doctrine or precept. For prophecy is but divine history, in which the narrative is before the fact.

History is "natural," "civil," "ecclesiastical," and "literary "; whereof the first three are extant, but the fourth is deficient. A true history of learning throughout the ages is wanting. History of Nature is of three sorts--of Nature in course, of Nature erring or varying, and of Nature altered or worked; that is, history of creatures, history of marvels, and history of arts. The first of these is extant in good perfection; the two others are handled so weakly that I note them as deficient. The history of arts is of great use towards natural philosophy such as shall be operative to the benefit of man's life. Civil history is of three kinds: "memorials," "perfect histories," and "antiquities," comparable to unfinished, perfect and defaced pictures. Just or perfect history represents a time, a person, or an action. The first we call "chronicles"; the second, "lives"; and the third, "narrations," or "relations."

Of modern histories the greater part are beneath mediocrity. Annals and journals are a kind of history not to be forgotten; and there is also ruminated history, wherein political discourse and observations are mingled with the history of the events themselves. The history of cosmography is compounded of natural history, civil history, and mathematics. Ecclesiastical history receives the same divisions with civil history, but may further be divided into history of the Church, history of prophecy, and history of Providence. The first of these is not deficient, only I would that the sincerity of it were proportionate to its mass and quantity. The history of prophecy, sorting every prophecy with the event fulfilling the same, is deficient; but the history of Providence, and the notable examples of God's judgments and deliverances have passed through the labour of many. Orations, letters, and brief sayings, or apophthegms, are appendices to history. Thus much concerning history, which answers to memory.

Poetry refers to the imagination. In respect of its words it is but a character of style, but in respect of its matter it is nothing else but feigned history, which may as well be in prose as in verse. The use of this feigned history is to give some shadow of satisfaction to the mind of man in those points wherein the nature of things denies it; poetry serves magnanimity, morality, and delectation. It is divided into narrative, representative, and allusive or parabolical poetry. In poetry I can report no deficience; it has sprung up and spread abroad more than any other kind of learning.

In philosophy, the contemplations of man either penetrate unto God, or are circumferred to Nature, or are reflected upon himself; whence arise three knowledges—divine philosophy, natural philosophy, and human philosophy or humanity. But it is good to erect one universal science, *Philosophia Prima,* "primitive" or "summary philosophy," before we come where the ways part and divide; and this universal philosophy is a receptacle for all such profitable observations and axioms as do not fall within the compass of any of the special parts of philosophy or sciences, but are common and of a higher stage. Divine philosophy, or natural theology, is that knowledge concerning God which may be obtained by the contemplation of His creatures; and in this I note an excess rather than a deficience, because of the extreme prejudice which both religion and philosophy have received by being mixed together, making an heretical religion and a fabulous philosophy.

Of natural philosophy there are two parts, the inquisition of causes and the production of effects; speculative and operative; natural science and natural prudence. Natural science is divided into physic and metaphysic. But since I have already defined a summary philosophy, and, again, a natural theology, both of which are commonly confounded with metaphysic, what is there remaining for metaphysic? This, that physic inquires concerning the material and efficient causes, but metaphysic handles the formal and final causes. So physic is in a middle term between natural history and metaphysic; for natural history describes the variety of things, physic the variable or respective causes, and metaphysic the fixed and constant causes. Of metaphysic I find that it is partly omitted and partly misplaced. In mathematics, which I place as a part of metaphysic, I can report no deficience. But natural prudence, or the operative part of natural philosophy, is very deficient. It were desirable that there should be a calendar or inventory made of all the inventions whereof man is possessed, with a note of useful things not yet invented. A calendar, also, of doubts, and another of popular errors, are to be desired.

We come now to the knowledge of ourselves--that is, to human philosophy or humanity. First, a general study of human nature will have regard to the sympathies and concordances between mind and body. Then, since the good of man's body is of four kinds--health, beauty, strength, and pleasure--the knowledge of the body is also of four kinds--medicine, decoration or cosmetic, athletic, and the art voluptuary. Medicine has been more professed than laboured, and more laboured than advanced, the labour having been rather in circle than in progression.

As for human knowledge concerning the mind, it has two parts, one inquiring of the substance or nature of the soul, and the other of its faculties or functions. I believe that the first of these may be more soundly inquired than it has been, yet I hold that in the end it must be bounded by religion. It has two appendices, concerning divination and fascination; these have rather vapoured forth fables than kindled truth. The knowledge respecting the faculties of the mind is of two kinds, the one respecting understanding and reason, and the other respecting will, appetite, and affection, the imagination being active in both provinces. The intellectual arts are four--inquiry or invention, examination or judgment, custody or memory, and elocution or tradition; and these are severally divided into various sciences and arts. The knowledge of the appetite and will, or moral philosophy, leading to the culture and regiment of the mind, is very deficient.

Civil knowledge has three parts--conversation, negotiation, and government--since man seeks in society comfort, use, and protection. The first of these is well laboured, the second and third are deficient. Thus we conclude human philosophy, and turn to the sacred and inspired divinity, the port of all men's labours and peregrinations.

Sacred theology, or divinity, is grounded only upon the word and oracle of God, and not upon the light of Nature. Herein there has not been sufficiently inquired the true limits and use of reason in spiritual things. Exposition of Scriptures, on the other hand, is not deficient. Divinity has four main branches--faith, manners, liturgy, and government--in which I can find no ground vacant and unsown, so diligent have men been, either in sowing of seed or tares.

GEORGE BERKELEY

Principles of Human Knowledge

George Berkeley, the metaphysician, was born on March 12, 1685, near Thomastown, Kilkenny, the son of a collector of revenue. He entered Trinity College, Dublin, at the age of fifteen, and was admitted Fellow in 1707. In that year he published two mathematical essays; two years later, his "Theory of Vision," and in 1710 his "Principles of Human Knowledge." In 1713, in London, where he had published further philosophical papers, he formed the acquaintance of Steele, Swift, and Pope. After travels in Europe he became chaplain to the Lord-Lieutenant of Ireland in 1721, and a few years after emigrated to Newport, Rhode Island, with a view to the establishment of a college in Bermuda for the education of Indians. This scheme fell through, because of the failure of the promised government support. Berkeley returned to London, and in 1734, by desire of Queen Caroline, was consecrated Bishop of Cloyne, in Ireland. Here he lived until 1752, but spent his last months in retirement at Oxford, where he died on January 14, 1753. Berkeley's "Principles of Human Knowledge" is one of the most eminent of that sequence of metaphysical systems which, beginning with Descartes, constitutes what is known as modern philosophy.

I.--The Analysis of Perception

It is evident to anyone who takes a survey of the objects of human knowledge that they are either ideas actually imprinted on the senses, or else such as are perceived by attending to the passions and operations of the mind; or, lastly, ideas formed by help of memory and imagination, either compounding, dividing, or representing those originally perceived in the aforesaid ways. By sight, touch, and other senses, I receive various sensations; and any group of sensations, frequently accompanying one another, come to be known as one thing. Thus a certain colour, taste, smell, figure, and consistence, having been observed to go together, are accounte done distinct thing--for instance, an apple.

But, besides this endless variety of objects of knowledge, there is also the "mind," "spirit," "soul," or "myself," which perceives them. Neither our thoughts or imaginations, nor even the sensations which compose the objects of perception, can exist otherwise than in a mind perceiving them. It is impossible that objects should have any existence out of the minds for which they exist; to conceive them as existing unperceived is a mere abstraction. Whence it follows that there is no other substance but spirit, or that which perceives.

Some, indeed, distinguish between "primary" and "secondary" qualities, and hold that the former, such as extension, figure, motion, and solidity, have some existence outside of the mind in an unthinking substance which they call "matter."

But extension, figure, and motion are only ideas existing in the mind, and neither these ideas nor their archetypes can exist in an unperceiving substance. The very notion of what is called "matter" involves a contradiction within it. Not only primary and secondary qualities alike, but also "great" and "small," "swift" and "slow," "extension," "number," and even "unity" itself, being all of them purely relative, exist only in the mind. The conception of "material substance" has no meaning but that of "being" in general.

Even if we were to give to the materialists their "external bodies," they are by their own confession no nearer to knowledge how our ideas are produced, since they own themselves unable to comprehend in what manner body can act upon spirit, or how it is possible that it should imprint any idea on the mind.

It is evident that the production of ideas in our minds can be no reason why we should suppose corporeal substances to exist, since the rise of those ideas is acknowledged to remain equally inexplicable with or without the supposition of material existences. In short, if there were external bodies, it is impossible that we should ever come to know it; and if there were not, we should have the same reasons to think there were, that we have now. We perceive a continual succession of ideas; some are anew excited, others are changed or totally disappear. There is, therefore, some cause of these ideas, whereon they depend, which produces and changes them. This cause must be a substance; but it has been shown that there is no corporeal or material substance. It remains, therefore, that the cause of ideas is an incorporeal active substance or spirit.

A spirit is one simple, undivided, active being; as it perceives ideas it is called the "understanding," and as it produces or otherwise operates about them, it is called the "will." Such is the nature of spirit that it cannot be of itself perceived, but only by the effects which it produceth.

The ideas of sense are more strong, lively, and distinct than those of the imagination; they have likewise a steadiness, order, and coherence, and are excited in a regular series, the admirable connection whereof sufficiently testifies the wisdom and benevolence of its Author. The set rules or established methods, wherein the mind that we depend on excites in us the ideas of sense, are called the "laws of Nature."

These we learn by experience, and so obtain a sort of foresight which enables us to regulate our actions for the benefit of life. In general, to obtain such or such ends such or such means are conducive; and all this we know, not by discovering any necessary connection between our ideas, but only by the observation of the laws of Nature.

And yet this constant uniform working, which so evidently displays the goodness and wisdom of that governing spirit whose will constitutes the laws of Nature, is so far from leading our thoughts to Him that it rather sends them wandering after second causes. For when we perceive certain ideas of sense constantly followed by other ideas, and we know that it is not of our own doing, we forthwith attribute power and agency to the ideas themselves, and make one the cause of another, than which nothing can be more absurd.

II.--The Roots of Scepticism

Several difficult and obscure questions, on which abundance of speculation hath been thrown away, are by our own principles entirely banished from philosophy. "Whether corporeal substance can think," "whether matter be infinitely divisible," "how matter operates on spirit"--these and the like inquiries have given infinfte amusement to philosophers in all ages. But since they depend on the existence of matter, they have no longer any place in our principles. It follows, also, that human knowledge may be reduced to two heads--knowledge of ideas, and knowledge of spirits. Our knowledge of the former hath been much obscured and confounded, and we have been led into very dangerous errors, by supposing a twofold existence of the objects of sense, the one "intelligible," or in the mind, the other "real," and without the mind; whereby unthinking things are thought to have a natural subsistence of their own, distinct from being perceived by spirits.

This is the very root of scepticism; for so long as men thought that real things subsisted without the mind, and that their knowledge was only so far "real" as it was conformable to "real things," they could not be certain that they had any real knowledge at all.

So long as we attribute a real existence to unthinking things, distinct from their being perceived, it is not only impossible for us to know the nature of any real unthinking being, but it is impossible for us even to know that it exists. Hence it is that we see philosophers distrust their senses, and doubt of the existence of heaven and earth, of everything they see or feel. But all this doubtfulness, which so bewilders and confounds the mind, vanishes if we annex a meaning to our words and do not amuse ourselves with the terms "absolute," "external," "exist," and such like, signifying we know not what. I can as well doubt of my own being as of the being of those things which I perceive by sense; the very existence of unthinking beings consists in their being perceived.

It were a mistake to think that what is here said derogates in the least from the reality of things. The unthinking beings perceived by sense exist in those unextended, indivisible substances, or spirits, which act, think, and perceive them; whereas philosophers vulgarly hold that the sensible qualities exist in an inert, extended, unperceiving substance, which they call "matter," to which they attribute a natural subsistence distinct from being perceived by any mind whatsoever, even the eternal mind of the Creator.

As we have shown the doctrine of matter to have been the main support of scepticism, so likewise upon the same foundation have been raised all the impious schemes of atheism and irreligion. All these monstrous systems have so visible and necessary a dependence on this supposed material substance that, when this cornerstone is once removed, the whole fabric cannot choose but fall to the ground.

On the same principle does not only fatalism but also idolatry depend in all its varying forms. Did men but consider that the sun, moon, and stars, and every other object of the senses, are only so many sensations in their minds, which have no other existence but barely being perceived, they would never fall down and worship their own ideas, but rather address their homage to that Eternal Invisible Mind which produces and sustains all things.

As in reading books, a wise man will choose to fix his thoughts on the sense rather than lay them out on grammatical remarks; so, in perusing the volume of Nature, it seems beneath the dignity of the mind to affect an exactness in reducing each particular phenomenon to general rules, or showing how it follows from them. We should propose to ourselves nobler views, such as to recreate and exalt the mind, with a prospect of the beauty, order, extent, and variety, of natural things; hence, by proper inferences, to enlarge our notions of the grandeur, wisdom, and beneficence of the Creator.

The reason that is assigned for our being thought ignorant of the nature of spirits is our not having an idea of them. But it is manifestly impossible that there should be any such idea. A spirit is the only substance or support wherein the unthinking beings or ideas can exist; but that this substance which supports or perceives ideas should itself be an idea is absurd.

From the opinion that spirits are to be known after the manner of an idea or sensation have arisen many heterodox tenets and much scepticism about the nature of the soul. It is even probable that this opinion may have produced a doubt in some whether they had any soul at all distinct from their body, since they could not find that they had an idea of it. But the spirit is a real thing, which is neither an idea nor like an idea. What I am myself, that which I denote by the term "I," is what we mean by soul or spiritual substance; and we know other spirits by means of our own soul, which in that sense is an image or idea of them.

By the natural immortality of the soul we mean that it is not liable to be either broken or dissolved by the ordinary laws of Nature or motion. The soul itself is indivisible, incorporeal, unextended, and is consequently incorruptible.

III.--Our Knowledge of God

Though there be some things which convince us that human agents are concerned in producing them, yet it is evident to everyone that those things which are called the works of Nature--that is, the far greater part of the ideas or sensations perceived by us--are not produced by, nor dependent on, the wills of men. There is, therefore, some other spirit that causes them, since they cannot subsist themselves.

If we attentively consider the constant regularity, order, and concatenation of natural things, the surprising magnificence, beauty, and perfection of the larger, and the exquisite contrivance of the smaller parts together with the exact harmony and correspondence of the whole--I say, if we consider all these things, and at the same time attend to the import of the attributes, one eternal, infinitely wise, good, and perfect, we shall clearly perceive that they belong to the aforesaid Spirit, who works all in all, and by whom all things consist.

Hence it is evident that God is known as certainly and immediately as any other mind or spirit whatsoever, distinct from ourselves. We may even assert that the existence of God is far more evidently perceived than the existence of men, because the effects of Nature are infinitely more numerous and considerable than those ascribed to human agents. There is not any one mark that denotes a man, or effect produced by him, which does not more strongly evince the being of that Spirit who is the Author of Nature.

It seems to be a general pretence of the unthinking herd that they cannot see God. Could we but see Him, say they, as we see a man, we should believe that He is, and, believing, obey His commands. But we need only open our eyes to see the sovereign Lord of all things with a more full and clear view than we do any one of our fellow-creatures. We do not see a man, ifby "man" is meant that which lives, moves, perceives, and thinks as we do; but only such a collection of ideas as directs us to think there is a distinct principle of thought and motion like to ourselves, accompanying and represented by it. And after the same manner we see God.

Men are surrounded with such clear manifestations of Deity, yet are so little affected by them that they seem, as it were, blinded with excess of light.

DESCARTES

Discourse on Method

René Descartes was born March 31, 1596, at La Haye, in the ancient province of Touraine, France, of a noble family of Touraine; and was educated at the College of La Flêche by the Jesuits. The decisive crisis of his life arrived in 1619, while he was serving as a volunteer with Prince Maurice of Nassau, and the next nine years may be regarded as the period of his formation. The most fruitful years of his life were spent in Holland, whence he made occasional excursions into France, and perhaps paid a visit to England. In 1633 he finished his treatise on "The World; or on Light," an epitome of his "Physics," which, however, he deemed it wise, in view of Galileo's fate, to withhold from publication during his lifetime. Besides the "Discourse on Method" (1637), with the treatises on dioptrics, meteors, and geometry, his principal works were his "Meditations" addressed to the Deans of the Faculty of Theology in the University of Paris; the "Principia Philosophiae," and the "Traité des Passions de L'Ame," in which, he handled morals. Descartes died at Stockholm, whither he had been summoned by Queen Christina, on February 11, 1649. His work stands a landmark in the modern history of philosophic thought.

I.--The Aim of this Discourse

Good sense or reason must be better distributed than anything else in the world, for no man desires more of it than he already has. This shows that reason is by nature equal in all men. If there is diversity of opinion, this arises from the fact that we conduct our thought by different ways, and consider not the same things. It does not suffice that the understanding be good--it must be well applied.

My mind is no better than another's, but I have been lucky enough to chance on certain ways, which have led me to a certain method by means of which it seems to me that I may by degrees augment my knowledge to the modest measure of my intellect and my length of days. I shall be very glad to make plain in this discourse the paths I have followed, and to picture my life so that all may judge of it, and by the setting forth of their opinions may furnish me with yet other means of improvement.

It is my design not to teach the method which each man ought to follow for the right guidance of his reason, but only to show in what manner I have tried to conduct my own.

I had been nourished on letters from my infancy, but as soon as I had finished the customary course of study, I found myself hampered by so many doubts and errors that I seemed to have reaped no benefits, except that I had observed more and more of my ignorance: Yet I was at one of the most celebrated schools in Europe, and I was not held inferior to my fellow-students, some of whom were destined to take the place of our masters; nor did our age seem less fruitful of good wits than any which had gone before. Though I did not cease to esteem the studies of the schools, I began to think that I had given enough time to languages, enough also to ancient books, their stories and their fables; for when a man spends too much time in travelling abroad he becomes a stranger in his own country; and so, when he is too curious concerning what went on in past ages, he is apt to remain ignorant of what is taking place in his own day. I set a high price on eloquence, and I was in love with poetry; above all, I rejoiced in mathematics, but I knew nothing of its true use.

I revered our theology, but, since the way to heaven lies open to the ignorant no less than to the learned, and the revealed truths which lead thither are beyond our intelligence, I did not dare to submit them to my feeble reasonings.

In philosophy there is no truth which is not disputed, and which, consequently, is not doubtful; and, as to the other sciences, they all borrow their principles from philosophy.

Therefore, I entirely gave up the study of letters, and employed the rest of my youth in travelling, being resolved to seek no other science than that which I might find within myself, or in the Great Book of the World.

Here the best lesson that I learned was not to believe too firmly anything of which I had learnt merely by example and custom; and thus little by little was delivered from many errors which are liable to obscure the light of nature, and to diminish our capacity of hearing reason. Finally, I resolved one day to study myself in the same way, and in this it seems to me I succeeded much better than if I had never departed from either my country or my books.

II.--The Intellectual Crisis

Being in Germany, on my way to rejoin the army after the coronation of the Emperor [Ferdinand II.], I was lying at an inn where, in default of other conversation, I was at liberty to entertain my own thoughts. Of these, one of the first was that often there is less perfection in works which are composite than in those which issue from a single hand. Such was the case with buildings, cities, states; for a people which has made its laws from time to time to meet particular occasions will enjoy a less perfect polity than a people which from the beginning has observed the constitution of a far-sighted legislator. This is very certain, that the estate of true religion, which God alone has ordained, must be incomparably better guided than any other. And again, I considered that as, during our childhood, we had been governed by our appetites and our tutors, which are often at variance, which neither of them perhaps always gave us the best counsel, it is almost impossible that our judgments should be so pure and so solid as they would have been if we had had the perfect use of our reason from the time of our birth, and had never been guided by anything else.

Hence, as regarded the opinions that I had received into my belief, I thought that, as a private person may pull down his own house to build a finer, so I could not do better than remove them therefrom in order to replace them by sounder, or, after I should have adjusted them to the level of reason, to establish the same once more.

When I was younger I had studied logic, analytical geometry, and algebra. Of these, I found that logic served rather for explaining things we already know; while of geometry and algebra, the former is so tied to the consideration of figures that it cannot exercise the understanding without wearying the imagination, and the latter is so bound down to certain rules and ciphers that it has been made a confused and obscure art which hampers the mind instead of a science which cultivates it. And as a state is better governed which has but few laws, and those laws strictly observed, I believed that I should find sufficient four precepts which follow.

The first was never to accept anything as true when I did not recognise it clearly to be so--that is to say, carefully to avoid precipitation and prejudice, but to include in my opinions nothing beyond that which should present itself so clearly and distinctly to my mind that I might have no occasion to doubt it.

The second was to divide up the difficulties which I should examine into as many parts as possible, and as should be required for their better solution.

The third was to conduct my thoughts in order, by beginning with the simplest objects and those most easy to know, so as to mount little by little, by stages, to the most complex knowledge, even supposing an order among things which did not naturally stand in an order of antecedent and consequent.

And the last was to make everywhere enumerations so complete, and surveys so wide, that I should be sure of omitting nothing.

Exact observation of these precepts gave me such facility in unravelling the questions comprehended in geometrical analysis and in algebra, that in two or three months not only did I find my way through many which I had formerly accounted too hard for me, but, towards the end, I seemed to be able to determine, in those which were new to me, by what means and to what extent it was possible to resolve them. And so I promised myself that I would apply my system with equal success to the difficulties of other sciences; but since their principles must all be borrowed from philosophy, in which I found no certain principles of its own, I thought that before all else I must try to establish some therein. By way of preparation (for I was then but twenty-three years old) I must root up from my mind my previous bad opinion of it, and must practise my method in order that I might be confirmed in it more and more.

III.--A Rule of Life

Meanwhile I must have a rule of life as a shelter while my new house was in building, and this consisted of three or four maxims.

The first was to conform myself to the laws and customs of my country, and to hold to the religion in which, by God's grace, I had been brought up; guiding myself, for the rest, by the least extreme opinions of the most intelligent. Among extremes I counted all promises by which a man curtails anything of his liberty; for I should have deemed it a grave fault against good sense if, because I approved something in a given moment, I had bound myself to accept it as good for ever after.

My second maxim was to follow resolutely even doubtful opinions when sure opinions were not available, just as the traveller, lost in some forest, had better walk straight forward, though in a chance direction; for thus he will arrive, if not precisely at the place where he desires to be, at least probably at a better place than the middle of a forest.

My third maxim was to endeavour always to conquer myself rather than fortune, and to change my desires rather than the order of the world, and in general to bring myself to believe that there is nothing wholly in our power except our thoughts. And I believe that herein lay the secret of those philosophers who, in the days of old, could withdraw from the domination of fortune, and, despite pain and poverty, challenge the felicity of their gods.

Finally, after looking out upon the divers occupations of men, I pondered that I could do no better than persevere in that which I had chosen--so deep was my content in discovering every day by its means truths which seemed to me important, yet were unknown to the world.

Having thus made myself sure of these maxims, and having set them apart together with the verities of faith, I judged that for the rest of my opinions I might set freely to work to divest myself of them. For nine years, therefore, I went up and down the world a spectator rather than an actor. These nine years slipped away before I had begun to seek for the foundations of any philosophy more certain, nor perhaps should I have dared to undertake the quest had it not been put about that I had already succeeded.

IV.--"I Think, Therefore I Am"

I had long since remarked that in matters of conduct it is necessary sometimes to follow opinions known to be uncertain, as if they were not subject to doubt; but, because now I was desirous to devote myself to the search after truth, I considered that I must do just the contrary, and reject as absolutely false everything concerning which I could imagine the least doubt to exist.

Thus, because our senses sometimes deceive us I would suppose that nothing is such as they make us to imagine it; and because I was as likely to err as another in reasoning, I rejected as false all the reasons which I had formerly accepted as demonstrative; and finally, considering that all the thoughts we have when awake can come to us also when we sleep without any of them being true, I resolved to feign that everything which had ever entered into my mind was no more truth than the illusion of my dreams.

But I observed that, while I was thus resolved to feign that everything was false, I who thought must of necessity be somewhat; and remarking this truth--"*I think, therefore I am*"--was so firm and so assured that all the most extravagant suppositions of the sceptics were unable to shake it, I judged that I could unhesitatingly accept it as the first principle of the philosophy I was seeking. I could feign that there was no world, I could not feign that I did not exist. And I judged that I might take it as a general rule that the things which we conceive very clearly and very distinctly are all true, and that the only difficulty lies in the way of discerning which those things are that we conceive distinctly.

After this, reflecting upon the fact that I doubted, and that consequently my being was not quite perfected (for I saw that to *know* is a greater perfection than to *doubt*), I bethought me to inquire whence I had learned to think of something more perfect than myself; and it was clear to me that this must come from some nature which was in fact more perfect. For other things I could regard as dependencies of my nature if they were real, and if they were not real they might proceed from nothing--that is to say, they might exist in me by way of defect. But it could not be the same with the idea of a being more perfect than my own; for to derive it from nothing was manifestly impossible; and, because it is no less repugnant that the more perfect should follow and depend upon the less perfect than that something should come forth out of nothing, I could not derive it from myself.

It remained, then, to conclude that it was put into me by a nature truly more perfect than was I, and possessing in itself all the perfections of what I could form an idea--in a word, by God. To which I added that, since I knew some perfections which I did not possess, I was not the only being who existed, but that there must of necessity be some other being, more perfect, on whom I depended, and from whom I had acquired all that I possessed; for if I had existed alone and independent of all other, so that I had of myself all this little whereby I participated in the Perfect Being, I should have been able to have in myself all those other qualities which I knew myself to lack, and so to be infinite, eternal, immutable, omniscient, almighty--in fine, to possess all the perfections which I could observe in God.

Proposing to myself the geometer's subject matter, and then turning again to examine my idea of a Perfect Being, I found that existence was comprehended in that idea just as, in the idea of a triangle is comprehended the notion that the sum of its angles is equal to two right angles; and that consequently it is as certain that God, this Perfect Being, is or exists, as any geometrical demonstration could be.

That there are many who persuade themselves that there is a difficulty in knowing Him is due to the scholastic maxim that there is nothing in the understanding which has not first been in the senses; where the ideas of God and the soul have never been.

Than the existence of God all other things, even those which it seems to a man extravagant to doubt, such as his having a body, are less certain. Nor is there any reason sufficient to remove such doubt but such as presupposes the existence of God. From His existence it follows that our ideas or notions, being real things, and coming from God, cannot but be true in so far as they are clear and distinct. In so far as they contain falsity, they are confused and obscure, there is in them an element of mere negation (*elles participent du néant*); that is to say, they are thus confused in us because we ourselves are not all perfect. And it is evident that falsity or imperfection can no more come forth from God than can perfection proceed from nothingness. But, did we not know that all which is in us of the real and the true comes from a perfect and infinite being, however clear and distinct our ideas might be, we should have no reason for assurance that they possessed the final perfection--truth.

Reason instructs us that all our ideas must have some foundation of truth, for it could not be that the All-Perfect and the All-True should otherwise have put them into us; and because our reasonings are never so evident or so complete when we sleep as when we wake, although sometimes during sleep our imagination may be more vivid and positive, it also instructs us that such truth as our thoughts have will assuredly be in our waking thoughts rather than in our dreams.

V.--Why I Do Not Publish "The World"

I have always remained firm in my resolve to assume no other principle than that which I have used to demonstrate the existence of God and of the soul, and to receive nothing which did not seem to me clearer and more certain than the demonstrations of the philosophers had seemed before; yet not only have I found means of satisfying myself with regard to the principal difficulties which are usually treated of in philosophy, but also I have remarked certain laws which God has so established in nature, and of which He has implanted such notions in our souls, that we cannot doubt that they are observed in all which happens in the world.

The principal truths which flow from these I have tried to unfold in a treatise ("On the World, or on Light"), which certain considerations prevent me from publishing. This I concluded three years ago, and had begun to revise it for the printer when I learned that certain persons to whom I defer had disapproved an opinion on physics published a short time before by a certain person [Galileo, condemned by the Roman Inquisition in 1633], in which opinion I had noticed nothing prejudicial to religion; and this made me fear that there might be some among my opinions in which I was mistaken.

I now believe that I ought to continue to write all the things which I judge of importance, but ought in no wise to consent to their publication during my life. For my experience of the objections which might be made forbids me to hope for any profit from them. I have tried both friends and enemies, yet it has seldom happened that they have offered any objection which I had not in some measure foreseen; so that I have never, I may say, found a critic who did not seem to be either less rigorous or less fair-minded than myself.

Whereupon I gladly take this opportunity to beg those who shall come after us never to believe that the things which they are told come from me unless I have divulged them myself; and I am in nowise astonished at the extravagances attributed to those old philosophers whose writings have not come down to us. They were the greatest minds of their time, but have been ill-reported. Why, I am sure that the most devoted of those who now follow Aristotle would esteem themselves happy if they had as much knowledge of nature as he had, even on the condition that they should never have more! They are like ivy, which never mounts higher than the trees which support it, and which even comes down again after it has attained their summit. So at least, it seems to me, do they who, not content with knowing all that is explained by their author, would find in him the solution also of many difficulties of which he says nothing, and of which, perhaps, he never thought.

Yet their method of philosophising is very convenient for those who have but middling minds, for the obscurity of the distinctions and principles which they employ enables them to speak of all things as boldly as if they had knowledge of them, and sustain all they have to say against the most subtle and skilful without there being any means of convincing them; wherein they seem to me like a blind man who, in order to fight on equal terms with a man who has his sight, invites him into the depths of a cavern. And I may say that it is to their interest that I should abstain from publishing the principles of the philosophy which I employ, for so simple and so evident are they that to publish them would be like opening windows into their caverns and letting in the day. But if they prefer acquaintance with a little truth, and desire to follow a plan like mine, there is no need for me to say to them any more in this discourse than I have already said.

For if they are capable of passing beyond what I have done, much rather will they be able to discover for themselves whatever I believe myself to have found out; besides which, the practice which they will acquire in seeking out easy things and thence passing to others which are more difficult, will stead them better than all my instructions.

But if some of the matters spoken about at the beginning of the "Dioptrics" and the "Meteors" [published with the "Discourse on Method"] should at first give offence because I have called them "suppositions," and have shown no desire to prove them, let the reader have patience to read the whole attentively, and I have hope that he will be satisfied.

The time remaining to me I have resolved to employ in trying to acquire some knowledge of nature, such that we may be able to draw from it more certain rules for medicine than those which up to the present we possess. And I hereby declare that I shall always hold myself more obliged to those by whose favour I enjoy my leisure undisturbed than I should be to any who should offer me the most esteemed employments in the world.

RALPH WALDO EMERSON

Nature

Ralph Waldo Emerson, the American writer and moralist, was born at Boston on May 25, 1803, of English stock and a family of preachers. He was educated at Harvard for the Unitarian ministry, and became a settled pastor in Boston before he was twenty-six. Three years later he resigned his charge owing to theological disagreements. In 1833 he visited Europe and England as a hero worshipper, his desire being to meet Landor, Coleridge, Wordsworth, and Carlyle. He saw them all, and formed a lifelong friendship with Carlyle. Returning to America, he settled at Concord, where he lived till his death, on April. 27, 1882. His public work took the form of lectures, of which his books are reproductions. In 1836 he published his first book, "Nature," anonymously. "Nature" was the germ essay from which all Emerson's later work sprang, a first expression of thoughts that were expanded and developed later. It was published in 1836, when its writer was thirty-three years of age, and known only as a preacher who had become a lecturer. Already Emerson had adopted the methods of a seer rather than those of the consecutive thinker. "Nature" was one of the first-written books of great writers that made a deep impression on the understanding few, but had only a few readers. It presaged the greatness to be; and indeed its poetical quality carries a charm, which Emerson sometimes failed to reproduce and never afterwards surpassed.

I.--To What End is Nature?

Our age is retrospective. It builds the sepulchres of the fathers. It writes biographies, histories, and criticisms. The foregoing generations beheld God face to face; we through their eyes. Why should not we also have an original relation to the universe? Why should we grope among the dry bones of the past, or put the living generation into masquerade out of its faded wardrobe? Let us interrogate the great apparition that shines so peacefully around us. Let us inquire to what end is Nature.

Philosophically considered, the universe is composed of Nature and Soul. Strictly speaking, therefore, all that is separate from us, all which philosophy distinguishes as *not me*, that is both Nature and Art, all other men and my own body, must be ranked under this name, Nature. Nature, in the common sense, refers to essences unchanged by man: space, the air, the river, the leaf. Art is applied to the mixture of his will with the same things, as in a house, a canal, a statue, a picture. But his operations, taken together, are so insignificant, a little chipping, baking, patching, and washing, that in an impression so grand as that of the world on the human mind they do not vary the result.

To go into solitude, a man needs to retire as much from his chamber as from society. But if a man would be alone let him look at the stars. The rays that come from those heavenly bodies will separate between him and what he touches. One might think the atmosphere was made transparent with this design, to give man in the heavenly bodies the perpetual presence of the sublime. Seen in the streets of cities, how great they are! If the stars should appear one night in a thousand years, how men would believe and adore, and preserve for many generations the remembrance of the city of God which had been shown! But every night come out these envoys of beauty, and light the universe with their admonishing smile.

Nature never wears a mean appearance. Neither does the wisest man extort her secret, and lose his curiosity by finding out all her perfection. When we speak of Nature in this manner we have a distinct but most poetical sense in the mind. We mean the integrity of impression made by manifold natural objects. The charming landscape which I saw this morning is indubitably made up of some twenty or thirty farms. Miller owns this field, Locke that, and Manning the woodland beyond. But none owns the landscape. There is a property in the horizon which no man has but he whose eye can integrate all the parts--that is, the poet. This is the best part of these men's farms, yet to this their warranty-deeds give no title.

II.--Her Delight

In the presence of Nature a wild delight runs through the man in spite of real sorrow. Not the sun or the summer alone, but every hour and season yields its tribute of delight; for every hour and change corresponds to and authorises a different state of mind, from breathless noon to grimmest midnight. Crossing a bare common, in snow puddles, at twilight, under a clouded sky, without having in my thoughts any occurrence of special good fortune, I have enjoyed a perfect exhilaration. I am glad to the brink of fear. In the woods, too, a man casts off his years as the snake his slough, and at what period soever of life is always a child. Within these plantations of God a decorum and sanctity reign, a perennial festival is dressed, and the guest sees not how he should tire of them in a thousand years. Standing on the bare ground, my head bathed in the blithe air, and uplifted into infinite space, all mean egotism vanishes. I become a transparent eyeball; I am nothing; I see all; the currents of universal being circulate through me; I am a part or particle of God. I am the lover of uncontained and immortal beauty.

Yet it is certain that the power to produce this delight does not reside in Nature, but in man, or in a harmony of both. It is necessary to use these pleasures with great temperance. For Nature is not always tricked in holiday attire, but the same scene which yesterday breathed perfume and glittered as for the frolic of nymphs is overspread with melancholy to-day. Nature always wears the colours of the spirit.

The misery of man appears like childish petulance when we explore the steady and prodigal provision that has been made for his support and delight on this green ball which floats him through the heavens. All the parts incessantly work into each other's hands for the profit of man. The wind sows the seed; the sun evaporates the sea; the wind blows the vapour to the field; the ice on the other side of the planet condenses the rain on this; the plant feeds the animal; and thus the endless circulations of the divine charity nourish man.

The useful arts are reproductions or new combinations by the wit of man of the same natural benefactors. The private poor man hath cities, ships, canals, bridges, built for him. He goes to the post-office, and the human race run on his errands; to the book-shop, and the human race read and write all that happens for him; to the court-house, and nations repair his wrongs.

III.--Her Loveliness

A nobler want of man is served by Nature, namely, the love of beauty. Such is the constitution of all things, or such the plastic power of the human eye, that the primary forms, as the sky, the mountain, the tree, the animal, give us a delight in and for themselves, a pleasure arising from art, line, colour, motion, and grouping. This seems partly owing to the eye itself. The eye is the best of artists, as light is the first of painters.

To the body and mind which have been cramped by noxious work or company Nature is medicinal, and restores their tone. But in other hours Nature satisfies by her loveliness and without any mixture of corporeal benefit. I see the spectacle of morning from the hilltop over against my house from daybreak to sunrise with emotion which an angel might share. How does Nature deify us with a few and cheap elements. Give me health and a day, and I will make the pomp of emperors ridiculous. The dawn is my Assyria; the sunset and moonrise my Paphos, and unimaginable realms of faerie; broad noon shall be my England of the senses and the understanding; the night shall be my Germany of mystic philosophy and dreams.

The inhabitants of cities suppose that the country landscape is pleasant only half the year. To the attentive eye each moment of the year has its own beauty, and in the same fields it beholds every hour a picture which was never seen before, and which shall never be seen again.

Every rational creature has all Nature for his dowry and estate. He may divest himself of it, he may creep into a corner and abdicate his kingdom, as most men do, but he is entitled to the world by his constitution. In proportion to the energy of his thought and will he takes up the world into himself.

IV.--Her Gift of Language

Language is another use which Nature subserves to man. Words are signs of natural facts. The use of natural history is to give us aid in supernatural history. Every word which is used to express a moral or intellectual fact, if traced to its root, is found to be borrowed from some material appearance. Right means straight; wrong means twisted; transgression the crossing of a line. Most of the process by which this transformation is made is hidden from us in the remote time when language was framed; but the same tendency may be daily observed in children.

It is not words only that are emblematic, it is things. Every appearance in Nature corresponds to some state of mind, and that state of mind can only be described by presenting that natural appearance as its picture. An enraged man is a lion, a cunning man is a fox, a firm man is a rock, a learned man is a torch. Visible distance behind and before us is respectively an image of memory and hope.

Man is conscious of a universal soul within or behind his individual life, wherein, as in a firmament, the natures of justice, truth, love, freedom, arise and shine. This universal soul he calls reason: it is not mine, or thine, or his, but we are its; we are its property and men. And the blue sky in which the private earth is buried, the sky with its eternal calm and full of everlasting orbs is the type of reason. That which, intellectually considered, we call reason, considered in relation to Nature we call spirit. Spirit is the creator. Spirit hath life in itself, and man in all ages and countries embodies it in his language as the Father.

As we go back in history language becomes more picturesque until its infancy, when it is all poetry. When simplicity of character and the sovereignty of ideas are broken up, new imagery ceases to be created and old words are perverted to stand for things which are not; a paper currency is employed when there is no bullion in the vaults.

V.--Her Moral Discipline

In view of the significance of Nature we arrive at the fact that Nature is a discipline. What tedious training, day after day, year after year, never ending, to form the common sense; what continual reproduction of annoyances, inconveniences, dilemmas; what rejoicing over us of little men, what disputing of prices, what reckoning of interest--and all to form the hand of the mind!

The exercise of will or the lesson of power is taught in every event. Nature is thoroughly mediate. It is made to serve. It receives the dominion of man as meekly as the ass on which the Saviour rode. It offers all its kingdoms to man as the raw material which he may mould into what is useful. And he is never weary of working it up. He forges the subtle and delicate air into wise and melodious words, and gives them wings as angels of persuasion and command. One after another his victorious thought comes up with and reduces all things, until the world becomes at last a realised will.

Every natural process is a version of a moral sentence. The moral law lies at the centre of Nature and radiates to the circumference. What is a farm but a mute gospel? The chaff and the wheat, weeds and plants, blight, rain, insects, sun--it is a sacred emblem from the first furrow of spring to the last stack which the snow of winter overtakes in the fields. Who can guess how much firmness the sea-beaten rock has taught the fisherman? How much tranquillity has been reflected to man from the azure sky? How much industry and providence and affection we have caught from the pantomime of brutes?

The unity of Nature meets us everywhere. Resemblances exist in things wherein there is great superficial unlikeness. Thus architecture is called "frozen music" by Goethe. "A Gothic church," said Coleridge, "is petrified religion." The law of harmonic sounds reappears in the harmonic colours. The granite is different in its laws only by the more or less of heat from the river that wears it away. The river, as it flows, resembles the air that flows over it; the air resembles the light that traverses it with more subtle currents.

Each creature is only a modification of the other, the likeness in them is more than the difference, and their radical law is one and the same. This unity pervades thought also.

VI.--Is Nature Real?

A noble doubt suggests itself whether discipline be not the final cause of the universe, and whether Nature outwardly exists. The frivolous make themselves merry with the ideal theory as if its consequences were burlesque, as if it affected the stability of Nature. It surely does not. The wheels and springs of man are all set to the hypothesis of the permanence of Nature.

But while we acquiesce entirely in the permanence of natural laws, the question of the absolute existence of Nature still remains open. It is the uniform effect of culture on the human mind to lead us to regard Nature as a phenomenon, not a substance; to attribute necessary existence to spirit.

Intellectual science fastens the attention upon immortal necessary uncreated natures, that is, upon ideas; and in their presence we feel that the outward circumstance is a dream and a shade. Whilst we wait in this Olympus of the gods we think of Nature as an appendix to the soul. Finally, religion and ethics, which may be fitly called the practice of ideas, have an analogous effect. The first and last lesson of religion is: "The things that are seen are temporal; the things that are unseen are eternal."

VII.--The Spirit Behind Nature

The aspect of Nature is devout. Like the figure of Jesus, she stands with bended head and hands folded on the breast. The happiest man is he who learns from Nature the lesson of worship. Of that ineffable essence we call spirit, he that thinks most will say least. We can foresee God in the coarse, as it were, distant phenomena of matter; but when we try to define and describe Himself, both language and thought desert us, and we are as helpless as fools and savages. The noblest ministry of Nature is to stand as the apparition of God. It is the organ through which the universal spirit speaks to the individual, and strives to bring back the individual to it.

I conclude this essay with some traditions of man and Nature which a certain poet sang to me.

The foundations of man are not in matter, but inspirit. And the element of spirit is eternity. To it, therefore, the longest series of events, the oldest chronologies are young and recent. A man is a god in ruins. When men are innocent, life shall be longer and shall pass into the immortal as gently as we awake from dreams. Infancy is the perpetual Messiah which comes into the arms of fallen men, and pleads with them to return to paradise. The problem of restoring to the world the original and eternal beauty is solved by the redemption of the soul. The ruin that we see when we look at Nature is in our own eye. Man cannot be a naturalist until he satisfies all the demands of the spirit. Love is as much its demand as perception. When a faithful thinker shall kindle science with the fire of the holiest affection, then will God go forth anew into the creation.

Nature is not fixed, but fluid. Spirit alters, moulds, makes it. The immobility, or bruteness, of Nature is the absence of spirit. Every spirit builds itself a house, and beyond its house a world, and beyond its world a heaven. What we are, that only can we see. All that Adam had, all that Caesar could, you have and can do. Adam called his house heaven and earth; Caesar called his house Rome; you, perhaps, call yours a cobbler's trade, a hundred acres of ploughed land, or a scholar's garret. Yet, line for line, and point for point, your dominion is as great as theirs, though without fine names. Build, therefore, your own world. As fast as you conform your life to the pure idea in your mind, that will unfold its great proportions.

EPICTETUS

Discourses and Encheiridion

The Stoic philosopher Epictetus was born about 50 A.D., at Hierapolis, in Phrygia, at that time a Roman province of Asia Minor, and was at first a slave in Rome. On being freed he devoted himself to philosophy, and thereafter lived and taught at Nicopolis, in Epirus (then a portion of Macedonia, corresponding to Albania to-day), from about 90 A.D. to 138 A.D. He left no works, but his utterances have been collected in four books of "Discourses" or "Dissertations" by his pupil and friend Arrian. In the "Encheiridion Epictete"--a "Handbook to Epictetus" compiled and condensed from the chaos of the almost verbatim "Discourses"--Arrian gives the most authentic account of the philosophy of the Greek and Roman Stoics, the sect founded by Zeno about 300 years before the Christian era, which flourished until the decline of Rome. Arrian himself was born about 90 A.D. at Nicomedia. He wrote in the style of Xenophon the "Anabasis of Alexander," a book on "Tactics," and several histories which have been lost. He is chiefly of note, however, as the Boswell of Epictetus. He died about 180 A.D.

I.--Of the Will, and of God

The reasoning faculty alone considers both itself and all other powers, and judges of the appearance of things. And, as was fit, this most excellent and superior faculty, the faculty of a right use of the appearances of things, is that alone which the gods have placed in our own power, while all the other matters they have placed not in our power. Was it because they would not? I rather think that if they could, they had granted us these, too; but they certainly could not. For, placed upon earth, and confined to such a body and such companions, how was it possible that we should not be hindered by things without us?

But what says Jupiter? "O Epictetus, if it were possible, I had made this little body and possession of thine free, and not liable to hindrance. But now do not mistake;it is not thine own, but only a finer mixture of clay. Since, then, I could not give thee this, I have given thee a certain portion of myself--this faculty of exerting the powers of pursuit and avoidance, of desire and aversion, and, in a word, the use of the appearances of things. Taking care of this point, and making what is thy own to consist in this, thou wilt never be restrained, never be hindered; thou wilt not groan, wilt not complain, wilt not flatter anyone. How then! Do all these advantages seem small to thee? Heaven forbid! Let them suffice thee, then, and thank the gods."

But now, when it is in our power to take care of one thing, and apply ourselves to it, we choose rather to encumber ourselves with many--body, property, brother, friend, child, slave--and thus we are burdened and weighed down. When the weather happens not to be fair for sailing, we sit screwing ourselves and perpetually looking out for the way of the wind.

What then is to be done?

To make the best of what is in our power, and take the rest as it naturally happens.

And how is that?

As it pleases God.

To a reasonable creature, that alone is unsupportable which is unreasonable; everything reasonable may be supported. When Vespasian had sent to forbid Priscus Helvidius going to the senate, he answered, "It is in your power to prevent my continuing a senator, but while I am one I must go."

"Well, then, at least be silent there."

"Do not ask my opinion, and I will be silent."

"But I must ask it."

"And I must speak what appears to me to be right."

"But if you do I will put you to death."

"Did I ever tell you that I was immortal? You will do your part, and I mine; it is yours to kill, and mine to die intrepid; yours to banish me, mine to depart untroubled." What good, then, did Priscus do, who was but a single person? Why, what good does the purple do to the garment? What but the being a shining character in himself, and setting a good example to others? Another, perhaps, if in such circumstances Caesar had forbidden his going to the senate, would have said, "I am obliged to you for excusing me." But such a one Caesar would not have forbidden, well knowing that he would either sit like a statue, or, if he spoke, he would say what he knew to be agreeable to Caesar.

Only consider at what price you sell your own will and choice, man--if for nothing else, that you may not sell it for a trifle.

If a person could be persuaded, as he ought of this principle, that we are all originally descended from God, and that He is the Father of gods and men, I conceive he never would think meanly or degenerately concerning himself. Suppose Caesar were to adopt you, there would be no bearing your haughty looks. Will you not be elated on knowing yourself to be the son of Jupiter, of God Himself? Yet, in fact, we are not elated; but having two things in our composition, intimately united, a body in common with the brutes, and reason and sentiment in common with the gods, many of us incline to this unhappy and mortal kindred, and only some few to the divine and happy one.

By means of this animal kindred some of us, deviating towards it, become like wolves, faithless and insidious and mischievous; others like lions, wild and savage and untamed; but most of us like foxes, wretches even among brutes. For what else is a slanderous and ill-natured man than a fox, or something still more wretched and mean?

To Triptolemus all men have raised temples and altars, because he gave us a milder kind of food; but to Him who has discovered and communicated to all thetruth, the means not of living but of living well, who ever raised an altar or built a statue?

If what philosophers say of the kindred between God and man be true, what has anyone to do but, like Socrates, when he is asked what countryman he is, never to say that he is a citizen of Athens, or of Corinth, but of the world? Why may not he who has learned that from God the seeds of being are descended, not only to my father or grandfather, but to all things that are produced and born on the earth--and especially to rational natures, as they alone are qualified to partake of a communication with the Deity, being connected with Him by reason--why may not such a one call himself a citizen of the world? Why not a son of God? And why shall he fear anything that happens among men? Shall kindred to Caesar, or any other of the great at Rome, enable a man to live secure, above contempt, and void of fear; and shall not the having God for our Maker and Father and Guardian free us from griefs and terrors?

II.--The Citizen of the World and his High Calling

You are a distinct portion of the essence of God, and contain a certain part of Him in yourself. Why do not you consider whence you came? You carry a god about with you, wretch, and know nothing of it. Do you suppose I mean some god without you, of gold or silver? It is within yourself you carry Him, and profane Him, without being sensible of it, by impure thoughts and unclean actions. If even the image of God were present, you would not dare to act as you do; when God Himself is within you, and hears and sees all, are not you ashamed to think and act thus, insensible of your own nature and hateful to God?

You are a citizen of the world, and a part of it; not a subservient, but a principal part. You are capable of comprehending the divine economy and of considering the connection of things. What, then, does the character of a citizen promise? To hold no private interest, to deliberate of nothing as a separate individual, but like the hand or the foot, which, if they had reason, and comprehended the constitution of nature, would never pursue, or desire, but with a reference to the whole.

"Ah, when shall I see Athens and the citadel again?" Wretch, are not you contented with what you see every day? Can you see anything better than the sun, the moon, the stars, the whole earth, the sea? If, besides, you comprehend Him who administers the whole, and carry Him about in yourself, do you still long after pebbles and a fine rock?

Boldly make a desperate push, man, for prosperity, for freedom, for magnanimity. Lift up your head at last as free from slavery. Dare to look up to God, and say,

"Make use of me for the future as Thou wilt. I am of the same mind; I am equal with Thee. I refuse nothing which seems good to Thee. Lead me whither Thou wilt. Clothe me in whatever dress Thou wilt. Is it Thy will that I should be in a public or a private condition, dwell here or be banished, be poor or rich? Under all these circumstances I will make Thy defence to men. I will show what the nature of everything is." No, rather sit alone in a warm place, and wait till your nurse comes to feed you. If Hercules had sat loitering at home, what would he have been? You are not Hercules, to extirpate the evils of others. Extirpate your own, then. Expel grief, fear, desire, envy, malevolence, avarice, effeminacy, intemperance, from your mind.

But these can be no otherwise expelled than by looking up to God alone as your pattern; by attaching yourself to Him alone and being consecrated to His commands. If you wish for anything else, you will, with sighs and groans, follow what is stronger than you, always seeking prosperity without, and never finding it. For you seek it where it is not, and neglect to seek itwhere it is.

III.--"His Will is My Will"

Have I ever been restrained from what I willed? Or compelled against my will? How is this possible? I have ranged my pursuits under the direction of God. Is it His will that I should have a fever? It is my will too. Is it His will that I should pursue anything? It is my will too. Is it His will that I should desire? It is my will too. Is it His will that I should obtain anything? It is mine too. Is it not His will? It is not mine. Is it His will that I should be tortured? Then it is my will to be tortured. Is it His will that I should die? Then it is my will to die.

He has given me whatever depends upon choice. The things in my power He has made incapable of hindrance or restraint. But how could He make a body of clay incapable of hindrance? Therefore He hath subjected my body, possessions, furniture, house, children, wife, to the revolution of the universe. He who gave takes away. For whence had I these things when I came into the world?

"But I would enjoy the feast still longer." So perhaps would the spectators at Olympia see more combatants. But the solemnity is over. Go away. Depart like a grateful and modest person; make room for others.

Do not you know that sickness and death must overtake us? At what employment? The husbandman at his plough; the sailor on his voyage. At what employment would you be taken? Indeed, at what employment ought you to be taken? For if there is any better employment at which you can be taken, follow that.

For my own part, I would be engaged in nothing but the care of my own faculty of choice, how to render it undisturbed, unrestrained, uncompelled, free. I would be found studying this, that I may be able to say to God, "Have I transgressed Thy commands? Have I perverted the powers, the senses, the preconceptions which Thou hast given me? Have I ever accused Thee or censured Thy dispensations?

I have been sick, because it was Thy pleasure. I have been poor, with joy. I have not been in power, because it was not Thy will, and power I have never desired. Have I not always approached Thee cheerfully, prepared to execute Thy commands? Is it Thy pleasure that I depart from this assembly? I depart. I give Thee thanks that Thou hast thought me worthy to have a share in it with Thee; to behold Thy works, and to join with Thee in comprehending Thy administration." Let death overtake me while I am thinking, writing, reading such things as these. Of things, some are in our power, others not. In our power are opinion, pursuit, desire, accession; in a word, whatever are our own actions. Not in our power are body, property, reputation, command; in a word, whatever are not our own actions.

Now, the things in our power are free, unrestrained, unhindered, while those not in our power are weak, slavish, restrained, belonging to others. Remember, then, that if you suppose these latter things free, and what belongs to others your own, you will be hindered; you will lament; you will be disturbed; you will find fault with both gods and men. But if you regard that only as your own which is your own, and what is others, as theirs, no one will ever compel you; no one will restrain you; you will find fault with no one; you will accuse no one; you will do nothing against your will; you will have no enemy and will suffer no harm.

Aiming, therefore, at great things, remember that you must not allow yourself to be carried out of your course, however slightly.

Study to be able to say to every hostile appearance, "You are but an appearance, and not the thing you appear to be." Then examine it by your rules, and first and chiefly by this: whether it concerns the things in your own power or those which are not. And if it concerns anything not in your own power, be prepared to say it is nothing to you.

With regard to whatever objects either delight the mind, or contribute to use, or are loved with fondness, remember to tell yourself of what nature they are, beginning from the most trifling things. If you are fond of an earthen cup, remind yourself it is an earthen cup of which you are fond; thus, if it be broken, you will not be disturbed. If you kiss your child, or your wife, remember you kiss a being subject to the accidents of humanity; thus you will not be disturbed if either die.

Men are disturbed, not by things, but by their own notions regarding them.

Be not elated over excellences not your own. If a horse should be elated and say, "I am handsome," it would be supportable. But when you are elated and say, "I have a handsome horse," know that you are elated on what is, in fact, only the good of the horse.

Require not things to happen as you wish, but wish them to happen as they do happen. Then all will go well.

In every happening, inquire of your mind how to turn it to proper account.

Never say of anything "I have lost it," but "I have restored it." Is your child dead? It is restored. Is your wife dead? She is restored. Is your estate taken away from you? Well, and is not that likewise restored? "But he who took it away is a bad man." What is it to you by whose hands He who gave it hath demanded it again? While He gives you to possess it, take care of it, but as of something not your own, like a passenger in an inn.

IV.--Of Tranquillity and the Means Thereto

If you would improve, lay aside such reasonings as prevent tranquillity. It is better to die with hunger, exempt from grief and fear, than to live in affluence with perturbation. It is better your servant should be bad than you unhappy. Is a little oil spilt? A little wine stolen? Say to yourself, "This is the purchase paid for peace, for tranquillity, and nothing is to be had for nothing." When you call your servant, consider it possible he may not come at your call; or if he doth, that he may not do what you would have him do. He is by no means of such importance that it should be in his power to give you disturbance.

Be content to be thought foolish and stupid with regard to externals and unessentials. Do not wish to be thought to know. And though you appear to others to be somebody, distrust yourself. For be assured it is not easy at once to preserve your faculty of choice in a state conformable to nature, and to secure externals, since while you are careful of the one you will neglect the other.

Behave in life as at an entertainment. Is anything brought round to you? Put out your hand and take your share, with moderation. Doth it pass by you? Do not stop it. Is it not yet come? Do not stretch forth your desire towards it, but wait till it reaches you. Thus do with regard to children, to a wife, to public posts, to riches, and you will be, some time or other, a worthy partner of the feasts of the gods. And if you do not so much as take the things set before you, but are able even to despise them, then you will not only be a partner of the gods' feasts, but of their empire.

Remember that you are an actor in a drama, of such a kind as the Author pleases to make it. If short, of a short one; if long, of a long one. If it be His pleasure you should act a poor man, a cripple, a governor, or a private person, see that you act it naturally. For this isyour business, to act well the character assigned you; to choose it is another's.

To me all the portents are lucky, if I will. For, whatever happens, it is in my power to derive advantage from it.

Remember that not he who gives ill language or a blow affronts, but the principle which represents these things as affronting. When, therefore, anyone provokes you, be assured that it is your own opinion which provokes you. Try in the first place not to be hurried away with the appearance. For if you once gain time and respite you will more easily command yourself.

Be assured that the essential property of piety towards the gods is to form right opinions concerning them as existing and as governing the universe with goodness and justice. And fix yourself in the resolution to obey them, and yield to them, and willingly follow them in all events, as produced by the most perfect understanding. For thus you will never find fault with the gods, nor accuse them of neglecting you. And it is not possible for this to be effected any other way than by withdrawing yourself from things not in your own power and placing good or evil in those only which are. For if you suppose any of the things not in your own power to be either good or evil, when you are disappointed at what you wish, or incur what you would avoid, you must necessarily find fault with and blame the authors.

Be for the most part silent, or speak merely what is necessary, and in few words. We may sparingly enter into discourse when occasion calls for it, but not on the vulgar topics of gladiators, horse-races, feasts, and so on; above all, not of men, so as either to blame, praise, or make comparisons.

If anyone tells you such a person speaks ill of you, make no excuses, but answer, "He does not know my other faults, or he would not have mentioned only these."

When you do anything from a clear judgment that I tought to be done, never shun the being seen to do it, even though the world should make a wrong supposition about it. For if you do not act right, shun the action itself; and if you do, why be afraid of mistaken censure?

When any person does ill by you, or speaks ill of you, remember that he acts or speaks from a supposition of its being his duty. Now, it is not possible that he should follow what appears right to you, but what appears so to himself. Therefore, if he misjudges, he is the person hurt, for he is the one deceived. Meekly bear, then, a person who reviles you, for you will say upon every occasion, "It seemed so to him."

The condition and characteristic of a vulgar person is that he never expects either benefit or hurt from himself, but from externals. The condition and characteristic of a philosopher is that he expects all hurt and benefit from himself. The marks of a proficient are that he censures no one, praises no one, blames no one, accuses no one, says nothing concerning himself as being anybody or knowing anything; when he is hindered or restrained, he accuses himself; when praised, he secretly laughs; if censured, he makes no defence. He suppresses all desire; transfers his aversion to things only which thwart the proper use of his own will; is gentle in all exercise of his powers; and does not care if he appears stupid and ignorant, but watches himself as an enemy, like one in ambush.

Whatever rules of life you have deliberately proposed to yourself, abide by them as laws, and as if it were impious to transgress them; and do not regard what anyone says of you; for this, after all, is no concern of yours. Let whatever appears to you to be the best be to you an inviolable law. Socrates became perfect, improving himself in everything by attending to reason only. And though you be not yet a Socrates, live as one who would become a Socrates.

Upon all occasions we ought to have ready at hand these three maxims:

> Conduct me, God, and thou, O Destiny,
> Wherever your decrees have fixed my station.
> I follow cheerfully. And did I not,
> Wicked and wretched, I must follow still.

> Whoe'er yields properly to Fate is deemed
> Wise among men and knows the laws of heaven.

"O Crito, if it thus pleases the gods, thus let it be. Anytus and Melitus may kill me indeed, but hurt my soul they cannot."